ADULT SIBLING RELATIONSHIPS

Adult Sibling Relationships

*Geoffrey L. Greif and
Michael E. Woolley*

 COLUMBIA UNIVERSITY PRESS   NEW YORK

COLUMBIA UNIVERSITY PRESS
Publishers Since 1893
New York   Chichester, West Sussex

cup.columbia.edu

Library of Congress Cataloging-in-Publication Data

Greif, Geoffrey L.
Adult sibling relationships / Geoffrey L. Greif and Michael E. Woolley.
     pages   cm
   Includes bibliographical references and index.
   ISBN 978-0-231-16516-7 (cloth : alk. paper) — ISBN 978-0-231-16517-4 (pbk.) —
ISBN 978-0-231-54080-3 (electronic)
   1. Brothers and sisters. 2. Sibling rivalry. 3. Developmental psychology.
4. Adulthood—Psychological aspects. 5. Brothers and sisters—Death.
I. Woolley, Michael E. II. Title.
   BF723.S43G74   2016
   155.6'46—dc23

                                                      2015009584

Columbia University Press books are printed on permanent and durable acid-free paper.
This book is printed on paper with recycled content.
Printed in the United States of America

c 10 9 8 7 6 5 4 3 2 1
p 10 9 8 7 6 5 4 3 2 1

Cover design: Catherine Casalino

References to websites (URLs) were accurate at the time of writing.
Neither the author nor Columbia University Press is responsible for URLs
that may have expired or changed since the manuscript was prepared.

CONTENTS

BETWEEN US, GEOFFREY GREIF AND MICHAEL WOOLLEY, we have seven siblings, which include full, step-, and half brothers and sisters. One of us (Geoff) is the youngest of three, and the other (Mike) is the second oldest of six. Our own sibling relationships range from the very close (Geoff), to quite distant (Mike has both). We have marveled at the sometimes very large differences in our sibling relationship experiences and how that reflects the range of experiences of the people we interviewed for this book. We grew up with two parents who were married once, to each other (Geoff), and with a constellation of parents who, counting just the two progenitor parents, were married seven times (Mike). We observed our parents and stepparents who had varying degrees of closeness to their own siblings, our aunts and uncles, whom we have come to see affect our own relationships with our siblings. Between us, we have experienced both parental support of and parental interference in our sibling relationships. Some of our parents have shown favoritism (Mike). Both of us have buried parents (Geoff one and Mike three, two biological and one step) and have participated in (Geoff) or acted as the sole executor of (Mike) their estates. The divisions of those estates ranged from the amicable (Geoff) to the complicated and conflictual (Mike). Our wives also have complicated relationships with their siblings and have sibling-like relationships with first cousins. One of us has both a sibling and a sibling-in-law with a disability (Mike). One of us (Geoff) has two children, and the other (Mike) has one child. Geoff keenly watches his adult children's relationships with one another develop, and we both observe how all three of our children interact with our siblings' children, their first cousins, and our sibling-like cousins' children (Mike).

Each of these three generations (and an emerging fourth; Geoff has young grandchildren) of sibling interactions stands on the shoulders of the previous generations and are interconnected in ways that we can see more clearly after undertaking the research we describe in this book.

This topic was of interest to us because of the important and understudied role of adult siblings in all our lives. In researching the topic, we could not escape seeing reflections in our own relationships, which has given us a new appreciation for our siblings as well as insight into problematic dynamics that clinicians may need to attend to in therapy. Those reflections, coupled with our experiences based on our gender, race, socioeconomic status, birth order, age, and our combined total of more than sixty-five years of teaching and practicing family, child, and group therapy, affected our conclusions and recommendations for improving those relationships. In turn, clinicians working in this area should be aware of their own projections onto their clients. Although vertical parent-child relationships have been the focus of most professional training, the horizontal relationships we describe in this book may be new territory for some readers and may present challenges, both personal and professional. (Sibling relationships have long been overlooked in mental health therapy, for reasons that we discuss in chapter 1.) A few decades ago, one of our clinical supervisors advised us that when we were working with a client who was struggling with an issue with which we also were struggling, "if you can stay one valley ahead of your client, who may be traveling the same road, you can be helpful." So while we therapists need to start focusing on our clients' sibling struggles, we first need to get on that road.

This book is based on interview and questionnaire data from 262 siblings aged forty and older, with at least one living sibling. For three years, from 2011 to 2013, trained master of social work (MSW) student interviewers located and interviewed people who fit our study criteria and interviewed one sibling from each family. Together, our respondents shed light on more than seven hundred sibling relationships, as most had multiple siblings. We expanded these interviews by conducting additional in-depth and follow-up interviews, plus interviews with a few siblings and sibling sets together. We have slightly changed some of the quotations to make them easier to read, and we have changed the names and identifying details of the interviewees to protect their confidentiality. We have been careful, though, not to change the intent of what was said. To ensure the accuracy of the in-depth interviews in chapters 7, 8, and 9, we had all the interviewees read what we had written.

Our exploration is both retrospective and oriented to the present. We provide a framework for viewing sibling relationships using family therapy theories. We offer in-depth examples of well-functioning relationships as well as examples of relationships ranging from unsatisfactory, or conflictual, to nonexistent. In addition, we present findings from our own survey of mental health practitioners and their views of sibling relationships in therapy. In our conclusion, we provide suggestions to clinicians, and others, for improving sibling-related struggles. Those insights and suggestions come directly from those we interviewed as well as from our analyses of those interviews using family therapy theories and a framework that considers the affection, ambivalence, and ambiguity inherent in these interactions.

Why are we focusing on siblings aged forty and older? Not only have other researchers used that age as a beginning point for adult research,[1] but we also believe that by forty, a midlife marker, most individuals, as well as sibling relationships, have run their initial course of ups and downs and have stabilized. We say "initial course" because these relationships still may change significantly after forty. But because by that age, people are more settled in their own life, their sibling relationships have likely become less mercurial. For example, most siblings have left home and established an identity outside the family. They have settled into other adult relationships with a partner and most likely have children, as 75 percent of our sample do. The influence of the family of origin, though often still strong, is not as strong as it once was.

Forty years of age is also when many children have to begin taking care of their parents, which forces siblings to interact on meaningful issues at a level and in a manner not often encountered since childhood. That means siblings not only must be adults but also must be adults *together*. No longer can siblings ignore or tolerate one another as easily when they must take care of a parent and make weighty, sometimes life-and-death, decisions together.

We hope that reading this book will lead to a new understanding of sibling relationships and to new insights into both therapeutic work and personal growth. To this end, chapter 1 looks broadly at sibling relationships to show how, in turn, clients might perceive them. We all decide how these relationships *should* operate by looking at how others in our immediate family and broader society, including friends, well-known sibling sets, and fictional characters depicted in literature and film, manage theirs. Chapter 2 focuses on research that we believe will be relevant to issues raised in therapy. We then present our research findings in the next four chapters, starting with a descriptive overview and zeroing in on the relationship of age to how these relationships are maintained. This is followed by the importance of parental influences on sibling interactions throughout the life span. The serious problems that many sibling relationships encounter are discussed in chapter 5, followed by a chapter on how having step- and half siblings influences closeness.

Part 3 of this book contains three in-depth case studies. The first is a heartbreaking account of a family in which the three siblings have had little to no contact for decades. The next two chapters offer healthy models for how siblings can cooperate and handle conflict; one is based on a group interview with three sisters following the death of a fourth sister, a twin. The other chapter is based on a group interview with three brothers shortly after their second parent died.

Part 4 begins with two guest chapters by experienced practitioners. The first, provided by the main partners in Aging Network Services, describes their ongoing clinical work with siblings struggling with their parents' aging issues. These skilled clinicians describe how treatment with siblings unfolds over weeks and months. The second chapter recounts what happens in an emergency when adult siblings need to be organized to respond to a parent who is entering a hospital burn unit and for which the clinical work is often brief and intense. The next chapter lays out our own recommendations for clinicians working to improve siblings' interactions and includes the results of our survey of mental health practitioners as well as our respondents' own suggestions, which are sure to resonate with many of the readers' own experiences. The concluding chapter offers our observations of where sibling relationships could be heading and includes general recommendations that may appeal to lay readers.

We could not cover all the topics related to siblings in our research. For example, we do not discuss in depth siblings with developmental disabilities or the increasing recognition of the influence of genes on sibling relationships. Finally, we offer one, in-depth case study of the unique influence of twins on family and sibling relationships that was not in the research chapters, as only three respondents (1 percent of our sample) had a living twin at the time of the interview.

We hope that our readers will gain a deeper appreciation for the complexity of sibling relationships, their centrality in the lives of adults across the life span, and how they may be approached in therapy. Just as important, we hope that readers will gain a better understanding of the role that siblings play in their own lives and in the lives of those whom they love.

ACKNOWLEDGMENTS

GRACE McMILLAN HAS BEEN A fabulous contributor to many facets of this book. As a research assistant, she helped code qualitative interviews, enter questionnaire responses into an Excel file, and parse the multiple meanings of what we found. She also brought a kind and thorough editing hand that made the writing much clearer. Without her brilliant, patient, and often humorous assistance, the end product would have been much poorer.

We would like to thank the MSW student interviewers who assisted with the three waves of research. They helped not only with conducting interviews but also with thinking through the questions we asked and the answers we received. Their diverse backgrounds gave us a variegated perspective on the lives of siblings. They are, in 2011, Elizabeth Brolund, Rebekah Coverston, Zinaida Curtis, Anna Dorsey (who also was wonderfully helpful in the spring of 2012 as a research assistant), Stephanie Dudley, Rita Nzuwah, Kendall Rose-Gregg, Shira Rothberg, Lisa Schulkowski, Jennifer Seger, Andrea Sherman, Liz Smith, Alyssa Tarlow, Sara Vazquez, Mary Vinograd, and Christina Williams; in 2012, Nicole Davis-Hether, Stacy Embrack, Michelle Glenn, Keya Johnson, Gilby Kim, Jamie Kuntz, Lori Lagrossa, Adrielly Maclas, Mollie McGann, David Oliner, Jailaxmi Rajan, Gay Shackelford, Sara Sheikh, and Luke Smith; in 2013, Marilyn Bailey, Jacob Buck, Lauren Carpenter, Letitia Conrad, Ciara Cooks, Nancy Espinal, Sarah Grum, Stacia Hines, Kelsey Hurlburt, Jennifer Jones, Robert Kearney, Risa Khalili, Kendall Klein, Sarah Lee, Brittany McGraw, Kathleen McLaughlin, Sinem Menses, Elise Minor, Matthew Quinlan, and Amanda Trejo.

Finally, we wish to thank our wives, Maureen and Deb, and all seven of our siblings, who have taught us so much about relationships, both those that are blood and those that, to our benefit, are by choice.

ADULT SIBLING RELATIONSHIPS

PART 1

Introduction to Adult Siblings

The World of
Adult Siblings

When I was growing up and I was starting to have new experiences—getting married, starting a family, having babies—it felt really nice to have older sisters that I could share with and get advice from and feel part of a bigger family. It felt like a safety net, and later, it felt like a safety net for my children that they had other people that loved them too.

Forty-nine-year-old white female, youngest of three sisters

Len's living here and I was over there [an hour's drive] for dinner one night last week, and he comes here probably once or twice a week for dinner, so we're very close. And my sister, who lives like five miles from me, I hardly ever see. She calls me. I really have to work up the courage to call her back because it's just an unpleasant relationship.

Fifty-nine-year-old white female, middle of three

My sister and I are polar opposites. She is a kind and loving person. I do not have any harsh things to say to describe her. However, she fails to honor the boundaries that should come with adult sibling relationships. More than I would like, we do not see eye to eye on various things that lead to patterns of harsh and disrespectful dialogues. It is common for us not to speak to each other for months following these exchanges, but we engage each other again as if nothing ever happened when there is a birthday or other family event that requires both of us to attend.

Forty-four-year-old African American male, younger of two

Well, I have [my husband] and our son, and my brother does not want children. He and his wife just have different goals for their lives. I think my family looks much more like what we had when we were kids, while I don't know what my brother is doing half the time. The point is that it doesn't matter; he's still my brother.

Forty-three-year-old white female, older of two

Although it [our relationship] is fairly close and fairly frequent, it is also complicated. My brother is three years younger than me . . . somebody who growing up would now be diagnosed with social anxiety and maybe oppositional defiant disorder. Been treated for depression. Been treated for anxiety, so there are lots of those issues in the background, but everyone is crazy to some extent, so I am sure he has some things to say about me. He can be sort of a wild card and get angry pretty quick, and because he has social anxiety and OCD, it has really prevented him from being successful, and he is pissed about that, not all the time but a fair amount.

Fifty-nine-year-old white male, older of two

When I first agreed to do the interview, I was hoping to have a little bit of closure with that situation, but I decided just to wait and see if my brother would contact me. And he hasn't. He travels for work and for pleasure and was recently in town twice. He had talked about us getting together—not talked so much as texted. And then never called me. So on the day that they were leaving, I didn't realize they were leaving, I called and got their voicemail. I was really surprised; I thought it was like the next week or something.

Fifty-one-year-old white female with an older sister and younger brother

I have never been nearly as close to the others [step-, half, and adopted sibling] as I was to Donald [only full brother, who died in 1967]. I can do the dinners and all the usual stuff, but I can't be totally honest with them. I can't live those inner spots with any of them the way that Donald and I did it.

Seventy-one-year-old white female, oldest of six

THESE SEVEN WOMEN AND MEN speak about the loving as well as the distant and strained nature of sibling relationships. They describe appreciating the protection that siblings provide, avoiding a sister while staying close to a brother, pretending to get along at family events despite significant differences, not understanding a brother's behavior but still accepting him, coping with a brother's lifelong mental illness, feeling sloughed off by a brother, and mourning the loss of a cherished full-sibling while maintaining pseudo-relationships with other half, step-, and adopted siblings. To varying degrees, these relationships are marked by affection, ambivalence, and ambiguity, feelings that permeate many sibling relationships.

It may be a cliché, but we all face the reality that we can choose our friends but not our family of origin, the family into which we are born. We are forever tethered to our siblings, longer even than to our parents or children. We can drop or change our friends and our partners, but we cannot fully discard, relationally or psychologically, a brother or sister.

One of our initial premises in writing this book was to *compare* sibling relationships with friendships. After considering the data and reading the interviews, we determined that a friendship lens was not the correct lens to use. While siblings often are friends, the bonds that connect siblings are quite different. More family history is shared from birth and across generations. More physical space (bedroom, bathroom, dinner table) and activities (watching television, playing with toys, attending holiday rituals) are shared. Finally, family members are not chosen.

In this book, we offer an understanding of the complexity of adult sibling relationships, describing how affection is fostered, how ambivalence is a normal but little-understood feeling, and how ambiguity about the past or the present may lead to miscommunication and distancing. Based on in-depth case studies, interviews with more than 260 adult siblings forty and older, a survey of therapists, and consultations with experts, we offer ways to consider these complex and often changing connections so that they can be appreciated when going well and reconfigured and improved when needed. Even though mental health practitioners are our primary audience, what we describe will also be useful to lay readers interested in understanding and improving their relationships with their siblings.

Adult sibling relationships have been understudied in both mental health and historical research and only fairly recently have attracted attention. In both fields, the focus on the parent-child relationship has overshadowed other relationships. According to psychoanalyst Joyce Edward, the field of psychoanalysis has ignored such relationships because of its focus on the Oedipal complex and because most analysts paid little attention to it in their own analytic training.[1] C. Dallett Hemphill, a history professor at

Ursinus College, explained that her discipline also has been late in coming to the topic: "Despite all the attention to early modern families produced by historical baby boomers, it is curious that sibling relations, a near universal and crucial axis of family relations, have been almost totally overlooked."[2] As we will see in chapter 2, it was not until relatively recently that sibling relationships began to stimulate the interest of researchers and clinicians.

Edward argues that there is a plus/minus component to sibling relationships—a strong attachment to siblings can sustain a person and lead to a good sense of self throughout life or, conversely, can hinder individuation and growth. Competition can be healthy and foster maturity, or it can be debilitating and foster hostility. The task, according to Edward, is for the mental health profession to explore more deeply these important family relationships and then put this newfound knowledge about siblings to use in clinical practice in a world in which family forms are becoming increasingly diverse.

Another reason to look at sibling relationships is the recognition of the benefits of a robust social network in which siblings can be a critical part, particularly as people age. People with friends live longer, healthier, and happier lives. The qualities that people look for in friendships—loyalty, dependability, trustworthiness, and frequent communication have been noted as key elements of friendships between adults[3]—are often the bulwark of good family relationships. When sibling relationships are at their best, the connection goes beyond being merely a sibling relationship; it also can be a friendship, a perhaps higher and more satisfying order of connection. In those cases, it is not just blood that binds siblings together; instead, both siblings implicitly feel they would have chosen each other as a friend even if they were not already connected by a mutual love marked by a powerful shared history. When siblings are close, considering each other friends as well as family, they can play a key role in the social support network.

Other health and family benefits may accrue when siblings get along well. As the divorce rate among baby boomers increases,[4] people are more likely to be single in later life. Many worry about aging alone and relying on strangers to take care of them. Siblings provide a trusted and reliable potential source of caregiving as we age. Our longer life spans bring siblings, as well as families in general, closer together.[5] It is estimated that 80 percent of Americans have siblings.[6] With increasing longevity, we will arguably need our siblings for our mutual good. Improving relations thus would seem to be imperative and might even reduce the need for government services to provide the caretaking that siblings may be able to do for one another if they are on good terms. Improving relations could also improve quality of life, which, at an advanced age, is often marked by social isolation and reclusiveness.

This is what we gain from growing up and growing old with siblings (whether they are biological, step-, half, or adoptive siblings) who can help us as we venture out into the world and build relationships with people outside our family. From siblings we learn how to

1. Cooperate and deal with competition.
2. Interact with the opposite sex (when there is an opposite-sex sibling).
3. Develop same-sex friendships (when there is a same-sex sibling).
4. Bond for protection from parents (when needed).
5. Stick up for one another to parents and peers, in school and other situations.
6. Negotiate the differences inherent in everyday life.
7. Navigate major decisions, such as taking care of aging parents.
8. Deal with the loss of parents and close relatives.
9. Maintain a lifelong relationship with a person closely matched to us in biological characteristics and family environment.

We begin with the assumption that people want a close and loving relationship with their brothers and sisters, even though they may settle for something different. We cannot escape *family*. It is emphasized in everyday life in the books and newspapers that we read and the television shows and movies that we watch. Work colleagues mention spending weekends with family, traveling for family reunions and vacations, and wanting to start a family. Emergency number requests ask for next of kin.

Google the word *family* and more than a billion hits come up. *Family* defines who is in and who is out of the first—and possibly only—lifelong system of which we are a part. Almost everyone wants a family, and those who don't want one often feel they have to justify why they do not. While family does not provide the same life-and-death environment that it did in medieval times and pioneer days when, if you were thrown out of the home, you were unlikely to survive, it is still one of the most powerful forces in our lives.

Siblings are family. They may be the siblings that we "never see," "never were close to," "had a major falling out with," or "stopped seeing after Mom (or Dad) died." Notwithstanding such disclaimers, they still are related to us despite the lack of connection and strain; they remain a part of our history and our identity. Just as music is defined by the silences and art by the space on the canvas, relationships with siblings can be defined by the absence of connection.

Bad relationships with siblings can haunt us. Daniel Buccino, a Baltimore-based clinical social worker and former chair of the Maryland Board of Social Work Examiners, told us that half of his time providing psychotherapy to adults is taken up with discussing sibling relationships. "The residue of childhood often remains," he explained. Whether someone was abused by a sibling or was treated poorly or favorably by a parent, those events have a clear impact on a person's adult relationships with siblings and what kind of help is sought in treatment. In support of Buccino's statement, numerous research studies have shown that sibling-to-sibling violence in childhood is a common form of family-based aggression.[7]

Favoritism (defined in various ways in the research to include receiving more affection, time resources, support,[8] and treatment that is perceived as consistently unfair and one sided),[9] as our own research found, also leaves fingerprints throughout the life span.

At their worst, sibling relationships can remain a source of stress for years, sometimes for a lifetime. They can be complicated, painful, hurtful, and conflicted. Sometimes there may be bitter fighting or simply no communication at all, which is handed down from one generation to the next. One woman whom we interviewed, who died at age eighty-five, asked her three daughters not to tell her sister when she died. She had stopped contact with her fifteen years earlier, and she wanted to maintain that separation after her death. Hence that legacy is carried to the next generation. Her daughters have no communication with their first cousins and have struggled at times with their own sister relationships, mimicking, though to a lesser degree, their mother and aunt's relationship.

Between the siblings with wonderful, loving relationships and those with highly troubled relationships are siblings who may have settled into a valley with some, but not too much, emotional distance. These people often have ambivalent feelings about one another. A typical description of a brother or sister in such a situation might be:

"We understand each other, but we are not especially close and never have been."

"She is my sister and I love her, but I wouldn't choose her as a friend."

"I will always be there for him, but he is such a pain."

"We were close when we were young, but we have families now and don't have time."

"Since she moved away, we haven't been as close."

"His politics changed, so we avoid talking about a lot of stuff."

The good news is that sibling relationships are not immutable. As we found in our research, some events may cause the dynamics to improve. People gain perspective. They mature.

A young Caribbean man that one of us was seeing in therapy realized as he was turning thirty that he needed to work harder to connect with his younger and older siblings, all of whom were still living in their home country. His father was aging; his mother had died fifteen years earlier, and he had fixated on that significant age marker as the time to get his familial relationships in shape. How did he do it at a younger age than did many in our study? He became emotionally less reactive when dealing with them and began, in his own eyes, to "act more maturely." "At thirty, I want them to know who I am, so I need to work on these relationships," he said.

AFFECTION, AMBIVALENCE, AND AMBIGUITY

How can we put a frame around these complicated relationships? In the past, a number of researchers studying sibling relationships divided them into categories.[10] We attempted this, too, which gave us a broad impression of the nature of the relationships in our sample. When we asked siblings to classify each of their sibling relationships, 62 percent agreed with a statement characterizing the relationships as highly satisfying. Another 17 percent regarded their relationships more dispassionately, agreeing with the statement that "sibling relationships are neither highly satisfying nor particularly strained." The remaining 21 percent agreed with a statement that said they had strained relationships.[11]

While the answers to these statements give an overview of our interviews, they do not cover the depth and dynamism of sibling interactions. We came to believe that a more complex and nuanced understanding of these relationships could better guide clinicians in their work. We concluded, therefore, that affection, ambivalence, and ambiguity are better guides for framing sibling relationships in adulthood.

Affection is primary, as attested to by the majority of the respondents agreeing to the characterization of the relationship as close, trusting, and highly satisfying. Although our book is for mental health practitioners and focuses more on troubled relationships, we should not forget that these close relationships, according to our research and that of others, are very satisfying and sustaining for the majority. Accordingly, we believe that these affectionate relationships can serve as useful guides to sibling relationships as a source of support that is often overlooked in therapy.

Ambivalence was apparent, however, in many of our interview transcripts, even for some of those who had satisfying, close relationships. Therefore, in crafting a therapeutic framework for guiding family-based interventions with sibling issues, we borrowed from the work of Indiana University psychology professor Victoria Hilkevitch Bedford[12] and University of Western Ontario sociology professor Ingrid Connidis,[13] who described the ambivalence inherent in sibling relationships. Conceptualized in sociology to understand intragenerational relationships, ambivalence has been defined by others as "the paradox between closeness and distance, the push and pull between intimacy and setting boundaries."[14] This definition, of course, fits nicely with what therapists do every day: we help disentangle relationships in which feelings about someone are mixed and intimacy can be conflictual.[15]

In her review of the literature, Bedford noted that while ambivalence between siblings exists in childhood, it is less clearly articulated in adulthood, when the highly skewed nature of studies of siblings characterizes their relationships as either very positive or very negative. It may be, she surmised, that adults usually are reluctant to focus on negative or even mixed feelings for their siblings. One of Bedford's research findings, based on projective tests given to sixty adults between the ages of thirty and sixty-nine, was that some siblings were, in fact, unaware of the range of their feelings about their siblings and that using ambivalence was a productive way of looking at their relationships.

Connidis set the stage for understanding sibling ties by first describing some of the inherent inequalities that develop between siblings during their lifetime. These differences occur in education, income, and occupation and could be tied historically to, for example, gender. Connidis noted that those with more education are more likely to live farther from their family of origin, which could leave the care of their parents to those siblings with less education who have not moved away. In the upcoming chapters, we will cite many instances of siblings who were in a one-down or one-up position based on their status or education within the family: A doctor is favored; a sister marries into money and wants to treat all the others to vacations; a sister, but not a brother, is expected to take care of ailing parents. Inequalities between siblings are greater, of course, in larger families that have more possible permutations for differences. Connidis argued that these inequalities between siblings lead to ambivalence in their relationships. "Viewing ambivalence as an ongoing feature of family ties that is never permanently resolved encourages a life course view of relationships as regularly renegotiated in response to changing circumstances."[16]

As family therapists and researchers trying to understand siblings, we add to these sociological and psychological views of ambivalence what we regard as additional necessary components, namely, family history and climate—for example, favoritism, protection, and interference—as well as the unique characteristics and capabilities of the individuals in the family. Together with culture, they create sibling relationships that turn into a complicated stew.

When the pot is stirred, an ambivalent relationship can appear in various forms. It could be one in which one sibling is rooting for the success of another but realizes that it will come at a cost if they have always competed with each other. It is possible to feel affection for a sibling but still take some pleasure in being slightly better in some way. An ambivalent relationship could result in one sibling struggling his whole life and being unreliable and untrustworthy yet still capable of love and being loved by another sibling. When a family has multiple siblings, one of them might have great affection for another, little connection with yet another, and anger at a third, leading to ambivalence about sibling relationships in general. These relationships are not fixed; they can change on a dime and lead to a new round of negotiation either internally or within the family system.

Ambiguity also appears in the transcripts from our study. We consider ambiguous relationships those in which siblings are unclear as to what has happened between them and the meaning of those events. It is not only that they have mixed feelings of closeness and distance for a sibling (which is their ambivalence); they do not understand *why* certain events have occurred or why the closeness/distance exists. For example, many of those we interviewed—including the forty-three-year-old describing her brother in one of the epigraphs that opens this chapter, Ron in chapter 7, and Willa in chapter 4—do not understand why things are the way they are, with siblings hostile to or cut off from the rest of their families.

Ambiguity and ambivalence may be connected. Pauline Boss, an emerita family therapy professor at the University of Minnesota, has done research on ambiguous loss, the grieving process that is often unresolved because too much is unknown.[17] Boss explained that when combined with ambivalence, ambiguity implies a lack of clarity, which in turn can feed ambivalent feelings. When people are pulled in two different directions, they are uncertain how to act toward each other.[18] Connidis clarified how differences between siblings may play out on a microlevel: "Efforts to negotiate ambivalence may involve action to change the situation through diplomacy, persuasion, appeals to collective problem solving, and confrontation, or relative inaction by accepting the status quo, distancing oneself from a situation or relationship, or acquiescing to another sibling's perspective."[19] This ambivalence-ambiguity dynamic is, in a way, cyclical. For example, if a younger sister is unclear about her feelings toward an older sister and does not understand that sister's behavior, she may send confusing and contradictory messages to her. That may lead the older sister to act in ways that will heighten both sisters' ambivalence toward each other.

To lay the groundwork for how feelings of affection, ambivalence, and ambiguity can be used to frame our understanding of sibling relationships, we need to set the context of siblings in their earliest environment, the home. This will lead into an introduction of family therapy theories that we can use in guiding practice with siblings who want to improve their relationships.

A LOOK BACK: WHEN WE FIRST LEARN ABOUT SIBLINGS

It is in childhood that our relationships with our siblings and parents are at their most intense. We live in immediate proximity to them, both physically and emotionally, during the most formative years of our life, and we have few avenues of escape that are adaptive. We are heavily influenced by our family, with little experience living away from them until we reach young adulthood. These relationships do not begin *de novo* but are formed, in part, by the relationships both parents had and have with their families of origin. Murray Bowen, whose work we will explain later in greater depth, pioneered the concept of the multigenerational transmission process in families in which patterns of interaction are handed down from one generation to the next. For example, the mother who was very close to her sister may hope that her own daughters will be close and may take a relaxed attitude toward the relationship, confident that theirs will work out as hers did. Thus her children are born into an existing network that supports their relationship. A family pattern of closeness is handed down to the next generation. But if the mother had a strained relationship with her sister, she may consciously or unconsciously discourage her children's sibling closeness, believing that siblings are not reliable. Conversely, she may try too hard to compensate for what she did not have and be hypervigilant about how they are getting along, which could have the opposite effect of her intentions.

Just as no two families are alike in how they raise their children, no two children will have the same experience growing up in the same family. Unless they are twins, children come along at different stages in their parents' lives. Financial resources, geographic location, the quality of the parents' relationship, the involvement of extended family, and the parents' emotional lives will change in part or entirely while children are growing up, likely in both positive and negative ways, and that will affect how each child is raised. Parents simply cannot raise children in exactly the same way, no matter how much they love them and no matter how hard they try. Throughout life, children receive varying amounts of attention, discipline, affection, and resources from parents.

Siblings also have different experiences growing up because their emotional dispositions and physical needs vary and interact in different ways with their parents' experiences and abilities.[20] The cycles of interaction between parents and children are established early and vary from one child to the next. Some people are born with sunnier dispositions than others, more evident talents, and greater social ease. These children need less attention from parents than do children who are born with more challenges.

At the same time, parents relate to their children differently based on their own upbringing and interactions with the world. For example, both of us have worked with parents who were uncomfortable talking to principals or school counselors when their children were having trouble with their schoolwork. If the parents had struggled themselves, it can be painful for them to have to confront these issues again twenty-five years later. The parents' reactions to dealing with these issues can reverberate throughout the sibling system as parents react with anger or sympathy to the child who is not a star pupil.

Of course, the mere addition of a new child to the family changes its dynamics forever. The firstborn, on whom everyone dotes initially, may end up competing with a younger sibling and may even be asked to help raise that sibling. With the addition of each new child, whether by birth, remarriage, adoption, or kin care, they all have one another's unique personalities to contend with which, by definition, makes their home life different as well.

Siblings may vie not only for their parents' (and relatives') affection and attention but also for the other siblings' affection when there are more than two children. Anyone who is part of a sibling set of three or more children has experienced being included or excluded by younger or older brothers and sisters when sides were chosen for games or during arguments. The dyad becomes a triad and, with each additional sibling, has exponentially more relationships to balance. If stepsiblings, half siblings, adopted siblings, or foster children are in the home, each child's experiences will vary even more as the number of people and the types and number of parent-child and sibling-sibling relationships become more complicated.

While most people adapt to differential parental treatment, some fallout from unequal treatment is inevitable. This point was illustrated in one study in which family researchers interviewed 151 pairs of siblings (average age twenty-four). Those siblings who perceived being less favored experienced more depression in young adulthood, and the greater the perceived imbalance in favoritism was, the less sibling closeness was reported.[21] These trends of favoritism may have a lasting impact, as we also found similar results in our research with an older sample of respondents.

Finally, it is not just the "home" that affects sibling relationships; factors outside the family also come into play. Traumatic events happen to families. Children are bullied in school for any number of reasons. They are randomly mugged in their neighborhood. They become seriously or chronically ill. They are injured by an incautious automobile driver. They witness violence or are abused. "Stuff" happens to them over which they and their parents had no control, and the events reverberate throughout the family system. Yes, parents help assemble adaptive responses to crises, but sometimes nature, nurture, and luck conspire to make life tougher for some than for others in the same family.

With all the obstacles to sibling closeness, it may be surprising that many brothers and sisters reach adulthood with a strong bond, a bond that, our research shows, often improves over time. Despite competition for attention and affection, differences in abilities, age gaps, gender match, home environment, and random traumatic events, siblings usually get along. We learned from our interviews that sibling relationships have a great deal of resilience and hope. Brothers and sisters *want* things to work out. They wish to have a relationship with one another that can sustain them. A good adult sibling relationship means having someone accept us for who we are, who knew us at our worst and best, and who will be there when needed, regardless of our age or situation.

A good sibling relationship in childhood can also be a template for other relationships. When things go well between siblings, according to University of Illinois psychologist Laurie Kramer,[22] it can bode well for future peer and romantic relations. As both Kramer and Lewis Bank, a clinical psychologist and research scientist, pointed out, a growing body of literature illustrates the myriad ways that our quality of life is affected by our siblings across the life span:

> It is our brothers and sisters who see us as no one else does, who are experts at how to both please and annoy us, and who bring out the best and worst in us . . . the sibling world provides a critical window for understanding the ways in which children's experiences with their brothers and sisters may foreshadow variations in individual well-being and adjustment later in childhood, adolescence, and well into adulthood.[23]

We found significant support for this in our research as well: if adults report that they did not feel jealousy between themselves and their siblings when they were young, they are more likely to be close to those siblings.

On the flip side, if our interactions with our siblings are unresolved or uncomfortable, we may question our dealings with our parents, our friends, and those with whom we are romantically involved. A question that might arise would be: If we can't get along with our siblings, with whom can we get along? The inability to sustain relationships may cut across all contexts. An early lack of connection, or attachment, to parents and siblings may be related to the distancing of other relationships. The hope is that resolving sibling relationships at any age can benefit any other troubled relationships.

The Shifts in Adulthood

As we age, a close relationship with a sibling is usually supplanted, or at least accompanied, by an adult love relationship with a partner. Relationships with siblings may then loom less large and become a sidebar to other relationships, including those formed with close friends. Unlike in childhood, in adulthood the presence and nature of sibling relationships become a choice we make, consciously or unconsciously. For example, if we have children, unless our siblings are intimately involved in raising them, our siblings may recede further from the prominent position they held when we were younger. It is not that our siblings become less important or less loved, it is that our relationships with them may become less central as we add other meaningful people to our lives.

One goal of adulthood is to integrate the family of origin, the one into which we were born, into our family of orientation, the people to whom we choose to be close. This does not always work out, of course. As we learned, the family of orientation can affect relationships with the family of origin in both positive and negative ways. We fall in love with people who are more (or less) interested in contact with their own family than we are with ours. Their desire to draw closer to their family or distance themselves in turn affects how close we feel to our family.

Having children can bring people closer to their siblings, as it did for the forty-nine-year-old woman in the epigraph beginning this chapter. After her children were born, she felt more vulnerable and in need of the safety net that her sisters could provide. In fact, one-fifth of those we interviewed said they became closer to their siblings through their children or their in-laws. When spouses of siblings become friends, it can help nieces, nephews, and cousins become closer, which in turn can help siblings become closer. But the family of orientation can also pull people away from siblings, as happened with the people we interviewed who reported that their family disapproved of their choice of a spouse because of that spouse's religion, race, or personality.

It is not only the addition of new loved ones—spouses, partners, children—that can affect adult sibling relationships. We grow up, change, and move on. We develop opposing political views, are drawn to different occupations or activities, convert to a new religion, or stop attending a house of worship. Great income disparities between siblings in adulthood may result in more or less expensive clothes, homes, education options, and vacations, which can breed resentment or avoidance. A power imbalance may develop between siblings if the wealthier sibling financially supports the less financially stable sibling, as we heard occasionally during our interviews.

A parent's or sibling's illness and death may play a significant role in bringing people together, though this may be temporary. In fact, of those who were not close to their siblings at some point during childhood or adulthood, which was the majority of our sample, one-quarter said that it was the parent's illness or death that eventually brought them back together.

What appears most likely to bring siblings together in middle and later adulthood is maturity, which was cited by half our sample and illustrated by our thirty-year-old client. As we age, we learn that perceived injustices from childhood or early adulthood are no longer important. We gain insight into our early history and come to view events differently as we talk to others, hear our siblings' perspectives, and have our own children. Mark Twain is purported to have observed, "When I was a boy of fourteen, my father was so ignorant I could hardly stand to have the old man around. But when I got to be twenty-one, I was astonished at how much the old man had learned in seven years." We view people differently through the lens of age. In most cases, our siblings become more tolerable and important to us and us to them. Ideally, we want to make the most of our connections and leave a legacy of family closeness for future generations. We become less emotionally reactive, less self-centered, and more open to difference.

HOW WE APPROACH WORK WITH SIBLINGS: THREE THERAPY LENSES

First we offer the overarching frame of looking at sibling relationships with an eye to ambivalence, ambiguity, and affection. While these can help orient work with clients and address the complexity of their relationships, specific theories can also help guide practice. For this we borrowed three theoretical perspectives from family therapy: family systems theory

(Murray Bowen), structural family therapy (Salvador Minuchin), and experiential family therapy (Virginia Satir). These three theories grew out of a tradition of viewing families as systems in which each family member has an influence on and is influenced by every other family member. A change in one member signals a change in the other members. We use these theories to examine how sibling relationships operate, to see how problems may develop, and to suggest how to improve family relationships. These are well-established theories that offer a range of temporal approaches, from viewing problems as having historic, intergenerational roots, to seeing problems as the result of current behavior patterns. Each theory is applicable, depending on the specific situation being addressed. While we acknowledge that other theories may be appropriate (e.g., attachment theory or feminist theory), we have chosen to narrow our focus to these three family theories, as together they cover the spectrum of how many family issues develop and how they can be approached. Since clinicians may appreciate a reminder and lay readers may find it helpful to know some of the premises developed by these theories when thinking about family change, we next offer a brief overview of the relevant points of each.

Family Systems Theory

Murray Bowen has written extensively about the importance of differentiation within families, the formation and dangers of triangles, how family patterns are replicated in subsequent generations, emotional cutoffs, and the relevance of birth order.[24] When appropriate, we use these terms throughout this book.

Differentiation refers to an individual's ability to think and act rationally in the context of the family. A high level of differentiation is related to greater individual autonomy. The less differentiated one is, the more that family members can exert their influence and the more emotionally reactive the individual will be. If a sibling is experiencing very strong negative feelings, it may cloud her judgment and be a reflection of less differentiation.

Triangles form, Bowen believed, when people are anxious and unable to resolve issues within a conflicted dyad and they (subconsciously or consciously) pull in a third person to help quell their anxiety. In triangles, by definition, one person, usually one of the original dyad, is excluded from or is in conflict with the other two. That person may feel especially anxious, either anticipating being rejected or actually being rejected. Triangles often include a parent and two siblings (when a parent tries to influence one child through another), two parents and one child (with the marital conflicts being detoured through the child), or three siblings. Triangles established in childhood can have a lifelong impact on sibling relationships.

Family patterns of behavior can be handed down from one generation to the next, which is why family history is so important. Without any differentiation in the family of origin, emotionally reactive children may emerge in the next generation. This can manifest itself in two ways: emotional overinvolvement by a parent or an emotional cutoff between family members.[25] In the case of emotional overinvolvement, a sibling may be too needy for another sibling's attention or for a parent's approval. When growing up, approximately one-quarter of the respondents in the first wave of our study said they felt caught between their parents and their siblings, a situation akin to triangulation.[26] As adults, one-third said they felt they were the mediator or the messenger between their parents and their siblings, a situation that should be avoided in favor of the parent and child communicating directly.

Cutoffs, which occur when people cannot tolerate being around each other and need to establish distance, are a major issue for siblings struggling with their relationships. In Bowen's thinking, they are a sign that emotions are too high and issues are unresolved; the person is still emotionally attached. Denial of the family's importance is another sign of a cutoff, even if there is some contact.[27] Reasonable contact, when people can interact comfortably, is the goal.

Birth order can affect sibling relationships, with siblings often playing complementary roles.[28] For example, oldest children may be raised to assume leadership positions and youngest to follow. Middle children may have characteristics of both, which may be tempered by gender. Younger siblings may be raised to not upstage their older siblings. In such a family environment, success can be difficult to achieve if the eldest has not already achieved it. The actor Leonard Nimoy, who played Mr. Spock in the original *Star Wars* series, once said how happy he was to have been nominated for an Emmy for best supporting actor, even though he had been in a lead role. He said he was raised to not upstage his older brother and being nominated for best actor, rather than supporting actor, would not have been consistent with his own family history.

But if an older sibling has too much success, it may overshadow a younger one's success. The parents' birth order also may influence their expectations for different siblings. If both parents were the youngest children in their families of origin, their oldest child may be given different expectations for leadership than if both parents were the oldest children.

Bowen also is well known for his use of genograms, or family trees, to study intergenerational connections. These genograms often include a brief description of the family member and her or his relationship with other family members. Drawing them can provide insight into how relationships in previous generations may be playing out in the current sibling interactions. A genogram can also show if there are sibling dyads, triads, or more multiple sibling subsystems operating.[29]

Salvador Minuchin and Structural Family Therapy

Some components of structural family therapy, particularly its focus on boundaries, are also helpful in thinking about adult sibling relationships. Developed initially by Salvador Minuchin and others to offer an action-oriented approach to families coping with poverty, structural family therapy has been adapted to work with chronic illness and, most notably, anorexia nervosa.[30] According to this theory, healthy functioning families have a parental executive system in place with a boundary around it so children cannot cross generations and intrude inappropriately into their parents' interactions. In childhood, the parent executive system is in charge of the children's subsystem. The children's subsystem also has a boundary around it that prevents inappropriate intrusion from parents. In addition, the family as a whole has its own identity, or boundary, that helps define who is in and out of the family.

Ideally, in later adulthood and as the parents become frail, the children assume more of a "parenting" role as they take care of their parents. The hierarchy within the sibling set, which is greatly determined by age during childhood, may flatten out in adulthood as siblings establish a more equal relationship and assume more equal responsibilities.

When the boundaries between family members are unclear, people can become enmeshed on one extreme or disengaged on the other. With enmeshment, it is as if they are velcroed to each other. Enmeshment implies extreme closeness with only a few degrees of freedom in which to operate independently and that could look like Bowen's concept of a family member who was not differentiated. Disengagement is the opposite of enmeshment, with too little connection between family members. Enmeshment in childhood and adolescence might lead to children's not making friends outside the family and being stunted socially.[31] Also, echoing Bowen, enmeshment can be connected to triangulation as parents divert their communication with each other through a child and establish a pattern with that child as part of the parental relationship. Disengagement can be characterized by a lack of nurturing, with family members having to fend for themselves rather than obtaining sufficient guidance from a parent.

Similar to Bowen's drawing genograms, structural family therapists use mapping to understand the current relationships and the dysfunctional boundaries between members.

Virginia Satir and Experiential Therapy

The third theory we use is a communications model developed by Virginia Satir. Families have difficulties communicating, Satir believed, when family members have low self-esteem and are not aware of, emotionally and physically, their own presentation style. Her growth-oriented, humanistic philosophy believes in the self-worth of all individuals and the importance of adaptability. She believes that everything can be talked about and that until issues are brought out into the open, they will continue to fester and threaten the family's health.

Destructive communication patterns need to be changed. Common dysfunctional patterns are the *placater*, *blamer*, *distracter*, and *computer*. The *placater* always tries to please and never says what he or she really means. The *blamer* points the finger at others and never takes responsibility for her or his own actions. The *distracter* never stays on message. The *computer* is emotionally removed. According to this theory, the ideal model for healthy communication is the *leveler*, the person who can say what she feels and accept and consider feedback.[32] This role may be helpful in families in which communication is indirect and members are not expressing what they feel.

Finally, a general caution for clinicians when working with clients and for individuals comparing their family dynamics with theoretical ideals, images in popular culture, or their own sibling relationships: Appropriate and healthy levels of closeness in a family vary from one culture to the next, with some cultures encouraging more family togetherness than others do. Any consideration of functional relationships, therefore, needs to pay attention to the cultural dimension of the particular family dynamic.

CONCLUSION

We believe it is important to keep the lenses of affection, ambivalence, and ambiguity front and center when considering the research findings and trying to understand these complex relationships. Affection is a hallmark of many good adult sibling relationships; yet even some of the best have elements of ambivalence and ambiguity. Almost all of the more mixed and the difficult relationships have significant and complicated feelings of ambivalence and ambiguity. In addition to our family therapy theories, we consider recognition of the presence, significance, and normalcy of these three elements essential to any nuanced understanding of adult sibling relationships.

Any book on siblings must encompass such a variety of variables that bringing a summative statement to these lifelong relationships is impossible. These relationships vary by gender, number of siblings, age range, birth order, and the presence of step- and half siblings within the same family. They vary across culture and family history. They also vary in that siblings are dealing with divergent relationships with different siblings at the same time—they feel closer to one sibling than to another—and have to learn how to juggle the often conflicting tugs on the heart that emerge as a result. These relationships are not easy, but they can improve, as we heard, affectionately, from so many.

To put it another way, siblings are like an airport landing strip, always there but more or less difficult to get a fix on, depending on the weather. Sometimes we can find the landing strip by feel, without any help; at other times we need radar for a smooth landing; and at still other times we need help from the control tower to find the airport. Through it all, whether we are circling in a waiting pattern, competing for an arrival slot, or gliding into place, our siblings are an essential part of what both keeps us on the ground and lets us take flight.

CHAPTER 2

Sibling Relationships

STUDIES FROM BIOLOGY, HISTORY, CULTURE, AND RESEARCH

THIS CHAPTER PROVIDES A BRIEF review of the sources of knowledge that may inform people's perceptions and expectations of sibling relationships. These sources are diverse and wide ranging; they include popular culture and social science research, history and nature, religion and politics, literature and biology. Although our focus in this book is on adult sibling relationships, in this chapter we look at studies and discussions of them across the life span because the research supports a developmental trajectory. These relationships progress over time as individuals and families grow and change. Our own study shows that childhood relationships affect adult relationships, and we recognize that a full understanding of any one sibling relationship requires a broad view as well as specific details of the particular siblings. Whereas many of our chapters offer case studies of individual families or siblings, this chapter provides a broader view that we hope will be of interest to siblings seeking to understand their own family and to clinicians working with siblings struggling with their relationships.

THE ORIGIN OF SIBLING RELATIONSHIPS

Other Living Creatures

To trace ecological imperatives related to survival, we begin with the animal kingdom. Douglas Mock, a professor of zoology at the University of Oklahoma, and Geoffrey Parker, a biologist at the University of Liverpool, described how birds, plants, beetles, and mammals negotiate sibling rivalry, reminding us that in a world of limited resources, rivalry is always present.

Altruism, the other side of rivalry and requiring that limited resources be shared, is often pushed aside so that the stronger can survive. Some off-spring sort things out through their competition. In large litters, the big-ger barnyard pigs get the better nursing spots on the mother. Smaller pigs lose and end up in the less productive nursing area and consequently have a shorter life span. In smaller litters, however, this is not an issue.[1] Even mothers play a role in the rivalry, making calculated choices to promote the survival of stronger offspring at the expense of weaker ones when resources are limited. "The daily needs of a young bird or mammal, for example, are often steep and much like those of its nest-mates. At times, the broods' net demands outstrip the parents' provisioning abilities to such a degree that the adults do best by cutting their losses, perhaps ending investment alto-gether."[2] It is not only that parents often produce more offspring than they can or choose to fully support.[3] Comparing mammals and birds, Mock and Parker found that rivalry between mammals is greater. It begins in utero, where more contact occurs than between birds, which are encased in shells with no contact. As both grow, birds take flight and are more apt to leave their home territory, whereas throughout their life, mammals stay closer to where they were born, thus prolonging a possible rivalry.

Moving now to the world in which human siblings live and therapists work, all of us who have grown up in a family can understand the evolu-tionary basis for why parents must balance available resources with their children's relative needs. Families with limited resources must apportion the available supply even more carefully. If there is not enough time, for example, for nurturing to go around or if one child has greater needs, how are resources distributed? Any sibling who has received less, for whatever reason, may question the equity in the division of resources and carry that memory of getting less into their sibling relationships as they age. As a result, for them, adulthood may be about getting back what they feel they are owed. The child who received the resources may not escape either. She may wish that the flow of resources had not come her way or may feel guilty for receiving them if they arrived with an emotional price tag.[4]

Biblical and Mythic Stories

The Bible and its lessons also teach us about sibling rivalry. The entire first book, Genesis, relates story after story of sibling rivalry. From Cain and

Abel we learn not to trust our sibling and not to expect a sibling to "have our back." Driven by jealousy of his God's parent-like favoritism, Cain kills his brother Abel and then is wracked by guilt, denying that he is his "brother's keeper." A few biblical generations later, twins Esau and Jacob, each the favorite of a different parent, compete with each other for a birthright. Then Jacob's favorite son, Joseph, is left for dead by his older brothers, who threw him into a pit far from home. But another lesson emerges here. One of Joseph's brothers breaks from the pack and negotiates for Joseph's survival, albeit by selling him into slavery, teaching us that relationships with our siblings can vary in their loyalty, affection, and level of protection. Rachel and Leah, the best-known first sisters, struggled with jealousy in their relationship when an initially barren Rachel was loved more by Jacob than was her fecund older sister. We learn then that siblings compete with one another for power, their parents' affection, and adult love. Whether or not these religious teachings were meant primarily as morality tales or were historically true, they are among the many traditions that shape Western understandings of age-old sibling travails.

The Bible's stories can be understood in much the same way as oral histories and other mythic tales, which carry powerful messages, are. Lenore Davidoff, a research professor in the Department of Sociology at the University of Essex, argued that brothers and sisters have always had symbolic meaning in folk tales, legends, and mythology. "They surface as a metaphor, as a way of thinking and talking about relatedness. Metaphors help to make sense of individuals' place in the social and natural world, as well as their attempts to come to terms with endlessly troubling psychic processes."[5] Fairy tales teach us about how siblings get along and protect each other (e.g., Hansel and Gretel).[6] They also teach us how stepsiblings can make life more difficult. In *Cinderella*, the heroine is made to work in the kitchen and is treated cruelly by her stepmother and stepsisters.

Literature and Pop Culture

We now move from stories embedded in cultural memory so far back that no one author is known to have shaped a given story, to the era of plays and novels written by individuals whose sibling relationships may be reflected in their creations. Great literature is rife with examples of siblings that have proved instructional for generations as to how they should or should not conduct themselves cooperatively or competitively. For sisters, consider the close-knit Meg, Jo, Beth, and Amy March in Louise May Alcott's *Little Women;* or Goneril, Regan, and Cordelia, King Lear's battling daughters in William Shakespeare's play. Toni Morrison's novels portray a series of strong relationships between sisters, some living and some dead, as well as between women who are considered "sisters" in the expansive definition of who is family in African American culture.[7] For brothers, Fyodor Dostoyevsky's *The Brothers Karamazov* comes to mind, in which four brothers of different origins, including half brothers, full brothers, with one raised in the shadows, compete with one another and even with their father. Sister-brother relationships are easy to find, too. Jem, the older brother, takes care of his sister, Scout, by saving her life in Harper Lee's *To Kill a Mockingbird*. In J. D. Salinger's *Catcher in the Rye,* Holden Caulfield is portrayed as a brother in, at times, an upside-down relationship with his younger sister Phoebe. At one point in the book, she serves as his connection to people, and in the end, he protects her from himself.[8]

This is only a cursory glance at sibling relationships in literature. Many other sources are available for further study, and clients struggling with their sibling relationships also may have their own view of how such interactions should function. Clients may bring up more recent examples from popular culture; for example, they may have just watched an episode of the television series *Downton Abbey* and be reminded of competition between sisters and the roles of the youngest and oldest. Or they may have watched *Modern Family* and thought about their own full-, half-, step-, and adopted-sibling relationships.

Popular culture also presents siblings in the limelight. Fans of the music duo the Everly Brothers may be interested in how Phil and Don's relationship endured after a well-publicized onstage breakup that led to a ten-year estrangement. People battling for custody of a deceased sibling's children may be reminded of the late Michael Jackson and his family. A Fred Astaire movie may remind clients of the dancing relationship between Fred and his sister Adele, who always worked so beautifully in tandem. Sports fans may be inspired by Serena and Venus Williams who formed a strong sister bond that even when they competed against each other, kept them close in the highly individualistic sport of singles tennis in which there can be only one winner. Also in professional tennis are the Bryant brothers, who are identical twins, as well as the Jensen brothers and the Gullikson brothers, who spent their entire careers on playing doubles with each other, with great success. Tennis commentators were likely to say of these brother doubles partners after particularly coordinated play, "It is as if they can read each other's mind."[9]

History and Politics

Less inspiring stories of sibling relationships appear, however, when we turn to the history of siblings in power. Competition for the prince and access to his throne may recall our earlier discussion of fairy tales, but this is not limited to literature. History is full of power plays between royal siblings. The right of accession, for centuries reserved for firstborn males in many cultures, did not prevent vicious challenges. To name only one Western example, in the 1200s, Richard the Lionheart fought in the Crusades while his younger brother clung to power in England and initially resisted returning the throne to him when he returned.

European countries are not unique in their histories of princes and princesses plotting against and even murdering one another to gain power. In Morocco, almost five hundred years ago, Sultan Mulai Ismael competed with his brother Rachid for the throne. After Rachid's death, Ismael then had to deal with Rachid's son, who unsuccessfully fought for power. The legacy that this familial struggle left? After Ismael died, his sons competed for the throne. Chinese emperors with their many concubines often left an unclear line of succession (particularly if the empress did not give birth), and rival sons by different mothers vied for power. The message for those in power? Be wary of your siblings. They are your competition and possibly your enemy.

More recently, in American history, democratic politics eliminated inherited rule and the risks of primogeniture. Nevertheless, sibling relationships always are present in political life. In the 1960s, President John F. Kennedy appointed his younger brother Robert Kennedy as his right-hand man as attorney general and helped his baby brother Teddy run for office. JFK surrounded himself with the most trusted people he knew, his brothers. Still more recently, President George H. W. Bush, the second son of a U.S. senator, preceded his eldest son in the Oval Office. Today, many speculate about whether President George W. Bush's younger brother, Jeb, a former governor of Florida, will compete to be the next Bush-in-chief. In Congress, Democrats Senator Carl Levin and his younger brother,

Representative Sandy Levin, both were members of the Michigan delega-
tion for more three decades. Congressman Joaquin Castro (D-TX) and
Julian Castro, mayor of San Antonio, are twin brothers, both of whom
have chosen political careers.

Cultural and Racial Diversity

Any discussion of cultural differences runs the risk of overgeneralization
and perceptual bias. Nevertheless, recognizing trends in the diverse cultures that have come together in the melting pot of U.S. culture is helpful as
we consider the broad view of sibling relationships. According to research
conducted by historian C. Dallett Hemphill, there are great variations
among ethnic groups in how sibling relationships were maintained at the
time of this country's formation. Europeans who immigrated to the United
States came from cultures with different rules of primogeniture. English
descendants expected their eldest son to inherit their property or, at least,
a portion that was double that inherited by all the other siblings. To keep
their property in the family, fathers would give the land to their sons and
the more impermanent items (cows and cash) to their daughters. In contrast, the early Dutch settlers in New York divided their property equally
among their children without regard to gender.[10] African American and
Native American families define siblings more broadly than do European
American families. For example, in some Native American tribes, such as
the New England Algonquins, cousins were considered siblings. West African societies,[11] from which many slaves came, also had a more horizontal
and less hierarchical family structure. Both Native Americans and African
Americans tended more toward "informal" adoption. Apparently, even
children captured by the Iroquois tribe during a battle with another tribe
could be considered as siblings of the victors.[12] During the United States'
early years, and consistent with its democratic values and the blending of
cultures, sibling relationships became more egalitarian.[13]

The number of children in a family tended to vary, with European
families having the largest number, which is believed to have bred more
competition among siblings.[14] Conversely, competition does not appear
to loom large in Latino families.[15] Even though people from Mexico are
different from those from Cuba and those from Puerto Rico, some commonalities exist in the value placed on family (*familismo*). Latino families

are often described as close-knit, with adult siblings staying in touch with one another and with their parents. Family cohesion is given primacy, and rivalry is discouraged.[16]

Race, of course, intersects with gender in sibling relationships to form a nuanced culture of the family. By the early and middle nineteenth century, a trend was building steam, according to Hemphill, that continues to unfold. Sisters began to play a more distinct gendered role. Hemphill found that older sisters were increasingly expected to take care of younger children until they reached adulthood. At adulthood, when age differences between siblings become less important, sisters were increasingly involved in maintaining relationships with all the siblings. Bonds between sisters became more open, unlike the retreat of men from emotional expressiveness. As Hemphill stated, "Brothers certainly loved each other and did things together, but they communicated less often when apart and tended to discuss the business of the purse rather than the heart."[17] Men invested less in their sibling relationships than did women. Instead, they served as the conduit to the outside world and often helped their siblings by finding them jobs and assisting in their educational and religious upbringing. A twenty-first-century view of men's and women's communication and interaction patterns with each other and with their siblings shows the vestiges of this, with men often characterized as having "shoulder-to-shoulder" friendships and women as having "face-to-face" friendships. Men get together and do things with their male friends, and women are more likely to get together to talk.[18] One study found sibling bonds to be closer, with more confiding and contact, when the sibling set contained at least one sister.[19]

Changes continued in our concept of sisters and brothers. As recently as fifty years ago, according to Davidoff, the civil rights movement, flower power, and feminism helped establish "sisterhood" as signifying unity. The terms *brother* and *sister* for nonrelatives came into the vernacular, especially for African Americans, and indicated equality between the genders.[20] Today, we even have the term *Bro-mance*, symbolizing closeness between unrelated men who are fond of each other in a nonsexual way. Even though the interplay of gender and sexuality is complex, society's greater acceptance of gays and lesbians reflects a less circumscribed understanding of traditional male and female sexual behavior. Likewise, the greater number of options for our intimate and familial behavior may continue to flatten the roles of brother and sister in the family.

Being aware of the history of sibling relationships, current news, and pop culture, as well as the complexity of rich cultural and gender differences, can be useful when helping clients understand their own relationships with their siblings. Whether it is actively bringing these relationships into the therapy or being able to respond to the associations made by the client who says, "I really envy how the Obama daughters get along," having an awareness of these relationships can enhance clients' connections to their past, present, and future ties to their siblings.

Finally, informed clinicians must be familiar with the current social science research related to their practice. Accordingly, the following literature review will be of most interest to them.

SOCIAL SCIENCE RESEARCH

From research on the nature and dynamics of sibling relationships, we know that individuals who report maintaining close, supportive, satisfactory relationships with their siblings throughout adulthood also have enhanced well-being. People who have difficult or stressful relationships with siblings may wonder why their relationships are not like those positive relationships. Typically, the adult client who is struggling with a sibling relationship, in addition to needing assistance with the unique aspects of that relationship, wonders whether any common sibling configurations, circumstances, or sibling and family structures play a part in the relationship difficulties. To that end, we offer an outline of what the research says about sibling relationships in regard to the impact of family structure (birth order and gender), family dynamics (parental favoritism and gender), and life circumstances (disability and loss) that can be sources of stress.

As noted, storytellers and writers have found the dynamics of sibling relationships worthy of attention for centuries, whereas social science scholars and clinicians have only recently turned their attention to the nature and impact of such relationships. Inspired for the past 125 years by Sigmund Freud's developmental theory, the main focus for both scholars and clinicians has been the parent-child relationship. From there, they turned to the spousal relationship, clearly a central relationship in the psychosocial lives of many adults. Only in the past fifty years have researchers begun to study the influence of sibling relationships on child development, around the same time they began seeing development as a lifelong process, which led to investigating sibling interactions and associated outcomes in adulthood.

In the early 1960s, Donald Irish, a sociologist, presaged this emerging attention on sibling dynamics when he lamented, "Thus far, social scientists have rarely attempted to conduct statistical studies to explore the significance that brothers and sisters have for each other."[21] A decade later, in 1971, Lillian Troll, a psychologist and scholar of life-span development in families, published a review of research on family relationships in middle age and beyond.[22] In this seminal review, she described both the longer life spans and the research comparing relationships between family members while observing that most such research mentioned adult sibling relationships only "in passing" or included them in the category of "other relatives." Troll also characterized this research as "preliminary" and noted the complex and equivocal pattern of findings in which the "obligatory" nature of kinship ties sometimes was stronger than that of friendships. In other studies, though, people reported their level of intimacy and mutual dependence to be higher for friends than siblings. Five years later, in 1976, Jane Pfouts, a social work scholar, complaining about the dearth of research on the nature and impact of sibling relationships, observed,

> For better or for worse, siblings must involuntarily spend long hours, days, and years together. Over these long years they help to build one another's identity through interaction . . . [which] is more likely to be stressful and volatile than that in most other human relationships because the sibling relationship is so firmly rooted in ambivalence.[23]

Pfouts's observation about the ambivalence that can characterize sibling relationships foreshadowed the findings of subsequent research, including our own. Irish's and Pfouts's intentions were to draw the interests of both researchers and practitioners to the importance of sibling relationships to psychosocial development and well-being.

It worked. In 1983, Judy Dunn wrote a review of the research on sibling relationships that had been published in the previous seven years.[24] Based on the findings of the ten studies that comprised this seminal cluster of scholarship, she identified several patterns of findings regarding sibling behavior in families. First, she detailed the observational research of families at home, which revealed that siblings are with, and interact with, one another as much or more frequently than with their mothers. These in-home observational studies also revealed the high number of infants imitating the behavior of older siblings (which, according to several important developmental theories, is how children learn how to think and behave). This observation foreshadowed subsequent studies looking at sibling relationships through an attachment lens.[25]

Dunn herself highlighted the attachment relationships of younger siblings with their older siblings, in which the younger sibling misses the older sibling when absent and seeks out the older sibling for comfort when distressed, especially when the mother is not present. Such findings suggest that younger siblings develop attachment bonds to their older siblings. Dunn also noted that some of the studies she reviewed had found what were termed *mismatched* interactions, typically observed as hostile behavior from an older sibling responding to warm behavior from a younger sibling. Such out-of-sync patterns, that is, a younger sibling seeking more or a different contact from an older sibling, often marked the overall interactional pattern in such sibling dyads. Neither these studies nor Dunn discussed birth-order-related attachment patterns in the context of mismatched interactions, but it is an interesting topic to consider when dealing with certain types of sibling relationships.

Nevertheless, and important to note, Dunn's literature review also found that a high level of affection had been observed among siblings. This finding contrasted with the common thinking about sibling rivalry, conflict, and aggression held by many at the time. This affection—characterized by friendly, cooperative, and reciprocal help-giving interactions—was also found to increase as children aged. Similar to Pfouts's recognition of ambivalence in sibling relationships, Dunn's finding that these studies shared observations of sibling-to-sibling affection is echoed in our findings about the majority of sibling relationships in adulthood.

From these initial studies grew a body of research exploring the nature and influence of sibling relationships across the life span. The preponderance of that research reveals that most sibling relationships are constructive: affectionate, supportive, and a source of consistent positive impact across time. These positive dynamics have been linked to increased well-being (higher self-esteem, less loneliness, and less depression) for the individuals who are fortunate to have healthy sibling relationships in childhood that have lasted into adulthood.

FAMILY STRUCTURE AND SIBLING RELATIONSHIPS

Next we review attachment theory, which has proved useful in understanding the impact of close, long-lasting relationships that provide psychological safety, security, and support. Several researchers have investigated sibling relationships by applying attachment theory, which was initially conceptualized in the study of the impact of parent-child bonds on psychosocial development.

Emerging from Freud's work on the parent-child relationship, John Bowlby and Mary Ainsworth delved deeper into the parent-child bond and furthered our understanding of how those early childhood attachments influence psychosocial development when such attachments are securely formed and maintained. Their attachment theory has also helped explain how other relationships that begin in childhood or are long-lasting may have significant positive or negative psychosocial developmental consequences in predicting life struggles.

In fact, some of the first research on adult sibling relationships in the 1980s built on Bowlby's and Ainsworth's work on the development of attachment theory.[26] Given the efficacy of attachment theory to inform both research and practice related to the parent-child bond, its application to sibling research made sense. Like parent-child relationships, sibling relationships typically begin in infancy or early childhood; are constant, consistent, and close (both in proximity and emotionally); last for decades (typically longer even than parents); and can be sources of safety and security in both childhood and later life. That research showed that attachment ties between siblings last across the life span.

Bowlby's foundation for the development of attachment theory was his decades of both clinical practice and research on children's mental health problems.[27] While in psychiatric training in the 1930s, working with children and youth with serious mental health issues, Bowlby rejected the then prevalent Freudian assumption that children's psychological problems originated in their own aggressive and libidinal drives. Rather, Bowlby suspected those struggles had originated in the real-life events and relationships in the children's lives.[28] For children to be healthy, those relationships should include nurturance, support, and safety. Those who developed serious mental health problems often had early childhood relationships characterized by loss, abandonment, neglect, or abuse. Informed by that thinking, Bowlby met with the parents of the children he treated to talk to them about their own lives and their struggles raising their "disturbed" child, with the goal of positively influencing the parent-child relationship in order to help all the children (and siblings) in that family.[29]

Most social scientists and mental health professionals would now strongly agree that early relationships have a critical influence on the development of psychological, social, emotional, and behavioral health and functioning. Clearly, the early relationships with parents and caregivers are the closest and most vital, and for those who grow up with siblings, those relationships are clearly both developmentally and proximally the next closest.

In 1989 Ainsworth applied attachment theory to relationships other than those with a parent or other primary caregiver, including those with siblings.[30] She created several scenarios in which siblings might develop attachment bonds. Most notably, older siblings in many families and cultures took on caretaking roles toward younger siblings, so younger siblings predictably might develop attachment bonds with their older sibling(s). Ainsworth further suggested that siblings separated from their parents may attach to one another for mutual security and support. She also noted the great closeness that develops among siblings as the earliest playmates and with whom they shared extensive life experiences. Finally, siblings can be helpful throughout life in times of struggle, stress, or loss and are the people with whom many develop "enduring affectional bonds," to use her phrase.[31]

Using attachment theory's core concepts of proximity seeking, safe haven, separation protest, and secure base, Australian psychologist Judith Feeney and others examined the attachment networks of adults, including those with siblings.[32] This research revealed that sibling relationships in adulthood clearly demonstrate attachment bonds. In a study of attachment relationships among young adults, the respondents reported that sibling relationships contain three out of four key elements of an attachment relationship: emotional closeness (an aspect of proximity seeking), feelings of comfort (an aspect of safe haven), and a relationship that provides feelings of security (secure base).

In a later study across the adult life span, Feeney and colleagues found that by far the strongest reported attachments were to the participants' spouse/partner. Attachment to children and friends came next, followed by mothers and siblings, with nearly the same strength of attachment. Another noteworthy finding from this study, which fits the perspective of seeing sibling relationships on a developmental trajectory, is that sibling attachment was highest for younger adults and single and single-parent adults, diminished for partnered and parenting middle-aged adults, and then stronger again for older adults. In fact, age and parent status revealed interactive effects with sibling attachment, with the strongest adult sibling attachments reported by childless middle-aged and older adults. Feeney and her colleagues also found differences by gender, with males reporting stronger attachments to fathers and friends and females reporting both more attachment relationships and stronger attachments to spouses, children, siblings, and mothers. In addition, both genders reported more attachments to females. This pattern suggests not only that females make more attachments but also that they are more attractive figures with which to form attachment relationships. This conclusion is most likely based on females providing the types of relationships characterized by comfort giving, support, and safety, which is what humans seek in attachment relationships. There are lessons here for brothers (and fathers and husbands).

Although affection and attachment are core characteristics of childhood sibling relationships, these relationships change over time during individual siblings' maturation, changing family circumstances, and the family's developmental stage. While childhood siblings spend a great deal of time together and often are affectionate, it is important to note that they too may experience significant conflict, even aggression. Such conflicts, however, tend to peak in adolescence and typically dissipate in young adulthood. For example, research shows that the psychological and physical distance created in young adulthood when siblings may no longer live together and develop their own identities leads to siblings rediscovering one another and developing more healthy relationships.[33] In fact, in re-forming their bonds, young adult siblings use the same kind of *commitment* behaviors with their siblings that they use with potential romantic partners.[34] Such commitment behaviors include various types of support, shared activities, protection, and intimate though nonsexual play and talk. On the cusp of adulthood, then, a typical child may have felt affection for and experienced rivalry with a sibling, gotten into teenage conflicts, and then outgrown the more negative aspects of relationships as he achieved greater autonomy and forged new relationships.

The sibling relationship research literature uncovered other significant patterns associated with gender. For example, Michelle Van Volkom and her colleagues examined the impact of family structure on sibling relationships, including gender, birth order, and age spacing among college students.[35] Sisters were much more likely than brothers to report that if their closest sibling were not their brother or sister, they still would be friends with him or her. Sisters were also more likely to report being friends with a sibling and turning to a sibling when needing support at a difficult time in their life. In regard to birth order, Van Volkom and colleagues found that youngest siblings were more likely to compare themselves with their nearest-age sibling than with their middle or oldest siblings. Partial support was found for comparison and for conflict between siblings being more likely when the age gap was smaller.

While much of the research has concentrated on children and young adults, Victor Cicirelli, studying families in the 1980s, was interested in attachments between older adults and their siblings. In interviews with eighty-three adults aged sixty-one to ninety-one, Cicirelli found that attachment to sisters led to greater well-being in later adulthood for both sisters and brothers, whereas attachment to brothers had no effect.[36] This echoes the preceding research supporting the benefits of having a sister. Cicirelli measured well-being as an absence of depressive symptoms, and he based the degree of attachment on reports of closeness, conflict, and indifference. So when adults reported being closer to sisters, they also reported less depression. If they reported conflict with or indifference to their sisters, they reported more depressive symptoms. It is important to note that sisters reported greater closeness to their sisters and only slightly less closeness to their brothers, with brothers who had no sisters having the least closeness. Interestingly, Cicirelli found no differences in regard to gender in the amount of conflict and indifference experienced.

Today, most people would define well-being as more than a lack of depression. Similarly, our understanding of attachment is now more complex than measures of closeness, conflict, and indifference. We could also anticipate that gender roles in families have changed from those thirty years ago for people now in their sixties, seventies, or eighties. Nonetheless, this seminal study shows that sibling relationships last across the life span and affect psychological functioning.

Parental Favoritism

Favoritism by parents is an issue that research has shown hurts the disfavored child. Less often studied is the adverse impact of favoritism on a favored child, on the relationship between the siblings, and on the relationships between each child and the parents. In many families in which parental favoritism is felt in childhood and adulthood, research suggests that the impact on sibling relationships is negative.

Social work professors Ricky Finzi-Dottan (Bar-Ilan University) and Orna Cohen (Tel Aviv University)[37] surveyed 202 young adults about their perceptions of being treated differently than their siblings by their parents. They found a consistent pattern by gender of the impact of parental favoritism. When mothers showed favoritism, respondents reported a decrease in warmth between siblings but no impact on sibling conflict. But when fathers showed favoritism, respondents reported increased conflict between siblings but no impact on warmth. They also found a difference in the magnitude of the effect, with a father's favoritism having a larger impact than a mother's favoritism. The authors recommended more research to determine why differences appeared between fathers and mothers.

Similarly, Alexander Jensen and colleagues,[38] whose work we mentioned in the first chapter, collected data from 151 pairs of young adult siblings on their treatment by their mothers and fathers, also asking about their sibling relationships and psychological well-being. When compared with siblings who felt that they and their siblings had received equal treatment from their parents, all those siblings who perceived differential treatment by their parents reported higher rates of depression. That was true for both those siblings who felt they received less support and for those who felt they received more support from their parents relative to their sibling. In addition, those who felt they received less support from their parents than their sibling also reported less intimacy in the sibling relationship in young adulthood. Furthermore, there were significant patterns in those findings by gender of both parent and sibling and the extent of the differential treatment reported. For example, when mothers treated their children very differently, both the more favored and the less favored siblings reported similarly greater depression. Yet when fathers showed favoritism, the psychological well-being of only same-gender sibling dyads (two brothers or two sisters) was hurt, especially the less favored. In short, young adult sibling relationships were best for all siblings when children perceived their parents as not showing favoritism.

In a study of 1,020 middle-aged adults, Thomas Boll and colleagues[39] similarly found that their respondents' perception of parental favoritism during middle adulthood had negative effects for both the favored and the disfavored on their emotions and behaviors toward siblings, with greater negative effects on those middle-aged adults who reported being the less favored. Favoritism also hurt these siblings' relationships with their parents, with the best relationships reported by those who felt a little favored. Parent-adult child relationships were considerably worse for the disfavored and only slightly better for those extremely favored than for those disfavored.

Finally, in a study based on 299 elderly mothers and 774 of their adult children, Sociologist Megan Gilligan and colleagues[40] found that parental favoritism affected adult siblings' conflict (tension and arguments) and closeness (loving and caring). Maternal favoritism remembered from childhood was associated with less closeness and more conflict between siblings, while reports of favoritism in adulthood predicted only less closeness.

Next we look at research regarding family situations that often lead to parents' differential treatment of siblings but that are not due to a clear case of favoritism. Rather, they are due to one sibling arguably needing more time, attention, and energy from the parents than the other sibling(s) do.

When One Sibling Struggles

Significant challenges for one sibling, for example, a traumatic brain injury, Down syndrome, or autism, can affect the entire family system. Research has zeroed in on how these and other health issues[41] in adulthood affect both the sibling who has the disability and the sibling who often received less attention from the parents in childhood and then may be called on in adulthood to be the sibling's protector and caretaker. Similar to all adult sibling relationships, the research suggests that the majority of adult siblings of individuals with disabilities maintain close, caring, and ongoing relationships with their struggling sibling.[42]

Adult siblings who have a brother or sister with a developmental disability often feel responsible for that sibling when the parents' abilities to care for that sibling diminish. This issue has increasing significance now that medical advancements have lengthened the lives of children born with developmental and other disabilities. Frequently, these responsibilities come just as the adult children also are having to care for parents and their own young children.

How do such issues affect siblings and their relationships? Disabilities researchers Gael Orsmond and Marsha Seltzer[43] surveyed 154 adults with siblings who had Down syndrome or autism spectrum disorder and uncovered several factors that affected these relationships. First, siblings' relationships were closer when the siblings providing care used a problem-solving approach with their sibling with a disability. Relationships were also closer, as predicted, when the siblings lived closer to one another. Interestingly, closer relationships were also reported when the caretaking sibling was more optimistic about the future of the disabled sibling and when they reported that the disabled sibling had not damaged their own relationship with their parents.

In another survey study of adult siblings of individuals with Down syndrome or autism spectrum disorder, Robert Hodapp and Richard Urbano, researchers from Vanderbilt Kennedy Center,[44] found that when caretaking siblings felt that there may be more rewards (e.g., becoming more compassionate, more understanding of differences, and more empathetic) from being the sibling of an individual with a disability, they reported closer relationships. Furthermore, such closer relationships predicted more frequent and lengthier contacts. Closer relationships also were reported when the sibling with the disability was more independent and had fewer behavioral problems. In addition, researchers have explored the effects on sibling relationships when a sibling has suffered a traumatic brain injury (TBI) that leads to disabilities. Although in many ways different from a developmental disability that has existed since infancy, some of the issues related to adult siblings who are responsible for caring for a sibling with a disability when parents are no longer able to provide that care are the same. Charles Degeneffe and Marjorie Olney, professors at San Diego State University, surveyed 280 adult siblings who were taking care of siblings who had been disabled by a TBI.[45] While expressing a commitment to caring for their sibling, these caretaking siblings were most concerned about the quality of care their siblings would receive in the future. They also were concerned about their sibling's relationships with other members of the family and about the sibling's ability to become independent, hoping that social services would increase the sibling's functional capacity and independence.

Charles Degeneffe and Ruth Lynch, drawing on the same sample of sibling caretakers,[46] found depressive symptoms in 39 percent of the caretaking siblings. Those with access to social support had fewer such symptoms. Also, contradicting their hypothesis, an increase in the caretaking burden was associated with a *reduction* in reported depression, suggesting that the depressive symptoms found were not due to the extent of caretaking they provided for a sibling. Instead, the greater number of reports of depression was due to the loss of valued family activities, something that could certainly be maintained with a conscious effort. Finally, in a qualitative study by Degeneffe and Olney,[47] again using the same sample and asking how the siblings' lives had changed since a sibling had incurred a TBI, they reported the biggest issue was that medical professionals did not recognize how much their sibling's injury and subsequent struggles had affected them personally; that is, whereas the parents and children of the injured person are attended to, the siblings often are not.

Sibling Loss and Bereavement

One final component of the sibling relationship needs to be addressed: loss as part of the natural life span. The loss of a sibling in infancy can produce what University of Wyoming social work professors Diane Kempson and Vicki Murdock referred to as the loss of a sibling "never known."[48] Similar to a TBI incurred by a sibling, in this case of loss the sibling grief is often invisible. In their interviews with fifteen surviving adult siblings who had lost a sibling in infancy, some before and some after they were born, Kempson and Murdock asked them to tell the story of their lost sibling. Three major themes emerged. First, all these siblings worked to keep the memory of their sibling alive. In this pursuit, some told stories about the sibling, had a party each year on the sibling's birthday, or visited the sibling's grave. Second, feelings of deep loss permeated their lives for years, a loss exacerbated by others who did not recognize or even know about the death. Third, most interviewees had trouble making sense of the loss, the loss of something they had never had (as Pauline Boss might say, an "ambiguous loss"). Because it occurred in childhood and was not acknowledged by others, it was particularly difficult to resolve.

University of Pennsylvania nursing professors Linda Robinson and Margaret Mahon[49] reviewed the research on the loss of a sibling in early adulthood and presented scenarios illustrating how siblings experience such a loss. In what they described as a typical case, the sibling is preoccupied with the loss, for example, has developed a fear when driving if the sibling died in a car accident and, while experiencing serious grief, takes on a supportive role with the parents as they struggle with the loss. In their example, the parents have moved away to avoid thinking about the loss, and the surviving sibling is having to clean out and sell the family home. Once again, the pattern of a sibling's grief being difficult continues, even though the social systems surrounding siblings do not seem to recognize or respond to the loss.[50]

These studies looked at loss from childhood to early adulthood, but in later life, loss of a sibling also can take an enormous toll, though it may be moderated by the surviving siblings' other relationships. The number of siblings and the nature of the relationship with each all can affect the surviving sibling's reaction. In a recent study of 150 people aged sixty-five to ninety-seven, Cicirelli found, as expected, that the fear of death increased with the loss of a sibling as the feeling of vulnerability grew. In addition, the closeness of the surviving siblings grew as other siblings died. Depressive symptoms were more common among surviving siblings who had lost a sibling with whom they had had an unsatisfactory relationship.[51] The pain of losing a sibling in later life also was shown in research undertaken almost twenty years ago at Duke University, in which 3,173 elders living in the community were found to suffer more from the loss of a sibling than from the loss of a spouse or close friend.[52]

Perhaps pointing to the complexity of this topic, a Swiss study of 717 people aged eighty to eighty-four put the loss in a different perspective. Those study participants who had lost a spouse or child suffered the most depressive symptoms, followed by those who had lost a close friend. The loss of a sibling, while upsetting, had the least effect. While family ties frequently strengthened after the loss of a child or spouse, no such strengthening was noted after the loss of a sibling. One result was that the suffering sibling was left without as much support as that given to someone who had lost a spouse or child. Gender was not a significant variable in how people reacted to the death of a loved one.[53]

CONCLUSION

At the risk of simplifying any of these findings, we will try to bring together a few of the key lessons that can be learned from this brief review. More extensive literature reviews are available, from both the studies we cited and other scholars.

First, for most adults with siblings, these relationships are vital sources of affection and support, which can enhance well-being throughout middle and later adulthood. Attachment theory is one approach to considering the strengths of these connections. For those who do not find their adult sibling relationships satisfying, the research suggests that efforts to form a more positive relationship with adult siblings lead to greater well-being; that is, getting along with one's siblings is good for one's health.

Second, older siblings should be mindful that younger siblings may look to them for comfort and support when they are in need, potentially a repeat of patterns from years before. Likewise, younger siblings should be mindful that older siblings may be seeking a more reciprocal relationship than the one developed in childhood.

Third, parental favoritism in its various forms can hurt both the favored *and* the unfavored and can damage their sibling relationships throughout their lives. We are just beginning to understand the impact of a father's, versus a mother's, showing favoritism, but discussing each separately and not as a unit in therapy could help in understanding their individual legacies.

Fourth, when children have significant life struggles, they may need help from their siblings in some form throughout their life, and this may create a positive bond if both have appropriate and sufficient additional supports. Recognition by professionals, as well as family members, of the impact on the caretaking siblings of their siblings' special needs helps support all siblings and their relationships.

Fifth, the loss of a sibling, particularly at a young age, leaves an enduring legacy. The impact and grief created by the loss of a sibling over the life span is often not recognized and frequently leaves the sibling(s) in an ambiguous state of grief.

Finally, according to many studies and across the life span, sisters are more emotionally connected to the family than brothers are. Brothers and sisters should therefore keep these differences in mind as they negotiate their adult relationships with their siblings.

PART 2

What We Learned About Siblings from Our Research

CHAPTER 3

Sibling Relationships in Middle to Late Adulthood

WHAT'S AGE GOT TO DO WITH IT?

HOW DO WE CAPTURE SOMETHING as multifaceted as a relationship with one sibling or a set of sibling relationships? Like a Lego set, these relationships build on one another, with each piece affecting the overall family structure and offering seemingly infinite possible configurations. We looked at adult sibling relationships in varying ways through the use of two tools: a questionnaire with a standardized scale and semistructured in-depth interviews with all respondents. We learned about siblings' satisfaction with their relationships, the importance of their relationships, the nature of those relationships now and in childhood, the frequency and type of contact between siblings, their geographic proximity, and the words they use to characterize their siblings. The scale used explores the feelings, behaviors, and beliefs in their relationships.[1] Together, these inquiries provide a complicated picture of the role of siblings in American family life that is often characterized by affection but also by ambivalence and ambiguity. Yes, sibling relationships are quite important to the majority of those we interviewed. But some of these relationships also appeared to be a balloon about to burst if just one more puff of air were to stress its tensile strength. And occasionally, as we wrote earlier, siblings can be like an airport landing strip, always there but difficult to find in stormy weather without some outside assistance.

In this chapter, we describe our sample's responses to our questions and look at them with a focus on the variable of age. Age and the period of time in which siblings were raised are important to understanding sibling relationships because a therapist treating a fifty-five-year-old who wants to work on her sibling relationships will be confronting familial experiences unlike those raised by a forty-year-old or a seventy-year-old. In addition to considering their unique family histories, clinicians benefit from understanding how the range of normative sibling experiences are shaped by both the different eras in which those three different clients were raised and the different life stages that they and their siblings currently are in.

Age is a difficult concept to gauge; it is more than a number because it encompasses both context and time period. Children of divorce are said to grow up a little faster, as are those born in war zones or pressed into battle in childhood. We all know children who grew up amid the trappings of comfort who nonetheless struggle as adults, as well as children who faced an array of challenges who grew up to be well-adjusted and successful adults. Experiences can age family members disproportionately or help them feel young and optimistic. Generational differences are a common topic for researchers to explore, and through the questionnaire responses and the qualitative interviews, we searched for clues to understanding what may appear in therapy in siblings seeking help.

We examined age from a number of perspectives. We first looked at the age of the sibling who was interviewed and compared young and old interviewees. To go further, we looked at the average age of a sibling set; that is, we considered the sibling who was interviewed and all his siblings and derived a mean age.[2] We also split the sample in half and compared youngest (forty to fifty-five) with oldest (fifty-six to ninety).

Finally, we grouped siblings into three age categories based on co-occurrence of life stage and cultural generation (which we discuss in the next section). The oldest siblings in our sample, those aged sixty-six and older, born between 1921 and 1945, have been referred to as the "silent generation."[3] They are retired, with grown children; most of their parents are dead; and they are facing their own and their siblings' mortality. The next group are the baby boomers, aged fifty-one to sixty-five.[4] They are often at or near the peak of their careers and are likely to be dealing with the care of infirm or dying parents or the aftermath of their parents' deaths while trying to support their own children in their late teens and early twenties. The odds of having a sibling who has died are greater in this than the next group, especially the older baby boomer siblings. The youngest siblings, labeled Generation X (Gen X), aged forty to fifty, usually have at least one parent, and often both parents, still alive and needing little assistance. Gen Xers are focused on raising their school-aged children and building or consolidating their careers. No matter how we consider age, these three sibling groups have come of age during vastly different eras and have families in dramatically different stages of growth and decline.

SIBLINGS IN CONTEXT

When considering sibling relationships, we cannot concentrate on only their chronological age and remove them from the broader social context in which they were raised. The times in which we live shape our view of the family's ecology and the connections that siblings feel toward one another. While those we interviewed ranged in age from forty to ninety (the oldest being born in 1922 and with a living sibling born in 1915), their full siblings, half and stepsiblings, and adopted siblings ranged from twenty-one to ninety-seven. Thus our sample includes at least three distinct cultural generations, as suggested by the names of these groups, who grew up in very different historical periods. While it is impossible to generalize the experiences of an entire generation, we can highlight certain events that likely influenced many members of that generation.

In his *Children of the Great Depression*, sociologist Glen Elder described a cohort of 167 people born in the early 1920s from Oakland, California, who were followed for forty years. Our oldest cohort contained people who were born between 1922 and 1945, and they could have shared much of the historical-cultural experience of Elder's cohort. Growing up when they did, their values regarding family were transformed multiple times. Almost all those whom Elder studied had served in World War I or II or had a close family member who did. As adults, many witnessed race riots, war protests, great economic booms, and, eventually, low unemployment rates. Gender roles changed when women went to factories and men to war. For much of their lives, races were separate and considered unequal; homosexuality was kept deep in the closet. Children were supposed to "mind their elders," and neighbors in urban and rural communities watched out for one another. The oldest in this cohort could have given birth to children who served in the Vietnam War or demonstrated against it. By their retirement in the 1980s and 1990s, home computers and cell phones had become commonplace. In the later stages of their lives, they might struggle to manipulate iPods, iPads, and iPhones, technologies that their children and grandchildren consider user friendly. What the members of this cohort brought to their sibling relationships was shaped by their family structure, their social and cultural environment, and the weight and buoyancy of growing up when they did. Someone born in 1925 might have been part of a newly arriving immigrant wave from Europe or Asia, the child of an immigrant, or the grandchild of an immigrant. An African American born in 1925 could have a grandparent born in slavery.

The boomers, born between 1946 and 1964, were raised in more prosperous, permissive, and potentially pessimistic times marked by greater upheaval in the nation. The strong postwar economic and education boom of the 1950s was coupled with the threat of annihilation from the Soviet Union. The powerlessness experienced with the assassinations of white and black leaders in the 1960s was coupled with civil rights and antiwar protests, urban riots spawned by decades of poverty and racism, the passage of voting rights bills, the resignation of a president, and the end of an unpopular war. Music dividing generations, the proliferation of birth control, the loosening of sexual mores, and spiking divorce rates affected the family's structure and communication patterns and the family members' treatment of one another.

The youngest siblings in our research, those born between 1964 and 1973,[5] came of age in the 1980s and early 1990s during a period of more incremental social change relative to that of previous eras. This generation grew up watching more television than previous generations, with the growth of cable TV networks and the advent of the twenty-four-hour news cycle. Politically, the country took a turn toward the more conservative, with twelve consecutive years of Presidents Ronald Reagan and George H. W. Bush in the White House. At the same time, serious drug abuse proliferated; AIDS exploded; and gay rights activism hit the ramparts. Dramatic population shifts, as epitomized earlier by the great migration of blacks from the South, began reversing, and urban centers lost residents. African Americans returned to the South, and older generations of all racial backgrounds moved south and west. New immigrant groups from Asia and Africa began arriving. Family members moved farther from one another, although improved means of communication kept distant members only a keystroke away.

Selective data provide a thumbnail sketch of just how dramatic these broader changes have been across these three cohorts' lifetimes. In the early 1930s, according to the U.S. Bureau of the Census, more than 82 percent of births were conceived after marriage, and by the 1990s, fewer than half were conceived after marriage. Between 1990 and 2010, the rates of both marriage and divorce fell. The census bureau also reported that in regard to our oldest cohort, by age forty, nearly 15 percent of women and men born between 1925 and 1934 had divorced. Of those born between 1945 and 1954, twice as many had split up by that age.[6] By the last half of the twentieth century, married-couple households had declined from 78 to 52 percent of all households. Although at the beginning of the twentieth century, the typical U.S. household contained seven or more people, by 1940 and through the end of the century, the typical household contained two people. And in 1970, women were householders in 21 percent of homes, but by 2000, they were householders in 36 percent of homes.[7]

As mentioned, many of the siblings in our study lived through an economic boom. Unemployment averaged 4 percent between 1948 and 1953. Fifty-five years later, it spiked to more than 9 percent. In 1920, approximately 20 percent of women were in the workforce; now it is close to 50 percent.[8] Over that same time period, religiosity declined. Various observers of religious trends cite the 1950s as a peak in attendance at religious services, with the vast majority of Americans stating an interest in some religious tradition. Religions' importance and attendance have dropped off since then. By 1970, the percentage of Americans believing that religion was in decline reached 70 percent, five times what it had been thirteen years earlier. This trend continued into the twenty-first century, with a Gallup poll finding a drop in religiosity from 73 percent in 2005 to 60 percent in 2012.

During our respondents' lifetimes, then, there were profound shifts in religious service attendance, women's participation in the workforce, marriage and divorce patterns, and residential mobility. Add to this the greater acceptance of gays and lesbians, people who choose not to marry, choose to intermarry, or choose to marry and not have children. We thus are presented with a panoramic view both of how siblings raised in the 1930s could construct sibling relationships different from those of siblings born two generations later and of how the time in which one is born shapes how family relationships are formed and evolve.

CASE STUDIES: SIBLING RELATIONSHIPS
IN DIFFERENT AGE GROUPS

While no one case can represent any age group, we offer the following three, one from the Gen Xers, one from the baby boomers, and one from the silent generation as a way to clarify some of our findings and also to point out the complexity and changing nature of sibling relationships.

Amelia, a Gen Xer

Amelia is a white, forty-seven-year-old illustrator with a brother four years her junior. She is unmarried and has no children. As she describes her relationship with her brother, we hear many common themes brought up by the siblings we interviewed. These include the joy that a parent, in this case Amelia's mother, feels when children are closer than the parent was to her siblings, the different roles played by older and younger siblings, how siblings work together to interpret and respond to their parents' behavior, and how relationships evolve with age.

> Our relationship is important because we only have each other. He's my only sibling. My mother has a very up-and-down relationship with her only sibling. She says to me now, "I am so happy that you and your brother get along." He and I don't talk on the phone all the time because we have opposite work schedules. We'll email occasionally. I realize we are going to have each other longer than we are going to have our parents. I think [because] I am single and he's divorced, it is particularly important to maintain some family bond.

Amelia's view, as we noted, is typical of the approximately four-fifths of our sample who said their relationship with siblings was important or very important, with sisters more likely than brothers to give this rating. That does not mean, however, that their relationships are always easy. As many others did, in her description of her relationship with her brother she cites both gender and age differences as challenges to their closeness. She also describes the paradox of protecting someone but also demanding adult behavior. In that part of her dynamic with her brother, we see two characteristics of this younger cohort: both parents are still alive, and one sibling is continuing to have trouble getting launched.

My brother's had kind of a struggle coming into adulthood. He's younger and I think those dynamics, I was a stereotypically bossy older sister. . . . He lived with my parents a lot longer and is still struggling in terms of deciding what he wants to be when he grows up. So I feel more the older sibling than us being on equal footing. I'm protective of him, but I am the one who expects more from him and wants him to take greater responsibility.

At the same time, and in a way that somewhat weakens the hierarchy of herself and her brother that Amelia describes, they are joined on the same plane in reference to their parents. From a structural family therapy viewpoint, she dynamically shifts from one subsystem, shared with her brother, to a parental one in which she takes care of him or sets expectations for him.

He's like the only witness to how crazy my parents are [laughs]. He'll call and say "We have to talk about Mom's hair. She dyed it a crazy color." We are able to laugh at my parents' quirks. I can take things kind of seriously, and he punctures that. If he is thinking about something jobwise, or I am going through something, we use each other as a sounding board.

The relationship teeters between Amelia's taking charge of him and being able to rely on him. They were not always as close as they are now. Some big sister–little brother relationships play out with the older one playing the benevolent caretaker role; others have the younger sibling depicted as a pest. Theirs had some of both but verged more on the caretaking role as they reached adulthood.

We fought a lot when we were kids until I was in my teens. I am not sure who my parents' favorite is, which is good. A parent's love for their kids is ideally limitless, but attention isn't limitless. It's a limited resource because there is only so much time and sometimes kids need more attention. There was a strong rivalry. Then I got to be a teenager, and he started to hang around with my friends a bit, and that was fine so we got close. But one difficulty was he lived with my parents until he was twenty-eight. He didn't want to go to college, and we sort of forced him to go. I found his not wanting to go hard to relate to. He also had a drinking problem for years. So there were times when he was engulfed in his own life and not taking responsibility.

There's a constant worry about someone who has a problem like that. He was just not into being part of the family, and I knew that caused my parents a lot of worry.

Her brother's behavior and withdrawal were a drag on their relationship. Despite the differences emerging from the differential maturation timetables, the relationship smoothed out with time, a characteristic for many in their forties.

We didn't have a lot in common. There were periods when we weren't in touch or I was upset with him for the way things were going in his life. But the last several years he's stopped drinking, and he's rebuilding his life and is much better about being in touch and sees my parents more often. He's more present. He can follow a conversation, which is easier when you are not drunk [laughs]. We are much more connected, but there were times when we were estranged, and I was wringing my hands about things. He didn't call me for six months after I had a serious car accident. We just got closer gradually.

EARLY HEALTH ISSUES LED TO GREATER PARENTAL INVOLVEMENT

Amelia believes her parents still focus more on her brother than on her, a vestige of Amelia's and her brother's early years. This would be consistent with Bowen's belief about parents' triangulating the child they feel the most concerned about. But Amelia does not see it as favoritism, more as greater concern. This difference is important when considering how parents raise their children, as we discuss in the next chapter. Some children need more than others, and if this is framed as favoritism, it means that another sibling was less favored. It also means that another sibling caused their parents less concern, a very different lens for viewing family interaction.

I always had the sniffles or some low-grade thing going on. But he would never get sick, and if he did, it was catastrophic. He'd be in the hospital for weeks. When he was really little, he almost died twice. He had some respiratory problem that was very frightening. So my parents had always been careful with him. I think they expected less of him and were very protective. They were thrilled that he was alive. I feel, sometimes, more was expected of me, or they weren't as careful with me. I feel that he was not more loved but [was] more on their minds. So I felt they had a different relationship with him than me.

While the brother was triangulated with the parents when he was young, elements of this pattern continued into adulthood and even now. Amelia gets drawn into speaking for him.

One thing my parents do is they will ask me, "Have you heard from him? What's going on? He was very quiet the last time he was here." I think he is a little more mysterious to them in some ways. I do sometimes find myself in the role of translator.

As Bowen captured in the "intergenerational transmission process," some familial patterns continue unconsciously, handed down from one generation to the next. Amelia's mother had a tempestuous relationship with her only sister, and they did not speak for periods of time. According to Amelia, their mother (Amelia's grandmother) pitted the sisters against each other, which discouraged their closeness. That experience is what drove Amelia's mother to encourage closeness between her own children. Their father had a less complicated relationship with his siblings, though not a totally satisfactory one.

I would say my dad loved his siblings and they loved him, but there was not a lot of intimacy. He complained that they kept him in the dark about things going on in their lives or in the family. Because of this, my mom is a believer in full disclosure, so we talk and talk. You can't say she keeps us in the dark.

THEIR RELATIONSHIP TODAY

Amelia and her brother are able to discuss most issues, including health, politics, and extended family. Sex is off the table, and discussions of money are difficult for them because Amelia makes more. Her comment about sex is typical for opposite-sex siblings and represents a boundary that many siblings draw—in fact, the least likely sibling dyad to talk about sex in our sample was a sister and her brother.

> We could talk about it in a limited way. There is only so much you really want to know about your sibling's sex life. Money is a continuing issue. There's that line between helping and not helping. In the past, I helped him financially, and it's not a great feeling. He hasn't asked in recent years, but there was a period when he was asking for help. I worry about his future and probably worry about his retirement more than mine [laughs]. We grew up in a lower-middle-class household, and I sometimes feel survivor's guilt. I want to make his life easier, but I don't want to take away his motivation or make him feel bad. It's the biggest thing challenging our relationship.

This situation is typical of many dynamics we see in our data that are complicated by intersecting variables. Money is the problematic issue when one sibling makes more than the other, and this is complicated by sibling order. When the older earns more, it adds to the preexisting power imbalance. This is further complicated by gender, with the sister earning more than the brother. Class issues between siblings came up throughout the interviews and became intertwined with the caretaking of their parents. Some siblings earned their own way, as Amelia has, whereas others married into money, as Willa's older sister did, and she uses that to treat the other sisters to dinner.

Based on her experience, Amelia has a healthy perspective on the long-term ups and downs of sibling relationships. Virginia Satir's clinical work on open communication would support a comment that Amelia made about her philosophy regarding her brother: "Your relationships will change at different times. Sometimes something that's really important now won't be in a few years. You have to be patient and keep the lines open."

Roger, a Baby Boomer

Roger is a white, forty-nine-year-old salesman who is also a stay-at-home father. Married to a pediatrician and with two young children, he is the youngest of six. Born in 1964, Roger is among the youngest of the baby boomers, even though having older siblings places him with the boomers.

His oldest sibling, a brother, is twelve years his senior, and each of his siblings (four brothers and one sister) was born approximately two years apart. Growing up, his home never felt safe. Their father, also a salesman, was an alcoholic. He usually came home at 6 P.M. and had his first martini. Every so often, he did not come home at all, or if he did, he would be drunk and abuse their mother. The oldest son would step in to protect her. The boundaries in the family were drawn in a way that the oldest brother was pulled into the parental subsystem, never a healthy dynamic. Roger was very young, so it was the oldest male's assumed role to protect their mother from their father. Such experiences can leave long-lasting dents in one's perception of life.

Roger's parents divorced when he was ten, at a time when divorce was becoming increasingly common. There was no question that the four youngest children, who were still young enough to be in the home, would stay with their mother. Six months later, when money was tight and they lost their home, they moved into an apartment. The three youngest children had to leave Catholic school and attended public school.

> By the time of the divorce, my oldest brother had escaped and went to Europe and grew his hair long. He then joined the air force. My sister left to find work. She and the oldest are my godparents. She used to get me dressed in the morning and take me to school when she was at home. The one next to me in age tried to commit suicide in the 1980s and had a drug problem. And then he got help and married a Jehovah's Witness. Our family had a hard time with it. We grew up Catholic and without much tolerance, so this did not go down well. They shut him [his brother] out.

Even though his parents were divorced, Roger's mother took their father back into her home when he became ill in 1984. He died three years later, and she died two years after that. The legacies of struggle and reconciliation epitomize the sibling relationships today. Roger would love to have closer relationships with his siblings, though they annoy and disappoint him at times, signs of the ambivalence he feels. His attempts to bond may mirror what his mother felt when she took his father back home—she longed for the connection and felt the obligation but may also have resented having to do it. Roger was the one who was still living at home when his mother died, having assumed a caretaker role similar to his mother's with his father.

He is the caretaker of the sibling relationships now, though the connections are sometimes strained.

> My relations with them could be better. No one lives within two hundred miles of me. But it seems like I am the only one in the family whom everyone talks to. Everything goes through me. That has been the case since our parents died. There is not a lot of respect there, and everyone feeds off the oldest and his attitude. We don't open up. Not a lot of heartfelt feelings out there. A middle brother had a heart problem, and I didn't know about it until two years later. They moved to a different city and didn't send a forwarding address or anything. Weird.

The oldest brother's style of interaction along with the ambiguity surrounding another brother's dropping out of touch cast a shadow on the family relationships as a whole. It also forced Roger to construct different relationships with each of his siblings.

> The oldest is strong willed and caring to a degree, meaning if it is convenient to him, he will be responsive. The next oldest brother—it is weird between us because of his politics. He is very right wing and doesn't want anything to do with me now if I don't believe what he believes. That is fine with me. The next oldest is fifty-five and an electrician. He's an interesting character. He wants to be a rock star still. I went to see him a few months ago, and he was immediately on top of me for something. "Hey, I didn't come here to be yelled at," I told him. He wants me to listen to or do something as soon as I arrive. Kind of intense. He wants things done only his way. My relationships with my sister and with the brother closest to me in age are the strongest.

SPECIFIC EVENTS WITH THE FAMILY

When asked to describe a difficult event, Roger mentioned a shared sad event, the death of his parents.

> We became less close after Mom died. We came together only for holidays or weddings. Christmas was fun, and then my oldest brother stopped coming and went to Mexico with his family instead. It was a slight to the family to never make time again to come, but that is just the way he is.

Roger's citing the decreasing closeness in his already strained sibling relationships after the death of their parents is typical for those in his life stage. As we mentioned earlier, some families are drawn together by this turning point, but others react the way that Roger's family did. That does not mean, however, that distant relationships are what people at this life stage want for the future.

WANTING MORE CLOSENESS

Roger would like to have more contact with his siblings and to have the kind of family whose members feel comfortable being themselves. "I try to be close, but I know you have to make calls to get calls. I'd make calls but I never got much back."

Roger's family had few role models for managing relationships. His mother had no siblings, and his father's relationships were like Roger's, strained and distant. They were never encouraged by their parents to be close.

> There are anger issues with all of us. No one did anything wrong, it is a self-ish anger that affects us all. . . . Give-and-take is not there, and that's a shame. I hope they respect me, but I don't feel like they do, even though I respect them.

It is not that the family has completely disintegrated. Contact continues at a safe distance, through the Internet, although that also presents its own challenges.

> Facebook is a big way for us all to stay close. Facebook helps a lot as long as you don't put out weird things, like one of my brothers defriended me because of my politics. Another brother put out bad feelings about something that happened in the family when we were young. "Oh, look, someone is bruised in this picture because Dad hit him or something." If you stay away from that type of stuff, it is just easier. You don't have to bring out something that happened forty years ago. Don't point out negativity.

As the youngest, Roger had the least control over what happened while he was growing up. He would like greater closeness in the family and the ability to talk about his feelings. He feels, though, that many of his siblings are not interested, and he is working to accept them for how they are. The residue of alcoholism, domestic abuse, divorce, and financial hardship when young has taken its toll on them. The siblings were never securely attached to one another except for a bond between Roger and his sister.

What Roger wants is instructive for all relationships. Theoretically, he wants more closeness to his siblings, but given their personalities, he really wants to be close to only some of his siblings. He wishes some of his siblings had different personalities and would change so that they could be closer. What is left is a loose confederation of relationships. How much of this is the result of the times in which they were growing up, with a cultural "Do your own thing" attitude, is hard to say. The family's hierarchy was turned upside down when one parent, the mother, needed protection by the oldest from their father and also when the youngest was left unsupported to care for their dying mother. Such experiences can leave even grown children unsure how to relate to one another.

At the same time, bad early experiences do not always lead to bad outcomes between siblings. Victoria Bedford and her colleagues observed that tensions among siblings, whether in early or later life, can challenge social skills that can ultimately lead to positive growth.[9] Support for this comes from a 2002–2004 Dutch study of 1,259 triads (two siblings and a parent). The authors found that siblings exchanged more support when the parent-child relationship was worse; that is, they worked hard to pull together when Mom or Dad was being difficult.[10] Many of the siblings we interviewed bonded after early trials rather than being left asunder.

The experiences of Roger and his family are in stark contrast with our final example of a larger and more closely knit family. The context and period in American history in which Roger and Sally grew up could not have been more different.

A Silent Generation Family

Sally, born in 1933 and the youngest of nine children, is a seventy-eight-year-old African American retired schoolteacher and educational administrator with a master's degree and credits toward a doctorate. Her second husband is a ninety-year-old retired school principal. They married ten years ago. Five of her siblings are still alive. Her three oldest, who were as much as twenty years her senior, have died.

When she completed the questionnaire, she started talking about her siblings. "My older sister expects us to listen to her, even now. I wish I could spend time with them because we are in different places, and we can't see each other as much. We telephone." She continues to go through the questionnaire and comes to the items written by Heidi Riggio,[11] whose scale we adapted for our research. "We are sort of open and share secrets . . . hmm . . . no, we don't borrow things from each other because we don't live near each other. Yes, we can talk about personal problems."

All of Sally's siblings finished high school. But only Sally and one other sibling finished college, and only she got a master's and began doctoral work.

> None of us was ever in prison. None of the kids or grandkids has ever been in trouble. That is the way we were raised by our parents. They put the oldest in charge of the youngest. Esther took care of me. She had to see my hair was combed and my clothes were clean. We had to do what the oldest told us to do. If you didn't, you heard from Mom and Dad, and you didn't talk back to them. We were a family that lived on a farm and we did farm things—pump water for cows and mules, feed the hogs and chickens. When there was time for chicken for dinner, we had to put the chickens up in a cage and give them corn to clean out their system. Three days later we had to kill them by wringing their necks. That was my job. We milked the cows by hand. My father farmed, and my mother took in laundry from white people.

Some of the other youngest siblings we interviewed for this book resented having a relationship in which their older siblings bossed them around, and they carried that resentment into adulthood. Not Sally—that was just how it was. The sibling hierarchy in her family was enforced by the parents.

> One day Esther sent me to a neighbor's house to borrow a hair iron to straighten my hair. Instead of coming back, I played with the girls in the other house for a while. When I started back home and got to the top of the field, Esther beat me. I told Momma, and Momma backed up Esther. That taught me a lesson. You did what your big sister told you to do because Momma will support her. I was seven, and that was a lesson learned I kept for life. If an older sister did something wrong, you didn't tell on them because they would get back at you when our parents weren't around.

Being the youngest in a large family, it was natural for Sally to have a favorite when growing up. One older brother worked in construction and would give her money, which she would spend on candy. Despite having a favorite, she quickly assured us that the family was a tight unit.

> If something happened to one of the siblings, everyone went to their rescue. A man took something from one of my brothers once, and I remember my father and brothers got in the car and went to get him. The whole family was like that. We were there for each other.

Sally spent her early life in North Carolina, where she was born. She married a minister, had one child, and became a teacher. A minister's life involved moving often to larger and larger parishes. Being away from her family was difficult. Eventually Sally and her husband returned to their hometown, and she ran for, and won, a seat on the county council and served for eight years. At one point, she was grand marshal of the town parade. Her husband died in the early 1990s, and ten years later she remarried and moved with her new husband to be closer to his family. She maintains contact with her hometown because some of her surviving siblings live there. In fact, she recently spoke at the swearing-in of the town's new mayor.

THE IMPORTANCE OF SIBLING RELATIONSHIPS

My brothers and sisters are very important to me. It is good to know what they are thinking and how they feel about things, especially my hometown. It is important for them to know what I am about and where I am. They call just to check on me. I am the baby, and I like that. It is not that they are catering to me. I just like being who I am. When the bishop would send my husband to different places to work, I stayed in constant contact with them and always came home for holidays.

The sister that took care of me, Esther, is still alive. I still listen to her—if she's right. She gambles and smokes and I don't smoke, but I let her smoke in my home. When she was here last, she wanted to smoke so I let her. I listen to my brother, too. He lives in New York. Big Jim. I like how he treats me because every time he sees me he has to give me something, like money. My husband asked me why I took it when we didn't need it, and I said, "He's my big brother." There is still a good relationship with my other sisters, too.

The close-knit and affectionate nature of Sally's family was handed down from a previous generation, as Sally's parents also were close to their siblings.

> Every year we would go visit my mother's sister. It was like vacation. My mom had a brother who would come visit every year. He was always well dressed and drove a Cadillac convertible. He was working in DC, and everyone respected him. My father was close with his family, too.

Sally's parents have been deceased for years. Their death did not bring the siblings closer, nor did the deaths of the oldest sibling a few years ago and a second sibling recently. "We were close already," Sally explained when we asked how those losses affected them.

Even though she is the youngest in the family, she feels respected, perhaps because she has accomplished so much educationally, professionally, and politically. Sally's strong relationship with her siblings connects her to good memories of her childhood. "They are proud of me as a person."

As they age, Sally and her siblings are finding it harder to stay in frequent contact. Death and dying never came up overtly during the interview, though there were references to God. "With two sisters being in the nursing home, it is a concern that we are not able to be in fellowship with them, but we think of them and are concerned about them."

This family has been close for generations, and the boundaries between the generations have always been clear. Sally is proud of what they have accomplished and of being so close-knit and supportive of one another. "I think our foundation from our mother and father steered us in the way we have lived our lives." While parents clearly played an important role, their small rural town, southern living, and the hierarchical nature of the church most likely helped foster family closeness. In addition, as one of the oldest in our sample and the youngest in her large family, she had relationships with siblings who were born almost one hundred years ago (at the time of the interview). Sally exemplifies a bygone time in American history. Parents ruled, the eldest helped out, and spirituality was a coherent force. That upbringing and sense of community shaped how close the siblings stayed throughout life.

HOW IMPORTANT AND HOW SUPPORTIVE
ARE SIBLING RELATIONSHIPS?

Victor Cicirelli, an early pioneer in studying adult sibling relationships, pointed out that the literature is inconsistent on the effect of age on sibling closeness. Cicirelli cited literature that described the relationship as being like an hourglass—close when young, less close in middle age, and close again in old age. Another study found that closeness increased with age as competition decreased. And according to one more study, contact, which is often related to closeness, diminished with age.[12]

But what is "close" and what constitutes "contact"? Some siblings, according to Duke University Researcher Deborah Gold, stay close out of obligation or loyalty and not out of a feeling of intimacy.[13] When interviewing sixty people sixty-five and older, Gold found that, depending on how closeness was conceptualized, relationships became closer with age.[14] Instrumental support, such as helping one another out, may diminish as a sibling's adult children take over that role. This would be a behavioral change and affect interactions and contact. Emotional support between siblings may increase, signaling a change in feelings. Scott Myers, a professor of communication studies at West Virginia University, wrote a wonderfully titled article, "I Have to Love Her, Even If Sometimes I May Not Like Her," in which he identifies "we are family" as one of the seven reasons why siblings maintain their relationships with one another. [15]

Robert Stewart, a psychology professor at Oakland University, and his colleagues found in their research that siblings have less conflict and act more positively toward one another with older age, similar to our findings. They believe that older people make a cognitive decision to avoid conflict because a sibling may be one of the few family members left and that it is risky to try to work through conflict if it might jeopardize the relationship.[16]

Clearly, sibling closeness is a difficult concept to define and capture and, even when captured, varies from one sibling, family, or generation to the next. In addition, it is dynamic. Many siblings we interviewed described feeling distant from a sibling until they reached adulthood. At the same time, other siblings grew apart after a significant event, like a parent's death and the division of the estate, ruined their relationship.

In our study, we asked about the importance of sibling relationships as a lead-in to the rest of the questions. A clear majority, approximately four-fifths, said they were very important (61 percent) or important (18 percent). One in six (16 percent) gave a neutral response, with one in sixteen (6 percent) saying they were not important. We also asked how comfortable they felt with the level of support from their siblings. Close to two-thirds (61 percent) were very comfortable, and one-quarter (28 percent) were somewhat comfortable. The rest (11 percent) said they would like more support.[17]

When comparing survey question response patterns among the groups in our overall sample of respondents or across two variables, we performed statistical tests of those differences or relationships. For example, we found no relationship between a sibling's age and how important sibling relationships were to him or her. We also found no relationship between age and how comfortable he or she felt about support from a sibling. Although these relationships may change over time, and, as we discuss in the next chapter, may vary as a function of how a sibling set is parented, these broad relationship dynamics among our respondents are often not subject to age and generation.

Sibling Relationship Quality as Measured by a Standardized Scale

These two questions were global and referred to all of a respondent's siblings, so we used a standardized measure to look at as many as two specific sibling relationships for each respondent.[18] We chose to use Heidi Riggio's Lifespan Sibling Relationship Scale (LSRS).[19] In this twenty-four-item scale measuring adult relationship quality, respondents are asked to think about a sibling who has had either a positive or a negative impact on their life and then to choose their level of agreement in three areas: feelings, beliefs, and behaviors. Examples of feelings statements are "My sibling makes me happy" and "My sibling frequently makes me very angry." Examples of beliefs statements are "My sibling is a good friend" and "My sibling and I have a lot in common." Examples of behaviors statements are "My sibling and I share secrets" and "I never talk about my problems with my sibling." The overall scores for the sample on these three subscales indicated positive relationship quality in the first two waves of the study and more variation in the third wave when we specifically asked the sibling to first indicate a sibling who had a positive relationship and then to indicate one who had a negative impact or to whom the sibling felt the least close.[20]

Overall, with all three waves, we found the pattern of responses to the three LSRS subscales matched the pattern of responses in the sample that Riggio used to validate her scale. In other words, the mean score on each of the feelings, behaviors, and beliefs subscales were very similar, indicating that the scales performed similarly with our respondents.[21] However, our sample, which was thirty years older, on average, than Riggio's, did report slightly more positive experiences in regard to feelings and beliefs and slightly less positive regarding behaviors. We also found, as did Riggio, that sisters report more positive feelings, beliefs, and behaviors about their sibling relationships than brothers do. When taking a more specific lens of gender *match* in sibling relationships, consistent with other research on female expressiveness, we found that sisters are more likely to share secrets and discuss problems with one another than brothers are.

Differences in our sample were in relation to age in the subscale for behaviors. The oldest siblings in our sample, those sixty-six and older, were less likely to report positive behaviors toward their siblings than were younger siblings. That difference was driven by two dynamics. First, the older respondents are less likely to share secrets or discuss personal problems, which, we suggest, fits the theme of this chapter and reflects the "silent generation" in which they were raised. The second dynamic seems more related to the exigencies of age; the older respondents reported being less likely to spend a lot of time with their sibling or to borrow things from them (also behaviorally related statements on the scale). These behaviors are consistent with the interpretation that older siblings are simply less mobile.

Some notable exceptions do exist among subsets, though. Older females, those older than fifty, are more likely to discuss problems and share secrets with their sisters and to call sisters more often than older brothers do with their brothers.[22] Differences did not appear with younger same-sex sibling dyads in regard to discussing problems and sharing secrets, suggesting that some gender differences between brothers and sisters are becoming less pronounced in the younger sibling set. In fact, younger brothers are more likely to report they spend more time with sisters, call their sisters frequently, and share secrets with their sisters than are older brothers and their sisters.

Furthermore, when we explored differences between younger and older gender-related dyads, older-sister dyads, compared with older-brother dyads, were more likely to report that their sibling made them happy; their sibling's feelings were important; they had more telephone and e-mail contact, shared secrets, and talked about problems; and that the relationship was important to them. The diminishing differences between genders in the younger part of our sample may have been driven by brothers becoming more like sisters in how they feel and behave toward their siblings.

Again in regard to the differences based on age, a logical hypothesis would be that if older siblings were less likely to share secrets or talk about personal problems, then more topics would be off limits for discussion. The next series of questions, information gathered during the interview process, confirmed this hypothesis.

Comfort in Discussing Topics

We wondered whether certain topics, some more highly charged than others, were easier for siblings to discuss. In the semistructured in-depth interviews, we asked, "Would you feel comfortable discussing the following topics with the sibling cited in the scale?" referring to the LSRS scale they had filled out on the questionnaire, followed by the topics listed in descending order in table 3.1.

Sex is obviously the most awkward or difficult topic for siblings to talk about, and we can see in the data that one of the reasons is cross-gender discomfort. In fact, brothers feel more comfortable talking about sex with one another than sisters do with one another. Age plays a part here, too. Younger brothers are also more likely to talk about sex and to talk about friends with their sisters than are older brothers and their sisters.[23] The

TABLE 3.1   Would You Feel Comfortable Talking About . . .

ISSUE	FEEL COMFORTABLE	DO NOT FEEL COMFORTABLE
Health problems	85%	15%
Family issues	78%	22%
Child's problems	77%	23%
Work issues	75%	25%
Religion	75%	25%
Politics	67%	33%
Friends	65%	35%
Money	58%	42%
Sex	33%	67%

topics of money, friends, and politics can be difficult, too, for a significant minority of the population to discuss with a sibling.

Differences did appear in relation to age in siblings' comfort in talking about these important issues. The silent and boomer generations are less likely to feel comfortable talking about sex, money, family, work, and friends than are the Gen Xers. Consistent with the results of the LSRS subscale referring to behaviors, this series of questions confirms that talking about certain topics—things people tend to keep secret or consider to be personal problems—is more difficult for the older generations.

Thus far, we have presented a picture of the importance of sibling relationships, the level of comfort with support received from one's sibling(s), the general level of relationship quality as measured by the LSRS, and some gender differences based on the LSRS. We also presented the general level of comfort with discussing various topics. The oldest group differed most notably from the younger ones on their level of interpersonal sharing and what they felt comfortable talking about.

To continue our level of inquiry and to flesh out these relationships, we next describe what the siblings had to say about each of their siblings and how much and what type of contact they maintain.

Describe Your Sibling(s) in a Few Words

To see the gray area between the global questions about the importance of all sibling relationships and the specific details about single siblings, we asked our interviewees to describe in a few words their relationships with each of their siblings. We then coded whether the descriptions were largely positive, mixed, or largely negative. Examples of positive descriptions were "I know she will be there for me," "We are close friends," and "We are good friends." Slightly more than half of all the descriptions of siblings were positive. Slightly more than one-fifth of all the descriptions were clearly negative, such as "overwhelming dictator" or "distant and uninvolved," and the rest, about one-quarter, were in the mixed or ambivalent category, with descriptions like "occasional conversations but not deep conversations," "superficial but pleasant, more distant than I would like," and "good to fair, feel inferior."[24]

Another way to look at these responses is to consider the extremes. Almost one-third of the siblings (30 percent) used only positive terms to describe their sibling set. Sally is one such example. In contrast, one in twelve

(8 percent) gave all negative terms to describe their siblings (in chapter 5 we discuss those families who seem to have very serious struggles with their sibling relationships). That leaves the majority, 62 percent, with some negative, some positive, or some mixed terms (neither positive nor negative) as descriptors. In fact, 8 percent used all mixed terms for their siblings. Hence, many siblings are balancing their relationships with their siblings, in which, if there is more than one sibling, feelings vary from one sibling to the next, reflecting possibly significantly different relationships with each sibling.

Again, age was a notable factor in responses to this question. The oldest group, the silent generation, was more likely to use positive terms to describe their siblings and less likely to use negative terms: two-thirds used positive terms, and only one-tenth used negative terms. When we compared this oldest group with the two younger groups, they were more likely to report only positive terms for their first two siblings. But when people had more than two siblings, the age-related pattern was no longer statistically significant. While the sample sizes do get smaller with each additional sibling,[25] it seems to be more a function of more ambivalent feelings for the sibling set as the number of siblings increases; the more siblings you may have, at any age or in any generation, the more likely you are to have one you do not get along well with.

Still, we want to highlight this series of responses, as they underscore how mixed (ambivalent) many of these relationships are and help us begin to paint a picture of the complexity of feelings that a sibling can have toward the same sibling and also toward different siblings. Remember, a brother can believe that his brother is a "loony toon" and still feel close to him and be willing to rush to his side in an emergency.

Contact Between Siblings

We asked about the frequency of telephone, Internet, and face-to-face contact, as well as the geographic distance from each sibling. According to the Pew Research Center, Internet use is common among older Americans, with 77 percent of people fifty to sixty-four and 52 percent of people sixty-five and older using it.[26] When looking at those in our sample who answered these questions, we found that more than one-third (37 percent) reported frequent contact by telephone, one in four (23 percent) frequent contact by Internet, and one in six (17 percent) frequent face-to-face contact.[27] Only 5 percent reported frequent contact with a sibling through all three means. At the other extreme, one-third said they had no Internet contact, one in five (19 percent) no face-to-face contact, and one in six (17 percent) no telephone contact. The remainder had occasional contact. We suspect these responses can be partly explained by the fact that having frequent contact via one means may mitigate the need for other types of contact. For example, two siblings who live together would see each other frequently but probably rarely, if ever, communicate by e-mail.

Approximately 10 percent indicated they had virtually no contact by any means with any of their siblings. This reflects what Murray Bowen would call a "cutoff" among these siblings and indicates an overall low level of differentiation in the family. In fact, across several parts of the survey and interview data, about one in ten respondents reported primarily problematic sibling relationships. Not all siblings who struggle with their relationships reach this kind of break. Having struggles with a sibling as part and parcel of the relationship was mentioned by 40 percent of those we interviewed, some noting a significant age gap, differences between the genders, and geography as reasons why siblings have not been able to get closer to one another or reconnect in adulthood.

When looking at frequency and types of contact through the lens of age, we again found differences. The oldest were more likely to say they had less face-to-face contact with siblings which, given their age and potential inability to travel easily, would be expected and which ties into our earlier discussion about this group having a lower score on the behaviors subscale of the LSRS. Interestingly, the oldest and youngest groups of siblings reported the same level of contact through the Internet and telephone.

What About Competition, Jealousy, and Trust Between Siblings?

We have discussed what siblings feel comfortable talking about and how often they communicate, but what is the underlying tone of their communications? Parents can play significant roles in affecting communication, often even into their children's adulthood. We discuss parental influence in the next chapter; here, we explore the internal sibling dynamic.

When asked about their childhood relationships with all their siblings, fighting and arguing were common in our sample: 46 percent reported that they fought and argued frequently when young. This could take the form of physical fighting between brothers and sisters as well as verbal aggression.

We found almost no instances when the fighting per se in childhood was the reason for a cutoff in adulthood, as most of it was seen as typical. A minority, 20 percent, believed they competed with their siblings *more* than most, and 16 percent believed they were jealous of one another *more* than most.[28] On the more positive side, the level of trust between siblings was high when young, with 71 percent believing they could trust one another. Only 15 percent said they could not, with the rest neither agreeing nor disagreeing.

These patterns of responses are important to consider in light of what types of feelings characterized the relationships now. By middle and late adulthood, competition dropped from 20 percent of the whole sample to 7 percent;[29] jealousy fell from 16 to 6 percent; and fighting and arguing dropped from 46 to 12 percent. The other key component touched on by these questions, trust, remained nearly static, up slightly at 73 percent trusting their sibling now.[30]

Through a developmental lens, we would expect jealousy and competition, common facets of any childhood, to be washed away by the acceptance of self and others that comes with maturity. While jealousy has rarely been characterized in a positive light, competition is more complex and contains elements that can be considered positive. Healthy competition can spur motivation and achievement; unhealthy competition can lead to resentment, anger, and hostility. For example, as we observed in chapter 1, the path taken by an older sibling often determines the path taken by a younger one. To avoid competition, some younger siblings may gravitate toward different activities (hobbies, sports) and careers, thinking the older sibling would always have a leg up if they chose the same trajectories. Competition in and of itself can be good, but as we show in the next chapter, the intricate interplay of competition with parental interference can lead to troubled sibling relationships in adulthood.

In tracking how people changed, most of those who felt jealous or competitive when young did not feel that way as adults. A few who indicated they were not jealous or competitive with their siblings when young felt jealous or competitive now. This could be the result of the respondent's achieving less as an adult in the work world, not having a partner or children, encountering significant mental health problems, or being treated differently by parents.

Approximately one-quarter of the siblings who did not trust their siblings when young trusted them now, a positive sign. A few who did not trust them when young moved to a neutral position, neither agreeing nor disagreeing with the question. The rest continued to not trust them. Of course, some siblings changed in the other direction—they trusted their siblings when young but did not trust them now. This dynamic seems to be the result of a regrettable event. For example, one such sibling stopped talking to his younger brother after that brother had an affair with his then (but no longer) fiancée.

Age is related to the responses to questions about past and present interactions between siblings. With age, the likelihood of competition, arguing, and jealousy characterizing childhood relationships diminishes, just as competition and arguing are less likely to occur in older adulthood. Two hypotheses may explain the differences here related to age. One is that people's memories become rosier with time and distance from childhood conflicts, and thus they let go of jealousy and competition. The second hypothesis is based on Glen Elder's thinking—these siblings of the silent generation grew up in a different time, a period when children were seen and not heard. It is well established that the parents of the baby boomer generation paid more attention to children and child rearing than the previous generations did. In contrast, parents of the silent generation may have put engagement with the emotional lives of children in the backseat while they struggled to meet the children's basic needs and fight foreign enemies. As we see in the next chapter, less parental involvement in children's relationships is often better for those relationships.

What Brings Us Together, What Pulls Us Apart?

Why people move beyond childhood jealousies and competition was revealed in the qualitative interviews. Certain specific events or factors that helped move them in positive directions with their siblings sometimes showed up more often in people in one life stage than another. Nonetheless, those same life events also were often cited as pulling families apart. We first describe people who found life-stage events or new awareness bringing them closer to their siblings. To obtain this information, we asked whether they had had a falling out and, if so, what, if anything, had brought the siblings close again.

As might be expected, the oldest generation talked most often about the illness or death of family members as a factor in bringing the siblings closer together. They all had usually dealt with the death of both parents and often of a sibling or spouse.

The baby boomers most frequently mentioned becoming more mature and seeing the existential importance of family as the reason for growing closer. Woven through some of the interviews was the awareness that siblings were the only guaranteed lifelong connection. Amelia cited this as a reason for getting closer, and it is related, in our view, to the cultural dictates in our society about the importance of family. Nearly half the siblings we interviewed said something to the effect that "at the end of day, whom do you have left but your family?" Typical of the responses was the realization that siblings would be together longer than they would be with their parents, spouses, or friends. Boomers also talked about, to a greater extent than did the other age groups, growing closer because their spouses and children got along with one another and because they had moved closer geographically.

Boomers were not immune from death and illness being reasons for getting closer. Deena, a fifty-four-year-old white factory worker baby boomer with a high school education and the middle of six siblings, provided an example of her generation's experience:

> I think we are all a lot closer now than we were before. My one sister, Cindy, she died about ten years ago from a drug overdose, and that was really hard on all the siblings. We all felt like maybe we could have done something to help her. That maybe we had failed her in some way. I think we all feel pretty guilty about her death, even now.

Gen Xers also frequently mentioned becoming more mature and realizing the importance of family as the reason they grew closer after the illness or death of a family member. Finding more commonalities in a sibling as a reason for growing closer was cited more frequently by this group than by those in the two older groups. By this stage in life, and having started most likely in their twenties, siblings begin to see one another in a new "adult" light as they face similar life events: leaving home, finding a partner, raising children, and solidifying careers.[31]

Yet other respondents gave some of the same reasons for being close that we heard in the interviews for why they became distant. Their parents' dying was either the end of closeness because the siblings had no reason to interact any more or it brought the siblings together.[32] A sibling's illness and death could result in a rift if the surviving siblings coped with it in different ways. Finally, growing older could cause some siblings to not want to spend time trying to repair ruptures with their siblings but, instead, to focus on their own partner, children, or close friends.

CONCLUSION

The majority of our sample believed that sibling relationships were important, felt supported by their siblings, and felt close to them. That said, though, differences in closeness appeared in the same family, and conflicting or mixed feelings were felt toward one sibling. This supports our using ambivalence as a defining feature of sibling relationships. With the caveat that questions are rarely asked by researchers in the same way and that samples are not gathered in the same manner and composed of the same age groups, our findings are similar to other research that explores siblings' support and closeness.[33] But the components of closeness need to be considered for a deeper understanding of how relationships operate. That entails looking at feelings, behaviors, and the age-related context. It also entails, as we discuss in our clinical chapter, finding out what a sibling wants from another sibling or siblings.

Is Age Relevant?

Based on other research, we had thought that with age, relationships might take on greater importance and that more support might be perceived. As we explained, this was not the case with our global questions. It could be because our sample began with forty-year-olds, when many of these relationships had been solidified, so fewer changes would be detected between the age groups. That possibility is supported by the differences we discussed between our sample and Riggio's sample on the LSRS, that our older sample had more positive feelings and beliefs about their siblings. We suggest that the changes that do occur after forty may be more subtle than those that occur earlier in life.

Age is a relevant consideration, given some of our findings. The older siblings feel less comfortable discussing personal issues; they are more positive in how they describe their siblings; and they report less arguing, jealousy, and competition in childhood and adulthood while also having less face-to-face contact.

Gender also appears as a relevant variable to consider when looking at relations between same-sex as well as opposite-sex siblings. Our findings suggest that younger brothers (forty- to fifty-year-olds) feel much more comfortable relating to brothers and sisters than do older brothers. This may bode well for the future of sibling relationships, as we discuss in the concluding chapter.

It is important to pay close attention to how a particular age group defines emotional support. Our findings showed that sharing secrets and talking about sex and money were not usually a part of the oldest group's relationships. Other researchers have found that emotional support among this oldest generation sometimes involves conscious choices to avoid conflict. Therefore, closeness should be gauged according to the range of ways in which it is maintained.

Perhaps of greatest importance is finding a lens for understanding that sibling relationships are not always simply good or bad. These often gray relationships have many ambivalent and ambiguous aspects during families' life spans. Only 22 percent of our respondents said they were always close; 70 percent said their sibling relationships waxed and waned over the years, meaning they had periods of emotional closeness and emotional distance; and just 8 percent said they were never close to their sibling(s). (These findings are remarkably similar to what another team of researchers reports.[34]) In addition, most of our sample had at least one sibling who was described in mixed or negative terms. It may be hard to reconcile two competing feelings: wanting more support yet not holding a wholly positive view of the sibling from whom one wants the support. And it is hard for those with many siblings if two of them are closer and a third or fourth is on the outs. But such is the nature of many sets of sibling relationships.

From the case studies, we see this relayed in the complicated stories that can pull a family apart, as in Roger's family, or hold it together, as in Sally's. Some, like Roger, long to be closer to their siblings yet do not expect it. Others, like Amelia, are able to continue working, with varying degrees of success, on both accepting and improving their sibling relationships. In the next chapter we turn to the profound influence that parents have on their children's relationships with one another.

CHAPTER | 4

The Perceived Impact of Parents on Sibling Relationships Across the Life Span

THERAPISTS TEND TO OPERATE FROM the assumption that the past shapes the present but does not predetermine it or force people to relive it. Nevertheless, it is inescapable or, at least, most people and most theories of human development believe that it is inescapable. *New York Times* science columnist Natalie Angier began a column on the evolutionary theory of the family with the joke: What do cul-de-sac, Jean-Paul Sartre, and the typical family have in common? The answer—no exit.[1] Most of us believe that if we understand the path we have traveled, we will be able to build a better path in the future. Because parents pave many of the paths their children take, in this chapter we look specifically at how perceptions of parents' behaviors in both childhood and adulthood affect siblings' interactions.

In our research, we found many significant and profound connections between how the siblings in our study perceived their parents' child-rearing behavior and their relationship with their siblings. Favoritism looms across the life span, and for a minority of respondents, their parents' interference often hovers nearby. We also found that the relationships our respondents' fathers had with their siblings shaped our subjects' relationship with their own siblings.

We began with the conviction that, to quote Shakespeare, the past is prologue. We asked a series of specific questions to try to understand how parents' behaviors and perceived attitudes may have affected their children's relationships with one another in the past and in adulthood. The picture

that emerged from the answers to those questions requires a few remind-
ers about individuality and family systems, as well as a couple of warnings
about methodological limitations.

First, and as we discussed in chapter 1, feelings toward siblings at any
time, but especially in middle and late adulthood, are shaped by much
more than parents' behavior in childhood and adulthood. Significant life
events continuously alter people's feelings about themselves and their relationships and also their perceptions of their parents. Second, parents and
children influence each other across the life span. Parents do not raise children in a vacuum; they constantly modify what they do based on the child's
nature and reaction to being parented. Aging parents with adult children
are no exception. Third, parents raise their children in slightly different
ways based on their own personality, parenting philosophy, and family history. When talking about parental behavior, the siblings we interviewed
sometimes spoke about one parent and, at other times, both. Each parent,
as our findings show, has different influences on children.

As for methodological warnings, in presenting our findings, we describe
what appears to be parents' influence on siblings' thoughts, feelings, and
behaviors toward one another, and we acknowledge that we may sometimes be describing correlation and not causation. We hope to draw attention to patterns that therapists can use in helping adult siblings sort out
their relationships.

In addition, any exploration of the relationship between childhood and
adult experiences must take into account that recall is tricky and that when
it is recall of childhood, it can be even trickier. One of our current clients in
psychotherapy is twenty years old and highly astute. He is in treatment to
resolve his relationships with his parents and grandparents and spends time
talking about his past, some of which is quite upsetting to him. He remem-
bers events that happened six, ten, twelve years ago and is not always sure
of the accuracy of his recall. Similarly, we asked the siblings in our sample,
all of whom were at least twice the age of our client, to remember back
twenty, forty, sixty, or even seventy years and to do so in a single research
interview, not in an ongoing therapeutic setting in which memory unfolds
over multiple sessions. What we report from our sample is their snapshot of
a complex series of interactions that unfolded over a lifetime, recognizing
the partial nature of their comments.

THE CONNECTIONS

We were surprised by the strength of some of our findings, given our training in family therapy and our quoting from Shakespeare's *Tempest*. Despite our theoretical orientation and clinical experience, we were surprised by *how* enduring the past is, that it can live on for generations. Decades later, the sting of childhood still aches for some and inhibits their sibling ties, just as the love and support from parents soothe others in adulthood. Shakespeare recognized these tethers, as did Freud, Bowen, Satir, Minuchin, and many others.

Favoritism

"Mom always liked you best." Tom Smothers's complaint to his brother Dick on 1960s *The Smothers Brothers* television program is not an unusual statement for a sibling to make when reminiscing about the past.[2] Indeed, Tom Smothers's complaint is amusing because many people recognize the truth in it. In interviews of children, adolescents, and young adults, the perception of favoritism is common, occurring, according to some research, in more than half of all families.[3] *Favoritism*, also called *parental differential treatment*, happens for a number of reasons. Parents may prefer a child based on gender, appearance, or birth order. A middle child who wanted to be rescued from his sibling position when he was young may favor his own middle child when he becomes a father. A child born at a propitious period in a parent's life may become favored. If, for example, the parent has just lost his or her own parent, the next child born to the family becomes a pleasant reminder and is named after the deceased. A deceased child may be favored; one fifty-seven-year-old woman we interviewed had had a full sister she never knew who died in the Holocaust. Her parents always honored the deceased sister in a way that made the living sister feel less loved.[4] Or similar personality traits may cause a parent to favor a child. These examples are based on the parent and, when taken to an extreme, indicate an unresolved issue in the parent that has little to do with any accomplishments or behaviors of the child.

Children's behaviors and accomplishments can also make a parent appear to favor a child through praise or attention lavished on one child. For a wealth of reasons, some children are easier to raise, and some children excel, thereby attracting more attention from the parent.

In the following example, both these issues collided in a forty-eight-year-old African American female medical assistant who felt that she was the more difficult child to raise and that her younger brother outshone her.

> I always felt like my mother favored my brother because he was always such a nice kid. He did his homework, was smart, respectful, and became a doctor. He did everything right. I was not so good in school. I skipped a lot as a teenager and switched schools a few times. She was very frustrated with me as a teenager. She could depend on him to be good, and not add to the stress of being a single parent.

Not only was this brother easier to raise, he achieved more and reinforced the mother's favoritism through his accomplishments. This chicken-and-egg situation echoes our earlier assertions that the parent-child influence is mutually causal. If one child excels much more than other, she or he is bound to garner positive attention.[5] But the attention that becomes unhealthy favoritism may be heaped on a child because a parent has not achieved much and is living through the child's reflected glory.

With favoritism, the accompanying perception of being the less favored child may be lurking in the shadows. In the study of young adults cited earlier, favoritism benefited the favored child and harmed the less favored child. Compared with siblings in families in which no favoritism was shown, researchers found that favored children had fewer signs of depression and that less favored children showed more signs of depression.[6]

That study was not a surprise to us, since our research found that parental favoritism that started in childhood often reached into middle and late adulthood. Other people we interviewed also observed that the favored child was the highest achiever, as in the following case of the family of this youngest of five, a fifty-two-year-old white female social worker. Here it may be that the parents' own need for a "doctor" drove the feeling of favoritism.

> We would all agree that my brother to whom I was close . . . the fifty-six-year-old, totally . . . my parents favored. So he grew up and he is the doctor in the family. He is a doctor of veterinary medicine, not people medicine, but he was *the* doctor. And so if you ask any of my siblings, we would all say that he is the favored one. If you ask him, he will say, "OK I used to be,"

but when he divorced his first wife, he feels that he fell out of favor because there has not ever been a divorce in the family. He felt like he scarred the family when that happened, but it's really not true. He is still the favorite.

Even though the brother felt he had fallen out of favor because of his divorce, the sibling we interviewed perceived the favoritism to be enduring. Despite her brother's vaunted position, she feels quite close to him and did not report any jealousy between them. This is typical of some families in which one child's status is higher in the parents' eyes, it is accepted, and it is not a source of conflict. Also, the fact that she is one of five and not one of two thus may make the situation less about her and more about him.

While these first two examples of favoritism are presented by a less favored child, the next example comes from Randy, a forty-two-year-old white software engineer (with an older sister and a slightly younger brother) who believed that he was the favorite. Randy came to rely on his parents' approval because he had always received it.

> I always felt as though I was the favorite. I don't think either of my siblings was a great student, and I was always the good kid. I don't know much about my sister when she was younger, but I always got the sense that my parents thought of me as the favorite, to the point where my brother was really the black sheep, and no matter what he did, it never seemed like it was good enough. It seemed like there was definitely comparison between me and my brother. Education seemed to be important to my mother, and I was good at that kind of thing.

Eventually, as many children do in adulthood, the brothers moved past the mother's biased behavior, even though it affected the sibling relationship for many years. Randy's brother, who sought the mother's approval but never received it, finally stopped seeking it, which Randy thinks may have been beneficial for the brother.

> My brother did name this feeling that he could never live up to the opinion my mother had of me, and eventually decided that it just wasn't worth trying. Later in life he joined the navy, and that was a point where he was trying to get some sense of acceptance from my mother because that's the

sort of thing that I would never do. It was like he was distinguishing him-self completely from me, his striving to create an identity for himself. In the navy, he really excelled and he moved up. But I don't think that he ever got the response from my mother that he was hoping for. To me, it never really seemed like she was proud of him, even though she is a real patriotic person. It really disappointed me that she didn't, because, to me, it seemed like my brother had gone out and created this new identity and was really successful, but it still didn't really seem to matter to her.

From Randy we have an illustration of how a parent, for reasons that are not clear, continues to not give a child the attention that he deserves and seeks. At the same time, we have an admission from Randy that he contin-ues to be favored by his mother.

I think that I am sometimes still looking for that approval from my mother, whereas my brother has just decided he doesn't care anymore, and I think that actually might make him a happier person because he is more just living for himself. And maybe I've been looking for more approval, so I've gotten more approval. So yeah, early on I think the favoritism may have played a role, but I don't think it affects our relationship now. And overall, our rela-tionships have really changed since we've become adults.

Randy's brother adapted to his mother never treating him fairly and moved on. In addition, though, Randy articulated a downside of being the favorite: he has come to rely too much on his mother's approval.

Interference

We also looked at a constellation of parental behaviors in addition to favor-itism. *Interference* is a *bête noire* in the family therapy field. Usually interfer-ence or intrusion refers to a child's being pulled in by one or both parents and triangulated into the parents' relationship (spousal subsystem) or a child's attempting to insert himself between the parents. Here, however, we are considering a variation on this theme, that is, a parent interfering inappropriately in the relationships children have with one another dur-ing either childhood or adulthood. Similar to a child's interference in the parental relationship, it may be a two-way street: the parent initiates the interference, or the children pull the parent into their relationship instead of resolving the issues themselves. Both also can happen simultaneously. Regardless of who sets up the interference, it creates problems, as structural family therapy explains, since a boundary has been crossed between the generations. Healthy family functioning has long been linked to boundaries around the sibling system.

Sometimes the parents' interference is blamed primarily on one parent. In the next case, Pat, a fifty-three-year-old white female parole officer with a brother eleven years younger, never quite understood why she was separated from him.

> They didn't like when I talked to him; they didn't like if I tried to help with him when he was young. They thought I would mess it up, I don't know. They just pushed me aside. Sometimes it still feels like they don't want us to be so close, but I think that's just my father. He's still such an angry man, I don't know if he'll ever change. I don't think so.

While Pat maintains contact with her mother, she and her father don't talk anymore. Despite the early separation from her brother, they have grown quite close as adults.

> We text each other every morning. He and I tell each other what is going on, what we're doing and stuff. I think it's really important to us both. It's important that we keep our relationship strong, because so much of our family isn't in touch. We don't talk to a lot of our family.

This adult brother and sister have taken control of their relationship, offering evidence of our assertion early in this chapter that as time passes, the parents' influence over sibling relationships can be replaced by other factors.

Jon, a fifty-nine-year-old white male photographer and the youngest of five, related how his unstable home life was fueled by his parents' behavior. Part of this he blamed on their culture and the era in which they were raised.

> My parents were fairly heavy drinkers for their entire lives. I think a lot of that was not just them particularly, it was that generation. They were

first-generation Polish American and it was after Prohibition, so I think that was their generation and the ethnic group they were in. Shortly after I was born, my father basically turned from being a drinker to an alcoholic. He was self-employed and he quit working; my mother had a good job. Very intensive arguments and fights started, and it was a classic toxic household.

Their treatment of their children was not a laissez-faire approach but, rather, a more active splitting of the children. When asked specifically about interference, Jon's response depicted this behavior as highly destructive and as taking a toll on the siblings' current relationship.

I think they interfered by not encouraging closeness among the siblings; the interfering manifested itself by excessive criticism of siblings, and the unstable home life interfered with the relationship among the siblings. Because it led us to be rather than a kind of typical or somehow cohesive family, we were driven to survive. I think we would have all been much closer if we did not have the home life we had.

In extreme situations, children grow up with parental violence. As one group of clinicians wrote, parents may "interfere" by consciously inciting violence among their children. Another form of interference is a parent and child failing to attach to each other. That lack of attachment affects the siblings' ability to relate to one another in a healthy way, as they never learned how to attach. The parent has disrupted, or interfered with, the normal course of development by failing to provide the necessary nurturing. In some instances of parental violence, children adaptively bond together as a defense against this behavior and learn to rely on one another instead of their parent.[7]

Parents can also "interfere" by leaving their wills or advance directives unclear, thereby saddling their children with an unresolved legacy at their death.[8] This family issue is taken up in detail in the next chapter.

Many siblings told us that their parents' interference was not problematical and came only when siblings were young and fighting too hard with one another and the parents needed to make sure that no one got hurt. Some types of interference carry a healthy message and are more in line with the role of the parent as a moral educator. One sibling, a fifty-three-year-old

Latino man with two brothers, one a year younger and one a year older, told us the following when we asked about interference:

> If we were arguing, my mom would separate us. She used to say that we are brothers and that we shouldn't fight because we come from the same blood. My mom always told us that we have to be together. She said that we should love each other, be close to each other and not fight.

We should note that there is a well-established cultural dynamic at work here, as the mother's lesson to her sons echoes the family-focused values of both *familisimo* and *respecto,* central to many Latino families, who place a high value on both strong multigenerational family ties and harmonious interpersonal relationships.[9] As we pointed out in the first chapter, the dynamics of what this mother said are universal, although the emphasis may vary across cultures.

Protection

Similar to the mother interfering with her sons to encourage their peaceful valuing of their relationship, we know that children should be raised in an environment in which they feel nurtured and protected by their parents. A one-year-old needs protection from her four-year-old sibling, and an elementary-aged younger sibling may need protection from older siblings who pick on him verbally too much. In a recent study, one-third of children aged three to six were reported to have been victimized by a sibling, according to parents' reports. Victimization included physical, property, and psychological aggression (e.g., verbal attacks), whether or not an injury occurred. One-eighth of adolescents reported being victimized by a sibling.[10] Unlike interference, which is seen mainly as toxic, protection can be looked at as functional: if it is needed, it should be supplied (although the fact that it is needed could be a sign of family dysfunction). Protection can look similar to interference, but it is more intentional and derives from a parent's believing that safety is at issue. In short, interference may derive from a parent's emotional need, whereas protection may derive from a parent's perception of a child's need.[11]

When it seems that something more serious and problematic is occurring between siblings in childhood or adolescence, protection may be needed to stop emotional, physical, and even sexual abuse. In these situations, the *lack* of protection is problematic and can lead to harm or abuse and affect the victim's psychological health and relationships throughout adulthood.

One seventy-six-year-old white woman wanted protection from her abusive older brother and resented her mother's ignoring her entreaties for help.

> He was really sometimes physically abusive, and he constantly derided me and made fun of me. And I would go to my mother sometimes and tell her that he was bullying me, and her attitude was "Don't let it bother you." And she never called him on it. Now maybe she did in private, and I didn't know it . . . but for me all I ever saw was "Just leave it alone . . . ignore it." And it was something that bothered me terribly. I didn't feel like there was anyone there to defend or support me.

Margaret Ballantine, a social worker in New York, described the case of a depressed, middle-aged mother of two whom she was treating who had been sexually abused by an older brother for six years, starting when she was ten. The abuse was precipitated by her seeking solace to escape her alcoholic father. Her mother was described as passive and unable to protect her from either her father or her brother.[12]

Kathleen Monahan, the director of the Family Violence Education and Research Center at Stonybrook, New York, wrote how issues around the death and dying of a parent brought eight different women between the ages of fifty-six and sixty-nine into therapy, in which previous issues related to incest at the hands of a brother during childhood emerged. Family isolation, violence, and discord are thought to spawn this type of behavior.[13] Although no instances of sexual abuse between siblings were reported during our interviews, a lack of protection can create long-term problems for the victim's emotional health and the sibling relationship.

Distress About the Sibling Relationship

We asked not only about parental favoritism, interference, and protection but also whether the parents were upset by the siblings' relationship. We knew, based on our knowledge of family functioning, that when parents are distressed about their children's relationship, a significant problem may exist. An example of a problem is siblings physically, emotionally, or sexually abusing one another (for one case study that illustrates this, see Ron in chapter 7). The parents in our research tended to be described as upset with their children's relationships when the children were not as close as the parents thought they should be in childhood or adulthood, based on the parents' own upbringing. That was the case for a fifty-six-year-old white female schoolteacher and the youngest of four.

> I know that when Mother would get an inkling that my sister and I weren't getting along, it really upset her. I think they always wanted us to get along and try our best to be harmonious, since, I think, that's what they grew up with. They spoke fondly about playing with their siblings, and they didn't have any money, but they had each other and they played ball outside. So they both talked about their growing-up time as nice times.

If this mother had forced her will on them, manipulated them, or insisted they modify their relationship, this would rise to the level of a clinical issue for the family. While distress over a lack of relationship is not uncommon, the actions a parent takes to correct this in childhood and adulthood have to strike a balance between speaking up and encouraging closeness and trusting that children will grow closer on their own and with time. As we show later, how parents, especially fathers, role-model closeness can be instructive.

Parental Disengagement

We have just described parents' active behaviors (showing favoritism, interfering, protecting, or voicing being upset). On the other end of the spectrum is disengagement. We asked if parents ignored the sibling relationship or if the respondent even knew how the parents felt. This is another way to try to understand the parents' roles in their children's relationships with one another, in both childhood and adulthood. For the silent generation, our pre–baby boomers, we assumed that parents would not be as hands-on and concerned with child development as they became in the 1960s and later.

Sometimes children don't know what their parents think. The parents may work long hours, not be emotionally available, or be too absorbed in their own life. The person we interviewed might also have never considered the question.

Support

Finally, we asked whether parents were supportive of their children's relationships. To get the full picture, we asked this question as a way of focusing on positive, strength-based behavior. Typical of what we heard are the following two brief comments, the first from a fifty-one-year-old African American female and the second from a sixty-one-year-old white male:

> Did we always support each other? Yes. That's a part of how we were raised, no matter what we were going through. Something happens to one of us, and everyone is right there.

> Well, my parents were very close to their siblings from what we understand, so maybe that's how they raised us to be, the same way. Because they were always very supportive of us being supportive of each other, so I guess that maybe trickled down.

THE PAST AND THE PRESENT

We asked about both the past and the present in relation to parents' behavior and also siblings' behaviors toward one another. As a reminder, even though our sample contained 262 persons, they were describing more than seven hundred relationships. Approximately 25 percent of the siblings had one living sibling; 30 percent had two siblings, the most common configuration; 16 percent had three siblings; and another 16 percent had four. The remaining respondents had five, six, or more, with a few having many more, including one who had twelve siblings.

To learn about childhood experiences, we asked siblings to rank their level of agreement with a series of statements about their parents' behavior both when the siblings were growing up and then when the siblings became

TABLE 4.1   To What Extent Do You Agree with These Statements About Your Parents When You Were Growing Up?

	STRONGLY AGREE/ AGREE (%)	NEITHER AGREE/ DISAGREE (%)	DISAGREE/ STRONGLY DISAGREE (%)
Our parents always played favorites	28	17	55
They interfered in our relationship	15	16	69
They often tried to protect one of us from the other	25	17	58
They were highly upset by it	11	17	72
They ignored our relationship	16	19	65
I don't know what they felt	22	22	56
They were supportive of it	79	14	7

Note: Percentages are rounded.

TABLE 4.2   To What Extent Do You Agree with These Statements About Your Parent(s) When You and Your Siblings Became Adults?

	STRONGLY AGREE/ AGREE (%)	NEITHER AGREE/ DISAGREE (%)	DISAGREE/ STRONGLY DISAGREE (%)
Our parents always played favorites[a]	27	16	58
They interfered in our relationship	12	16	72
They often tried/try to protect one of us from the other	13	18	69
They were/are highly upset by it	10	20	70
They ignore(d) our relationship	13	22	64
I don't know what they felt/ feel about it	14	27	59
They were/are supportive of it	83	11	6

Statements that do not apply to responses have been removed, and percentages are rounded.

[a]   This asked about favoritism *now*.

adults. In this way, we were able to track perceptions of parental behaviors over the parent–sibling life span.

What is interesting about the two time intervals is how consistent the perceptions stay across the years in relation to a number of parental behaviors. For example, 28 percent believed that favoritism was shown when young, and 27 percent believed that it was continuing. These are almost always the same people—only 3 percent of those who did not believe favoritism was shown when they were young now believe it is being shown, and about 12 percent who thought it was being shown when young do not perceive it in adulthood. In a further analysis, two-thirds of the group who thought favoritism was shown believed he or she was *not* the favorite when growing up or in adulthood! Perceptions of parental interference and the belief that parents are upset about the sibling relationship also stayed consistent. On a good note, parental protection dropped to half of what it was in childhood, and the respondents were more likely to know how their parents felt about their relationship when they became adults. Finally, support for the sibling relationships ticked slightly upward. It is hard to know with respect to these subtle changes how much was due to the siblings maturing and seeing things differently and how much was due to changes in the parents' behavior.

In our first wave of interviews, to detect any triangulation, we also asked if siblings ever felt caught between their parents and siblings growing up or if they felt caught now. As we mentioned in our discussion of parental interference, according to the family therapy literature, triangulation is most common when a child is caught between parents, but we were looking at triangulation that occurs when parents interfere with siblings. While growing up, 23 percent reported feeling caught and, of those with living parents, 38 percent said they felt caught now. Once caught always caught? Not necessarily. Half the people with living parents who felt caught when young do not feel caught now, whereas a new crop of adults are feeling caught who did not feel caught when young. When they feel caught as an adult, it is most likely in the role of mediator or messenger between siblings; less often, they feel caught because the parents are actively interfering.

One example of how being caught feels as an adult was provided by Linda, who has not seen one brother for twenty-five years, and one sister, Kay, for seven years. Linda first talked about feeling caught trying to protect a sister, Sarah, and then described feeling caught because her father interfered with her relationship with Kay. These are two different but related and, in the second situation, overlapping mechanisms, one protecting a sibling from judgmental parents and another dealing with a parent inserting himself into a relationship.

> My oldest sister's divorce, for example. My parents really liked Sarah's ex-husband, and they felt that the divorce was my sister's fault. And to me, it wasn't really anyone's fault. Or at least, it didn't matter to me. I wanted to protect my sister from my parents' comments. And my parents were pressuring me to say something to get her to consider reconciling. I liked the guy, too, so it was tough.

In the next situation, the father was upset and interfered, seemingly trying to protect Kay and her relationship with Linda while causing Linda to feel caught between her feelings about her sibling and wanting to please her father.

> At one point, my father tried to interfere in my relationship with Kay, and I went along with it to try to make him happy, even though I knew better. He wanted to repair the relationship, but I knew it just wouldn't work. I went along with his wishes for almost two years. He finally saw that she was the crazy one and that there wasn't anything I can do about it.

It is more common, though, to see families in which concern is shown by a parent but does not result in a sibling's feeling caught in the middle. This can be due to the overall tone set in a family. Note that in the following example, of a fifty-four-year-old white businesswoman, the oldest of four daughters, a sibling's divorce is involved, but the mother's concern does not entangle the other sisters:

> That's not how my family is. The one thing we would do was band together if our parents were mad at us or just one of us. We would cry to each other when we were kids, but my parents didn't put any of us in the middle of something going on with a different sister. My one sister went through a really nasty divorce, and my mom was very worried about her. We would talk about it, but I never felt as though I was caught in the middle. It was more that my mom was just a worried mother and needed to express her concerns.

MAKING MEANING

We next discuss our findings about perceptions of parenting in childhood and in adulthood. First, the perception of parental favoritism is alive and well in a quarter of these adult families. Favoritism can be difficult to live with, whether one is the most favored or the least favored. Some siblings blamed it on their gender or their culture but were not overly upset by it. It could be overt, and the siblings would smile and say, "Oh, we knew that Sarah was always the favorite." Others, though, stated that it was more subterranean and occasionally degenerated into physical, emotional, or sexual abuse.[14]

Sometimes the least favorite becomes the target, as was the case in Willa's family. Willa, a white social worker born in 1943 and the middle of six, observed that her only brother was drawn into conflict with their father, an alcoholic who sometimes abused their mother. The brother reacted by dropping out of contact with most of the family when he became an adult.

Why was the brother the most affected of all the siblings? Bowen would suggest that it could be related to sibling position, the specific needs of a child and parent, or gender. In Willa's family, he was the only male sibling and may have identified with the father the most, or been triangulated by the father and the mother, causing conflict between father and son. He may also have feared becoming like his father and so ran away from that fear, literally and figuratively. In addition, as the only male child, he might have felt a greater need than did the sisters to protect his mother physically. He also, by his nature, may have been the most sensitive to parental conflict. Willa offered her impression:

> Our father was not a violent gentleman. When he was sober, he was very sweet, kind, loved kids. He'd play ball with us, do all those kinds of things. But when he drank, he got verbally very awful towards my mother, who would take his stuff and pour it down the sink, so there was a lot of verbal anger. This was a struggle for my brother because he felt he had to protect my mother. That's how he got into the middle of it and how he sort of ended up running away. He would just try to get between them. And of course father being male and he being male, father could pick on him. He could pick on his son.

Second, parental interference can have different meanings in different families. The family therapy literature views interference as a negative action, driven by parental need, a generations-long way of handling conflict, and a lack of boundaries. But as we see in chapter 7 in our interview with Ron, who was raised in a troubled family, interference, protection, and being upset all may be necessary reactions to what a parent is observing, based on the behavior of one of the siblings. In Ron's case, his older brother was abusive to Ron and his sister when they were young. For our sample, parental interference in childhood sometimes (about 45 percent of the time) continued in adulthood. It is rare (4 percent of the time) for it to begin in adulthood if the sibling reports that it did not occur in childhood.[15] Some family patterns can be hard to break once they are established and become rigidified over the years, but it is not a given that this pattern will continue. If parental interference appears for the first time only in adulthood, it may be precipitated by the behavior of one sibling who needs more financial or emotional help than the other siblings and is being taken care of by the parents. Protection and favoritism sometimes accompany interference here, too.

As noted, we included the question about a parent's being upset as a way to identify families that may be at risk. Willa's family is one example in which a sibling believes, especially in adulthood, that a parent is upset about what has happened between her son and her daughters. Before her death, Willa's mother reestablished contact with her son, but he did not reestablish contact with all his sisters, which, Willa believed, was upsetting to their mother.

Third, in our multiculture society, views of parents' and siblings' roles are bound to differ. For example, oldest sons may automatically receive the most benefits or have the parents' authority bestowed on them. Protection and interference may play out in idiosyncratic ways in a culture in which, for example, an older daughter is supposed to marry before a younger daughter does. Such an expectation could result in more protection and interference in sibling behavior.

Fourth, and we say this more to frame this discussion, feelings of closeness and how much closeness any one sibling or sibling group wants varies. Sibling closeness in adulthood may be driven consciously or unconsciously by the past in conjunction with the current spousal/partner relationship with the sibling. One woman we spoke with grew up in a family in which the parents were never emotionally available, so she and her siblings had to learn to fend for themselves. She married a man who is quite close to his family members. She sees her siblings three times a year and communicates with them occasionally. While she is comfortable with that level of closeness, she believes her husband is much too close to his family, as he communicates with them constantly and wants to move closer to them. His wanting to relocate is a threat to her sense of independence. Her upbringing in regard to sibling and parental closeness affects her current relationship with her husband and also illustrates how feelings of closeness vary from one family to the next.

A Brief Word on Age and Parental Behavior

Let us briefly return to the theme of age that we introduced in chapter 3, in which significant differences appeared in the perception of parental behaviors. When growing up, the older siblings in our survey were less likely than their younger siblings to say their parents protected them or were upset by their relationship. Older siblings were also less likely to know how their parents felt about these relationships. The older siblings in our sample were more likely to be left on their own when young: seen but not heard. As adults, older siblings were less likely to report that their parents interfered or protected a sibling.[16] As adults, older siblings were also less likely to know how their parents felt about the relationship.

These findings are consistent with what we know about the pressures on the silent generation. These less-child-centric behaviors indicate a general lack of attention to and awareness of children. In turn, the children were either less tuned in to their parents, as evidenced by their not knowing how their parents felt, or raised to be more independent.

PERCEPTIONS OF PARENT BEHAVIOR AND SIBLING RELATIONSHIPS

In chapter 3, we looked at competition and jealousy, as well as trust, between siblings. Now we look at how parents may influence these feelings. We say "may influence" because as we mentioned, these are systemic actions. It could be that parents stir the pot but also that children become highly competitive through circumstances other than the parents' actions and that the parents interfere or protect as a result of the competition (or jealousy) that they observe.

When parents act toward their children in ways that the family therapy literature has identified as being problematic (show favoritism, interfere, are not supportive of the relationship, and fail to protect when they should), the outcomes are troubled. Because of the overlap of many of the findings, we use two examples to explain.

Favoritism and Support When Young and Favoritism and Support Now

Perceived parental favoritism and perceived parental support of sibling relationships are mirror images of each other. For both issues, we asked subjects to rate how likely they were to trust, help, compete with, be jealous of, and argue with their siblings both now and when they were young. In both time frames, if the parents were perceived as showing favoritism, the siblings were *less likely* to trust and help one another and were more likely to compete with, be jealous of, and argue with their siblings. Conversely, if the parents were perceived as being supportive of sibling relationships, the siblings were *more likely* to trust and help one another and were less likely to compete with, be jealous of, and argue with their siblings in the past and now.

Scores on the Lifespan Sibling Relationship Scale (LSRS), which looks at feelings, behaviors, and beliefs about the relationships, support these responses. Siblings who perceived favoritism during both childhood and the present scored lower on the scale, and siblings who perceived parental support during both childhood and the present scored higher on the scale.

In other words, even if their parents showed favoritism when the subjects were children but no longer do, siblings in those families continued to have less positive relationships as adults than did siblings whose parents had not shown favoritism in either the past or the present. Conversely, siblings whose parents were supportive of their relationships with their brothers and sisters when they were children were more likely to have had, and to continue to have, positive sibling relationships.

Interestingly, siblings whose parents apparently started showing favoritism when their children were adults also had less positive relationships with their siblings now, even though they had more trusting, cooperative, and less negative relationships when they were children. Moreover, parents who more recently became more supportive of the sibling relationships helped make those sibling relationships more positive now.

When we looked at the presence or absence of parental interference, parental protection, and parents being upset, the results were in the same direction. In other words, when parents were and are interfering and protecting and are upset by the relationship, siblings have less positive relationships in childhood and adulthood.

These findings illustrate how profoundly parents can influence sibling relationships, shaping them from childhood and still being able to damage or improve them in adulthood.[17]

The final parental variable to consider is those parents perceived as ignoring the sibling relationship. Here again, although the findings are not quite as strong from a statistical perspective, when parents are perceived as not paying attention to their children's sibling relationships while the children are growing up, that is, they are ignoring them, the children get along less well in childhood and adulthood. They are more jealous and less likely to trust one another both then and now. In childhood, they are also less likely to help one another, and in adulthood they are more likely to compete.

These are not new findings, as we have indicated from our liberal use of family therapy theory to understand interference and support. In addition, the showing of both favoritism and "disfavoritism" has been linked by others to strained adult sibling relationships.[18] Favoritism is difficult to escape and possible to excuse up to a point. As a team led by professors at Purdue University stated, our culture encourages the equal treatment of children, yet such treatment is impossible, given the vagaries that children present.[19] Still, the lessons for parents seem clear: if you want your children to get along as adults, it is vital to support those relationships as they are being formed in childhood and minimize parental actions that will be felt as favoritism or as interference throughout their children's lives.

At the end of the parents' lives, the investment they made in avoiding favoritism and respecting generational boundaries will likely pay off when their children become their caretakers. We looked at these parenting behaviors and whether siblings as adults agree on the care of aging parents and found important connections. When parents showed favoritism in either childhood or adulthood, siblings were less likely to agree on care. Likewise, when parents interfered in sibling relationships in either childhood or adulthood, those siblings were less likely to agree on the care of their parents. When parents ignored the relationships while the children were growing up or were perceived as upset about the siblings' relationships now or then, the siblings were less likely to agree on the care of their parents.

AN IMPORTANT WORD ON THE INFLUENCE OF THE FATHER'S AND THE MOTHER'S OWN SIBLING RELATIONSHIPS

We wondered what influence the parents' relationships with their own siblings (our respondents' aunts and uncles) might have on our respondents' relationships with their siblings. On the questionnaire, each parent was described as having a "very close," "somewhat close/mixed," or "not close" relationship with her or his siblings, with "does not apply" for those who did not have siblings. The few mothers and fathers who were only children were excluded from the following analysis. For mothers, 53 percent were viewed as having a very close relationship, 37 percent a somewhat close/mixed relationship, and 10 percent a not close relationship. For fathers, 36 percent were reported as having a very close relationship, 43 percent a somewhat close/mixed relationship, and 21 percent a not close relationship. As reflected throughout the literature, sisters tend to have closer relationships than brothers and this was the perception of their children, our respondents.[20]

Of great interest, we found a close connection between fathers who were perceived as having been close to their siblings and our respondents' answers regarding their greater trust of and help for one another when young. For example, if our respondents perceived their fathers as being very close to their siblings, they were twice as likely to say they trusted their siblings when young. In addition, if fathers were perceived as being close to their siblings, both parents were perceived as being supportive of the sibling relationships. Fathers who were close to their siblings also positively affected sibling relationships now. Our respondents who perceived their fathers as being close to their siblings reported being supported by their siblings now, having greater agreement on taking care of parents now, scoring more positively on the LSRS, and receiving more support from their parents for their sibling relationships. In sum, having a father who is close to his siblings is strongly associated with the next generation's having more positive sibling relationships in childhood and adulthood. A mother's closeness to her siblings was not a predictor.

Why might this example of intergenerational transmission be true? Our hypothesis is that it was unusual for men born in the first forty years of the twentieth century, when the bulk of our respondents' fathers and mothers were born, to maintain very outwardly expressive relationships with their siblings, especially their brothers. Indeed, their sisters might have facilitated much of the closeness if it existed. Many men did, of course, have strong bonds with their siblings, but they might not have appeared to be as physically or emotionally expressive as might be the norm today, when men are more open. If the father was perceived as being close to his siblings, it would send a powerful message to his children, our respondents, about the importance of siblings' closeness. Because mothers were expected to be close and to be the switchboard for much of the communication between siblings, the message of her closeness to her siblings would be less powerful.[21] Fathers in general may also be less engaged with the "feelings" side of the family, so when a father does show great warmth, it has a powerful impact on the other family members.[22]

An example of how some fathers showed their affection for their siblings, albeit in a somewhat restrained way, was provided by this fifty-one-year-old woman, the middle of ten, who reported being close to her siblings:

My father loved all his siblings, but he had a very reserved relationship with them. There was very little show of affection, but there was a very great show of love in the way of constant contact and supporting each other. I mean, he had lunch with his mother and father every day. Every day of his life and all his brothers and sisters, all of them, did different roles in taking care of their parents their whole life. His father lived to be ninety-nine, and his mother lived to be ninety-six. Everybody had a role, and everybody did their part to take care of them. I think I got that from him, that sense of being responsible for your family members, your siblings and family. Everybody helping each other.

RAISING CHILDREN

The results of this research offer clear as well as nuanced ways of child rearing for parents who wish to raise siblings to feel close to one another. Undoubtedly, families in which there is the perception of favoritism, interference, and protection generate greater competition and jealousy and less trust and help for one another. Arguing among siblings is greater, too, in both childhood and adulthood. If a child is unclear about where his parents stand, if the parents ignore the relationships, or if they are upset about the relationships, more problematic sibling interactions are likely as well.

The nuance comes in the implementation of these results. Interference, as the clinical psychologist Stephen Bank suggests, causes problems in the sibling subsystem when identification of the parent with the child or children leads to a loss of boundaries. If the parent is fulfilling his or her own needs, damage is occurring. Furthermore, as Bank pointed out, problems arise when parents cannot monitor their children's behavior appropriately.[23] So our findings need to be considered carefully.

On the one hand, if parents do not interfere, relationships appear to be positive. But on the other hand, if they ignore the relationships and the situations that need parental intervention, they tend to be less positive. The art of parenting lies in knowing when to do enough but not too much. As Mark Twain said, "The difference between the right word and the almost right word is the difference between lightning and a lightning bug." Watchful waiting by a parent may send the message that the sibling relationship needs to find its own way in childhood, yet it cannot be ignored. In fact, supporting it in a positive way without, again, interfering or trying too hard to engineer it may be the best course for parents, based on what we have learned.

The message can be sent that closeness is valued and that the children will be trusted to make that work without their parents' interference. The metaphor of the orchestra conductor seems to apply here: the parent is the conductor of the sibling relationships, providing guidance and suggestions while trusting the children to find their way, but the parents should not try to play any of the instruments; the children make the music.

Every parent knows that showing favoritism is a no-no. If one child needs more concern or attention, we believe it should be talked about and balanced to the extent it can be with time and attention spent with the other children also. There is some evidence that favoritism is easier for children when siblings understand that one sibling is more needy.[24] This, we realize, puts demands on the parents' time and attention when the number of single parents and families with both parents working is on the rise. Still, when parents see that one child needs more attention, it requires a conscious effort to attend to the other children while also attending to the struggling child. When people talk about favoritism, it should be considered separately from parental concern (or what might be protection), as the two are different behaviors. As Amelia suggested in chapter 3, parents might perceive that one child needs more than another because of genetics, nature, or the context in which they were raised. A child struggling in school may need more time with and assistance from a parent. That would not necessarily be favoritism, even though it could manifest itself as such. In short, when children feel that parents are showing favoritism, it is the combination of how the parents treat the child who is perceived to be favored and how the parents treat the children who feel not favored.

Competition and jealousy between children, a normal part of childhood, should not be encouraged by parents or it will increase. We are not so concerned about competition and jealousy in childhood, nor are we concerned by arguing (within reason), as these are typical behaviors and feelings at that stage of life. Arguing and holding strong feelings of jealousy and competition in middle and later adulthood, while also normal to some extent,[25] are areas in which interventions directed at adults and their parents could be useful. As one woman told us, "I was jealous of my brother until our parents died." These ten words nicely and sadly encapsulate a lifetime of bad feelings on her part and how she viewed her parents' participation in stimulating those feelings. Appropriate parenting behaviors, which we discuss again in the last chapter, are needed throughout the life span, not just when children are young.

Change can occur, as is evidenced by the next example of someone who learned by experience. This sixty-six-year-old white schoolteacher and the oldest of four often felt caught between her parents and her siblings as both a child and an adult. She took specific measures not to duplicate that pattern with her children.

> I kind of get it, like when my kids go off together, like to a bar or something, it's very hard for me to let them do that without me. However, I do, I let them go, partially because I think I realize how important it is for them to have relationships that don't include me.

In addition, and this is a message especially for fathers, parents' closeness to their own siblings does matter. In particular, when fathers are perceived as being close to their siblings, their children get along better. Fathers therefore should consider the message they are sending to their children when they are struggling with or show little interest in their siblings.[26] Past research describes the brother-to-brother bond as not being as close as a bond with a sister, who is more likely to provide emotional support.[27] It therefore may take particular effort to establish a bond if brothers are the only siblings. But as we explain in a later chapter, past assumptions about sibling behavior based on gender may no longer apply to the generation now raising young children to the extent they once were.

Murray Bowen and Salvador Minuchin were correct in many of their core teachings about the family. We found support for both the intergenerational process and the importance of boundaries. How these are applied to any one family hoping to raise children with healthy sibling relationships will vary based on the family's culture and their own particular nature. We believe our discussion of interference, protection, and favoritism, as well as parents supporting sibling relationships, can help therapists frame questions for adult clients now and that our findings on fathers' role modeling with their siblings can help build future family support.

CHAPTER 5

When Sibling Relationships Are in Serious Trouble

I have four siblings and a relationship with only one, my sister, who is four years older. The other three, I don't have a relationship, partly from being in the military. Being away from them probably made it easier. When we've had interactions, it has always been disruptive, drama, deceit, that kind of stuff. Life is hard enough—why do I need that in my life?

Fifty-five-year-old white male, youngest of five and a store manager

IN THE PREVIOUS CHAPTER WE examined how parental behavior can influence sibling relationships starting in childhood and lasting into adulthood. We discussed how a sibling relationship, even in middle and late adulthood, can continue to suffer from the residue of family interactions during childhood, in particular parent favoritism or interference in sibling relationships. In this chapter we focus on relationships that have entirely or largely ended because of events that occurred in adulthood, often to people in their fifties or sixties, and that have resulted in a significant or total breach in the relationship. In some instances, siblings no longer have any direct contact, creating what Murray Bowen termed a *cutoff*. In a few instances, siblings have rare and restrained contact with no meaningful communication.

In our qualitative interviews, we found examples of significant events that led to cutoffs. Sometimes the cutoff was from the respondent's only sibling, or at other times, as in the example that begins this chapter, the cutoff is from multiple siblings. Sometimes it is one sibling out of several who is the target of the cutoff. We want to emphasize that not all relationship cutoffs in middle and later adulthood are the culmination of a lifelong pattern. Although relationships are usually settled by this point in adult development, some events or behaviors can be so far from one sibling's understanding or limits of acceptance of another sibling that their relationship breaks down. Siblings can do things to one another that are not part of any past pattern of behavior and could not have been anticipated. (Remember Fredo going against the Corleone family in *Godfather II* and getting bumped off by his brother Michael at the end of the movie?) Once that happens, it is just too painful or upsetting for one or both siblings to move beyond the resulting pain or anger to then interact further, even in simply a civil manner.

In all the cases discussed in this chapter, without a significant event the siblings' relationship might have muddled along and been sufficiently satisfactory to not cause great angst to any of them. Indeed, it might even have improved with growing maturity and distance from early conflicts, as such improvement over time across adulthood is often seen in the research. In some of the cases we describe, the roots of disjuncture have been sown in the family's early history, but that history did not cause the cutoff until a more cataclysmic event triggered a break in the relationship. Even if that break occurred at a less than now visible but long-standing crack in the relationship, the event became the tipping point, ending a relationship that, in retrospect, had identifiable tension but would still be intact if the event (or a series of escalating events) had not occurred. In other families, events in adulthood cause a rupture in families in which there was little or no reported parental interference or favoritism and no other identifiable history that might, in hindsight, have predicted a cutoff based on their childhood relationships and family dynamics.

In most family therapy literature, family estrangement refers to splits between parent and child. In highlighting the work of other theorists (including Bowen), Kylie Agllias, an Australian social worker, noted that estrangement between a parent and an adult child may not mean there is less emotional or psychological involvement but that their relationship is stuck in a hostile mode. We suggest such hostility is often secondary to a underlying painful wound. The relationship can become rigidified in that hostile state, with one or both parties believing it unlikely, even impossible, that the relationship can be improved. Furthermore, they sense that something is wrong, that the family is not conforming to social expectations of closeness and mutual support, which may raise feelings of guilt, shame, or sadness. Finally, Agllias wrote, estrangement is often not the result of a single event but a pattern of conflicts.[1] Sometimes, if enough time has passed, cutoff members of a family cannot even remember specifically what triggered the cutoff. It becomes a self-sustaining state after the original insult or injury has faded from conscious memory. We agree that while many cutoffs are due to an accumulation of events started in childhood, some can begin in adulthood.

In order to select from our sample the most troubled relationships, we looked at various responses both on the questionnaire and in the qualitative interviews. We excluded those with step- and half siblings because their particular dynamics merit separate discussion, which we provide in the next chapter. Instead, we looked for siblings who disagreed with the statement "We trust each other (now)" (11 percent disagreed). We also looked at people who described all or almost all their siblings in negative terms when asked to describe the relationship in their own words (10 percent used primarily negative terms). We looked at respondents who, when asked during the interview if there was a change in how close they were to their siblings, replied that they were never close (9 percent). Finally, we looked at the 10 percent of those we surveyed[2] who indicated they had no e-mail, telephone, or face-to-face contact with their siblings, which is essentially what a cutoff is, no contact. In reading through the qualitative interviews for these cases, many of whose responses overlapped, we found a range of reasons, given by the respondents, for why their relationships were highly conflictual or cut off in adulthood.

We contacted the researchers Scott Myers and Victoria Hilkevitch Bedford, both of whom have written extensively on siblings. While neither has looked specifically at this type of relationship, they each offered an opinion from their years of work in the area. Myers, at West Virginia University, believes that while emotional distance in middle and late adulthood can be a carryover from childhood, it could also be caused by "some sort of chronic issue/addiction/condition that makes sustained interaction (frequency, breadth, depth) difficult or undesirable."[3] Bedford, a professor emerita at the University of Indianapolis, remarked that siblings can get stuck in their relationships throughout their life. Some people drift apart from one another but are not "officially" cut off. Perhaps they just have dissimilar interests, beliefs, and social networks or, as illustrated in this chapter's opening example, do not live physically close to each other. They therefore do not see each other except at infrequent yet important joyous (a wedding) or stressful (the death of a family member) events that bring them to the same place and time, and that is when their lack of relationship becomes problematic.[4]

WHY ADULT SIBLINGS HAVE SIGNIFICANT CUTOFFS

We have broken these events into two ways of thinking that may be helpful to clinicians in organizing their work: breakups in adulthood after a seminal event and breakups in adulthood after a series of events that have a cumulative effect over time.

Events Surrounding a Seminal Event

DEATH AND DYING ISSUES

The dying and death of a parent is usually an upsetting time for even the most sanguine families. "It's extremely difficult for a family to have to acknowledge the demise of its elders, evoking buried fears of death and abandonment. Often, the grown children don't feel ready for the changing of the guard," therapist Laura Markowitz wrote.[5] If siblings have not been on the best of terms, they can use the opportunity to put aside differences and unite for the first time or reunite in a manner that honors the dead. But that seems to be the exception. In one large survey of families, both a parent's illness and death were related to siblings' subsequently not getting along as well.[6] Sometimes while alive a parent can—like Mother Russia in the old Soviet Union—hold the sibling relationships together. The death may be a time when the threads that have been tenuously held together by the parent completely tear apart and the family fabric takes on a new form of individual strands.

Clearly, if siblings agree on the caregiving of a dying parent, the time surrounding the death will be easier. An equitable distribution of caretaking also can make this time easier. The perception of equity in care can vary: In our study, the majority (57 percent) said that they shared the care of their parents, whereas in another study based on focus group interviews, 65 percent indicated that the distribution of caregiving was inequitable.[7]

The meaning of a parent's death is usually so significant that no matter what the circumstances surrounding it are, miscommunication, hurt feelings, and the regeneration of unresolved issues ensue.

We first offer two examples of siblings whose relationships broke apart because of the treatment that a parent received at the hands of another sibling. The assumption here is that if the treatment had been better—in the eyes of the sibling we interviewed—the sibling relationship would not have broken down.

Letty, a fifty-two-year-old Native American, believed her sister's selfishness led to their father's death. Letty then talked about actions taken immediately following the death that poured fuel on that fire.

> My father died three years ago after a trip to Florida. He had passed out in North Carolina on the way here, and my sister, who was driving him, let him sign out AMA [against medical advice] to get on with the trip. They had stopped at a flea market on one of the hottest days in Florida, despite his condition. When they finally got to my house, my husband and brother-in-law had to carry him out of the van to bring him inside. He started having seizures as soon as he got in. We called 911. He never recovered and died in the hospital. I blame her for being so selfish. But more than that, she did some really trifling things after he died. It was really bad. I already didn't like her, but I tolerated her, since she was close to him. But she showed her true colors, and I know I will never speak to her again. She's just dishonest, and she's always been that way. She will get what is coming to her. I am sure of that.

A clinician's natural tendency when hearing (or reading) her description of what happened and her strongly held feelings about it is to start thinking about a strategy to help these sisters heal this cutoff. It seems clear such a strategy needs to proceed slowly and focus on Letty's feelings before any motion is made to include her sister in that process.

Jane, a forty-eight-year-old white female, the youngest of six, told us that even though she was a tax attorney and familiar with wills and estates, she was removed as one of the executors of her mother's estate, which she learned before her mother's death. In an example of conflict that does not arise as the result of the parents' treatment, these siblings fought, even though they described their mother as not interfering. Money disputes haunted the family, and as a result, the sister who was responsible for caring for their mother was unwilling to pay for nursing care, which, apparently, led directly to the mother's gruesome death.

> My oldest sister . . . the last straw with her was that she wouldn't release the money for someone to be there overnight. My mom ended up getting out of bed and falling, and she suffocated to death. That really took a lot. My sister Jennifer, unfortunately, told me that. She [the sister in charge] never shared with anybody else how it happened. She's a geriatric RN, works in a convalescent home. Another sister discovered my mom. She'd been dead for like eight hours. And she called Jennifer, Jennifer came over, cleaned up the body, washed her from head to toe. Cleaned up all of the feces and everything else. Cleaned up the bedroom. Put her in her favorite pink nightgown and put her to bed. And then called the police.

We asked Jane if having a night aide would have prevented her mother's death: "Absolutely. It wouldn't have happened. It's a blessing that she's gone, but the way . . . is horrible. I'll never speak to that sister again. That was the final straw."

As in Letty's case, what followed the death was one sibling blaming another sibling for hastening the death of the parent, an event-based cutoff that will be difficult to bridge. Conflict over the disposition of the estate also fed the flames. Jane offered these observations: "A lot of the relationships change after parent deaths. . . . In the relationship, not only do the children have to grieve, but they have to take care of the parent's stuff. . . . Even if everyone gets the same thing, it still sets up disagreements. They fight because they're grieving."

ESTATE AND MONEY ISSUES

The preceding examples focus on how events immediately before the death and, in Jane's and Letty's cases, disputes about the execution of the will only add to what is already a traumatic family loss. Some families agree on their coming to terms with their parent's death but run into trouble with the disposition of the estate. A parent does not even have to die for disputes over property to arise, which high school students learn if they read *King Lear*. In real life, siblings Brent and Shari Redstone have battled for a piece of their father Sumner's empire, even though he is still alive. More common are the posthumous battles. For example, Bernice, Dexter, and Martin Luther King III fought over Martin Luther King Jr.'s Nobel Peace Prize and personal Bible, both of which have enormous sentimental and financial value. Baseball legend Ted Williams's children even fought over whether he should be cryogenically preserved.

Jane was cut out of the opportunity to use her professional training and experience as a tax attorney to help with the division of her mother's estate. It was both a professional and a personal insult. In the next example, Jerome, a fifty-nine-year-old white male and the oldest of three, was excluded by his two younger sisters.

> The time that I became completely distant from them was after the death of my mother. In an attempt to reconcile her estate, they became what I considered to be very proprietary and exclusionary with respect to me and the handling of the estate, and as a result, tempers rose, and emotions rose, and "Bye. See ya." It all started about eight years ago.

Sometimes one sibling ends communication. Jerome went back and forth on how their relationship ended: "It was probably somewhat mutual, but my feelings were hurt the most and so I said, 'I quit.' I didn't want to keep going back into the same stressful situation, and so I stopped."

Even though his sisters tried to patch things up, Jerome did not think they were sincere: "Sandy did try once or twice to reconcile, spread some years after the fact. But I didn't sense any change in her attitude towards the previous situation or anything and so I said, 'It hasn't changed.' I still got nothing going, nothing in common."

Jerome, who felt closer to his father than his mother, believed that his mother's death uncovered a rigidly bounded and enmeshed relationship among the women in the family that excluded him. It also confirmed a pattern, established in adulthood, that one sibling, Janice, needed more support than the other children.

> My mother's death led to the destruction of the relationship. It was the whole, the girls getting together and conspiring with my mother to change her will and to modify the content to the benefit of Janice over me and Sandy, because Janice had struggled with finances her entire adult life and was leeching off my mother until the day she died, and the support that the

two sisters gave each other in opposition to me, how the estate should be handled, the changing of the will, and all of those things. I felt that it was conspiratorial among the two siblings, against me, and their actions more or less demonstrated that. The funny thing was, at the funeral, I was of a mind-set to forgive and forget, make peace, even though the relationship had become strained at that point. Yet shortly after the funeral, when it was time to actually start discussing the estate, it became very obvious that they were of a similar mind and against me, and at that point I just couldn't take it, wouldn't accept the fact that what was supposed to be "Share and share alike" was very tilted against me. They basically cut me out of the whole thing, and so I said, "The heck with it."

Whereas Jane and Jerome resented being cut out of the executor role, sometimes being the executor has problems, too. A fifty-eight-year-old eldest of three who took care of her siblings most of their lives was resented when she was made the executor, even though that was a continuation of her earlier role.

We're not as close as we were. My sister and I used to be best friends. But when I was put in charge of my grandmother, I was made executor, and they found out about it. And she was paying me to take care of her. When the family found out all of this, it caused problems when she passed and I was in charge of everything. So that put a strain on my relationship with my brother and my sister. . . . Because even when people die and they give money to this person, or you're in charge of this, it causes turmoil. They wanted to contest the will. When I found out my grandmother had put me in charge I didn't want it, I tried to get my name off, but when a will is in place, you can't do anything about it.

All these examples center on the death of a parent or grandparent. Those persons we interviewed were often trying to reconcile their sadness at their parent's death with the anger and sadness they felt toward their siblings. Sometimes a signal event that does not involve death and its aftermath can also cause rifts. A financial theft from a family business ends a relationship. A sibling offers alcohol or drugs to another sibling's child. As we mentioned in chapter 3, one brother had an affair with another brother's fiancé.

A Series of Negative Events

Whereas the previous examples seem to entail the "straw that breaks the camel's back," other cutoffs come after an accumulation of intersibling slights or disappointments that are often coupled with the conviction that little will change. Often an abundance of events accumulates, and finally one or all of them end their relationship. It has become too painful or too difficult to keep the relationship going.

MENTAL HEALTH AND SUBSTANCE ABUSE DISORDERS

Serious psychological issues, those related to substance abuse or mental health disorders, often emerge in the late teens and early twenties. Siblings earlier may have had serious concerns that a brother or sister was having trouble. They may have tried to help by planning an intervention, attending family therapy or a support group, or getting their own help to cope. As the years went on, they may have watched their parents anguish over the sibling and provide financial or residential support. The siblings also may have helped out in similar ways. Twenty or even thirty years after the onset of the illness or addiction, a sibling, who may be attempting to play a caregiving role, may be worn down and thus will distance herself or himself.

Kyle, a fifty-year-old African American FedEx driver described his relationship with his troubled fifty-eight-year-old only brother. Listening to him speak, a clear picture emerges of what life with his brother has been like and how Kyle must set clear boundaries to preserve his own well-being.

> My relationship with my brother is very distant and strained. He struggles with a mental illness and has been addicted to drugs for as long as I can remember, and that has caused major issues between us and our relationship as well as for the family. I don't remember a time when he didn't cause turmoil.

In trying to understand the high points of his roller-coaster relationship, we asked for a description of a particularly enjoyable time that the two siblings had together. Most respondents can offer many; Kyle was unable to offer even one: "I can't think of an enjoyable event or time with my brother. I don't know if I've blocked it out, or if there simply weren't any. He's suffered from mental illness since we were children. He's always been different."

Recalling a difficult event was much easier.

> There are many. One that sticks in my mind the most was one Thanksgiving when he came to dinner high. The minute he walked in the door, he was very combative and cursed everyone in the house out, including the children. He then began to knock all of the food off the dinner table. We ended up having to call the cops because he was out of control.

Kyle expects any interactions with his brother to be difficult to traumatic. There is no trust in the relationship, and there is no topic that Kyle would feel comfortable discussing with his brother. Indeed, Kyle may feel relief at not having to deal with his brother anymore. The relationship is not, however, categorized as strained; instead, it is intentionally distant, as Kyle keeps his brother at bay to the extent that he can. Still, given the cultural obligation that most adults feel toward their siblings, deciding to set such clear boundaries can be painful. "He's not in his right mind, so he's very unpredictable."

A forty-nine-year-old white loan officer, Leonard, who has a younger brother and sister, described his struggles with his brother. The brother's mental health problems emerged later in life than usual. Although Kyle is not interested in building a relationship with his only sibling, Leonard, who is close to his sister, would consider reaching out to his brother but feels that it would not be reciprocated. Out of exasperation, he seems to have decided to push his brother away. When asked about the importance of a relationship with him, Leonard replied angrily, "I could give a rat's ass." In Leonard's description, we hear the toll that the years have taken and the important position that his sister occupies.

> My brother has been living with my mom now for three years. Basically my mother is taking care of my fifty-one-year-old brother. He has bipolar issues and drug issues, so to be able to know what's going on and be able to confide in my sister about the situation is important. I can't talk to my brother in the same way I talk to her. That's because I don't think having a relationship with me means anything to him. He's sometimes here, and sometimes he's not. I think the drugs and the bipolar make it so he's barely there. . . .

Basically he can't work, but he keeps getting turned down for disability. He goes from manic to depressed, and you never know what you're going to get with him. It's really taken a toll on the family. With my sister, I can call her up and talk to her about anything. She's easygoing. She wants to please people. My brother, you never know who's gonna be there. The good brother or the sick brother.

Leonard separates his early years in the family from his adult years by describing his childhood as idyllic, surrounded by loving parents and grandparents.

I listen to other people talk about their childhood and their upbringing, and I think my childhood was magnificent in comparison to what other people experienced. I was closer to my brother growing up, but that has changed dramatically because it's impossible to have a relationship with him now because of his sickness. My brother has been this way only for the last eight years or so. And the relationship with my sister improved long before my and my brother's deteriorated.

In Leonard's description of his brother, we see an example of an "ambiguous loss," similar to ambiguity, that can happen with a sibling with a mental health disorder. The term was originally coined by Pauline Boss for abducted children and soldiers missing in action with no physical proof of what happened to them or their whereabouts.[8] They are absent physically but are alive psychologically in the thoughts of the loved ones who both struggle with the loss while holding on to hope of their return. The term has evolved to be applied to people with Alzheimer's disease or substance abuse issues who are physically present but psychologically absent. Leonard insisted that it was impossible to have a relationship with his brother now because of his emotional and substance problems, and this represents a combination of loss and ambiguity for Leonard and his family.

A third example is offered by Marvin, a fifty-year-old white male with a fifty-six-year-old sister. Whereas Kyle and Leonard described mental health challenges with other siblings, Marvin is the one with the history of substance abuse. He was interviewed at an outpatient facility where he was in rehabilitation. He and his sister maintain what he considers a "fake" or superficial relationship.

The first time that I crashed and burned and I needed to get some help, she allowed me to live with her for a while and she was there for me. I don't know. Maybe I just wore out my welcome. I don't know if that's a part of it because we're still a big. . . . We still visit each other, and she's never voiced it again because there's no honesty. I'm really speculating but she's . . . I've just been more intimate and revealing about who I am to you [the interviewer] than I would be with my sister.

Marvin wants a deeper, more meaningful relationship than his sister wants. She may very well be keeping her distance as a self-care strategy, given his history, and may want only minimal contact. He may be at a place in treatment at which he is trying to repair relationships and is asking for more connection to all his friends and family.

There's always this underlying stress underneath our relationship when we talk because of these unresolved issues. A lot of times, though I would prefer to just have a conversation like you and I are having, her voice will grow a little tense on the phone and I call it "playing house." She'll "play house" and ask me those kinds of "house-y" kind of questions. Some of the patterns in her behavior I was just finding unacceptable beyond the lack of intimacy. . . . My daughter would go up there to visit for summer camp and she would try to solicit stuff secretly out of my daughter during the week that she was up there year after year when she was a kid. I was like, "Oh no. That's unacceptable."

Marvin's sister may have been keeping an eye on his daughter to ensure her well-being, a concern that he rejects. Despite his wanting to be closer to his sister, he also believes that she is struggling with issues common to family members of people struggling with substance abuse.

I talked to you earlier about how we're the perfect cliché. You got two kids growing up in this incredibly toxic alcoholic environment, right? One of them goes off and becomes an alcoholic just like that, right? The other one becomes like the poster child for codependency, OK? I don't believe she's dealt with any of that crap because she and her husband are like codependency flags all over the place. A codependent is just as sick, they may not die from it, but they're just as sick emotionally and socially.

Marvin's attempts to get close to his sister have had little success. Ultimately, he would rather let the relationship end than maintain one with little meaning.

> Another big breaking point was all this stuff began to build up, and I'm living in [names town] maybe eight years ago, and I put it on the line. We had a real conversation because some of those issues on the surface came up, and it got more heated. I have been saying to my wife I might as well have no relationship because this is a fake relationship. I called my sister out on some of the things that I had observed going on and I said, "Unless you and I can work on improving our relationship, I don't want to talk to you anymore. I would prefer not to have a relationship." I said, "It saddens me because I love you, but I will not have you use my daughter as a proxy. I will not have you say negative things about me in front of her."
>
> She ultimately got back to me after like. . . . We had some letters and stuff and back and forth, and we patched things up. Things got a little better for a while, and then we kind of fell back into our old patterns of no intimacy. I've already given up on them ever being what I would want them to be and have tried to accept the fact that at least I have a sister whom I love and who I know loves me. We have some involvement in each other's lives. This is one of the greatest struggles in my life because she's my only living sibling or family member.

This is Marvin's perspective, and it is tinged with ambivalence. We do not know if his sister is like him, given their history. She may be as cautious or as withheld with him as Leonard and Kyle are when dealing with their siblings.

FAILURE TO ACCEPT A SPOUSE

When siblings marry or partner, they bring another person into the family that, for better or worse, affects the preexisting sibling relationships. If a spouse fits in well, siblings often become closer as they socialize as couples or a group and may share child-rearing experiences. But even when siblings get along famously, as they do in the lengthy case example in chapter 9, a spouse can become an obstacle to that closeness if, for example, he or she does not treat a sibling well. One sibling being partnered and another not partnered can cause an imbalance in the extent to which siblings need each other, such as when a widow or divorced woman may stay close to a sister for the instrumental help her sister's husband can provide.[9] Research has found that those who are not married or do not have a partner are more likely than those who are married or have a partner to consider their siblings as important confidants, especially if they live close by.[10]

The epigraph that begins this chapter is from a military man who in adulthood never became closer to his siblings. Walter had been close to his siblings when he was young, but then he joined the military, established an adult life away from and independent of the family, and married someone who did not fit into a mold that one of his sisters had constructed for the family. As he said, "When we've had interactions, it has always been disruptive, drama, deceit."

> Things were going well until Lynn and I got married. It's funny, I think the year before we married I was stationed in Omaha, and Lynn was in LA. My older sister was in Omaha. Lynn came up to visit, and I think my sister had an expectation; she's very much like my mother. My mother expected that when her mother died, all of the siblings would revolve around her—she's the oldest girl in the family. That didn't happen. When my grandmother died, all the siblings went their separate ways. My mother thought she'd be the matriarch and she wasn't, so she became a very angry person. My sister was kind of the same way. She thought she'd be the matriarch of all of the siblings. Lynn came into her life, as my bride-to-be, and she realized Lynn was not going to be able to be manipulated. That changed the dynamics. When Lynn was supposed to meet my parents, about six months after my sister met her, Lynn stayed with my sister, and all sorts of problems came up. My sister wanted to be able to run everyone's life, but she couldn't do that with Lynn, and so she lost her power, her throne, basically.

Here we see the power of family history that Bowen uncovered. In the sister's mind, the eldest child is supposed to be treated with deference and respect, and when the new person entering the family did not, she rejected her in an attempt to recreate the previous generation's dynamics.

> When I got back from my deployment, my sister told me her daughters can't be in the wedding. It'd just be too much for them. They were five- and three-year-old girls. They loved Lynn when they met her. "Well, it'd just be too

much. They wouldn't be able to focus on schoolwork." Well, one's three! They don't have to focus on schoolwork. So it was really kind of bizarre stuff. I called her one time, one of the nieces was sitting with Lynn on the couch and my sister was sitting next to her and the niece said to Lynn, "Aunt Lynn, I love you," and my sister just snapped at her, "You love your mother more." Mature adults don't do that kind of stuff. I think that was the trigger.

Walter and his sister went for seventeen years without talking. They spoke to each other at their mother's funeral but have not spoken since. The division of property after the funeral pushed them even further apart.

> When we got to the house, all of these official documents, the will and everything were all missing. We know now that because the family members have told us, the granddaughter, Jessica, and my older brother's son both had access to the house and the combination to the safe and they took everything out. Not only did they take out her will and other things, they took her valuables.

Walter's wife was not accepted by Walter's sister, and that lack of acceptance had helped poison Walter's relationships with his other siblings. The grandchildren's bad behavior may have had other causes and might have caused a rift even without the difficulty between Walter's wife and his sister, but the combination has meant that Walter does not have a good relationship with any of his siblings.

Another example of a spouse being rejected comes from a fifty-one-year-old white social worker with four siblings. Her brother's wife had been a close friend but then changed after a few years of marriage.

> When they first got married, she was my sorority sister. We all hung out, my husband and I and the two of them. But after they had kids, she got really weird, very anxious/OCD-ish, and we started not enjoying their company. After the kids started growing up a little bit, initially we played together and all that, but as they started to get a little bit older, she started getting very strange and we kind of parted ways.

Of course, partners may be rejected even when people are not married. Selma, a single, white, fifty-seven-year-old chemist, felt that her only sibling, an older sister, was rejecting a part of her when she was critical of all the men with whom she had ever had a relationship.

> My sister has never liked any of the men in my life—never likes the men in my relationships. She didn't like my first husband but likes him now that we're divorced [laughs]. She doesn't like my fiancé, who has been in my life for twenty years. That's a bone of contention. It made me unhappy because she can be very mean, and she doesn't even want to be in the same room with my husband, so she would just snub him during get-togethers. Or she would ignore him and pretend he wasn't even in the room. Or if he said something she didn't like, she'd make a nasty comment.

Although Selma wanted a relationship with her sister, she was not willing to give up her fiancé to be with her.

> It hurts me. She's made some pretty crappy choices in her life when it came to men. She's divorced from her first husband and has a contentious relationship with one of her sons. But I keep my mouth shut. She lives in Georgia, and there are times I would like to visit her with my fiancé, but I won't because she treats him like dirt. This summer we were two hours away, and I didn't go see her because I was with my fiancé. I've come to the realization that I have to have a relationship with her that doesn't include my fiancé because it's better for my health and well-being.

CHILDREN IN THE MIX

Issues between siblings can sometimes be taken up by their children who want to defend them; Bowen might call this a "multigenerational transmission" of *conflict*. Perhaps the children have heard stories about how their parent was treated by a sibling and take an opportunity to take their side. From Bowen's perspective, this would be an example of a lack of differentiation between generations when a child "goes to battle" for a parent. In the next two examples, adult children argued with a sibling, in the first case an uncle and in the second an aunt, which resulted in a break in the sibling relationship. In both cases, the children could have been acting consciously or unconsciously as protectors of a parent but, by speaking up, may have pushed the siblings further apart.

A sixty-six-year-old white retired CEO told us about a fight that her son had had with her brother a year before our interview with her.

My twenty-nine-year-old son had words with him. I don't know exactly what happened, as I wasn't in the room. My brother took great umbrage with my son, and my son, he was disgusted. And then my brother left the house in a huff, and I haven't heard from him since. Apparently he disrespected my son [which started the fight]. He has always had such hostility towards me. It was just awful. I wish it could have been different, but it was better in that moment that he left.

This respondent is upset by the loss of the relationship with her brother. In fact, she began therapy partly because of the loss of this relationship.

The second example raises the question of whether any other family member can block access to a sibling. (Chapter 8 analyzes three sisters who have a model relationship but believe that their stepmother has blocked access to their father.) Here, a sixty-three-year-old African American, a school principal with two older siblings, feels that her nephew blocked her from access to her sister, despite having driven for six hours to visit her in the hospital.

When I got to the hospital for my sister, her son was there, his ex-girlfriend was there, and my sister's girlfriend was there. But her son puts up a finger and tells me to wait before I can go in, though all those other people were there. And I am like, "This is my sister! And who are these other people that can stay and I don't." I was highly offended. So her son and I talked and I said, "I am going to a hotel to shower and go to sleep and go back home in the morning." But he said I was on the night shift, and I said, "If that is what you want, I will sleep here." I said, I am going back home tomorrow because she clearly doesn't need me here. All my sister heard was that I had offended her son, his girlfriend, and her girlfriend. That was major. So she and I had a big blowout. She was very sick. She got out of the hospital a few days later. When she got back home is when she laid me out. I told myself, she's oxygen deprived, but I was not going to accept her being offended because of some misunderstanding between her son and me. And then I became offended even more when my brother's wife was asked by my sister to act as a mediator between us.

Another type of hurt can result when a sibling does not attend a significant event for a child of a sibling. In this next example, when a brother skips another brother's daughter's wedding, it is the final straw in their deteriorating relationship.

Alan, a sixty-nine-year-old white higher education consultant, has a younger brother, sixty-seven, and two younger sisters, fifty-five and sixty-one. He first described the normal ups and downs that relationships go through over a lifetime. He then zeroed in on his brother's hurtful behavior that severely strained their relationship.

> My brother is bizarre. I really don't understand what's going on with him. We never had much in common. All four of us had very different experiences of our parents. My youngest sister is the one I feel fondest of, and the only one I felt somewhat guilty about leaving when I left home for college. My other sister I was having an increasingly good relationship with until two years ago, not great but better, and not as much fun as with my other sister. Then, starting around a year ago, it got harder. Now, it got really unpleasant around the time of our mother's dying [four months ago], and I feel like she and I are both working carefully to mend the relationship.

Alan was working to keep the lines of communication open with his brother but felt that he had rejected him when Alan's daughter was getting married.

> With my brother, it was after our mother died. My brother's decision not to bring his wife and daughters to my daughter's wedding. And then I called him, and that phone conversation was extremely unpleasant. My brother may have literally said, every time I saw him with our mother, "Who's your favorite? Must be me," or he would say to our mother, "I'm your favorite, right?" He even raised it at the funeral. My inference from that is whatever was going on, he was worried about being the favorite in ways that I don't really know why or what.

The rift that resulted in the brother's skipping the wedding had begun a few months earlier, but Alan was still caught by surprise by his refusal to attend the wedding.

My brother called me less than a year ago and started talking for like thirty minutes, telling me how terribly I had treated him when we were growing up, and he didn't understand how I had, or why I had started being nice later, and why did I treat him so terribly, and he had a terrible growing up. Until a year ago, it was common for our brother to say how wonderful a childhood he had, and how perfect our mother was and everything was great. What that all means I don't really know.

This case epitomizes one of our central themes: the ambiguity of a sibling's behavior. Alan does not understand what is going on with his brother and cannot talk about it with him because of their cutoff.

DIFFERENCES

A few siblings have ended their relationships because of political or philosophical differences. These usually fall along classic liberal and conservative lines. As we noted in chapter 3, 29 percent of our respondents do not feel comfortable talking about politics with at least one of their siblings. Political differences that ultimately cause a relationship to end usually emerged from a culmination of other differences between siblings, which may include child rearing, treatment of parents, and a general distancing that had begun many years earlier.

A fifty-eight-year-old white male, the middle of five sons in a family with large age gaps among the children, described the infusion of politics into their relationships:

I don't know right now. I just feel very unaccepting of three of my brothers' political views that it's difficult to feel close to them. If I were a different person I would transcend that side of things and remember that they are my brothers. But we never were that close.

Differences in sexual orientation have also resulted in the siblings' distancing from one another. Paul, a health care worker, is white, forty-one years old, HIV positive, and gay. He has a forty-four-year-old brother and a forty-two-year-old sister. He struggles with his relationships with both; one relationship he characterizes as apathetic and the other as hostile.

My family is important, but obviously not equally. My brother and I do not communicate well or often, and my sister and I tend to function poorly at best. Our relationships are really broken. We are not friends, but we are siblings. My brother just does not care; I doubt he would care at all if I stopped being his brother. He is disinterested, very self-sufficient and independent. My sister is a yes-and-no situation. We communicate more, but it is not comfortable, it is forced most of the time.

Like other situations we have cited, the family maintains quasi relationships to give the appearance that they get along: "We do not communicate in a friendly way. We will check in but not about anything substantial, more like updates. I think we talk because we think we are supposed to, not because we want to at all."

Part of the front they have maintained for years was based on Paul's sexuality. It was a family secret that eventually took its toll.

Oh my God yes . . . you know my gayness was a huge one [secret] [becomes quiet and his voice breaks]. We are a military family; we don't make "gays" especially really gay gays. I danced. I went to Europe to dance and lived out and open, and it was fabulous, and I also served my country. But it was such a point of discomfort for my father, not my mom. I remember when I was five or so, I was watching her get ready to go out with my dad. And she was painting her nails, and I was so excited and my sister was getting nail polish too, and I wanted it so badly. I begged for it, and my sister looked at me like I was crazy. I asked my mom again and again, and she finally said, OK just my big toes. My sister did not tell my dad. I am not sure if she even understood, but somehow . . . [begins to tear up]. Maybe my mom said something. I don't know. Maybe she felt like protecting me from my father and brother [crying]. Maybe she knew what would happen if "John Wayne" found out his son had a pedicure. So we do have secrets, and I feel like most are about me, my life, and my choices. Especially my choices. My HIV status, I mean, how much more gay do you get, right? It cost me my military career . . . thank you "Don't Ask Don't Tell," which was a hard secret to keep. It got to be way too much, and I had to tell them all. That did not go well, I was in a dark place then, but that was almost a decade ago, and it is a little better now. My mom tries the hardest to let me know it is OK. She loves me no matter what, and my father seems to have come around. My brother and I rarely speak, and my sister and I tend to communicate in letters/e-mails mostly.

YOU CALL FIRST

Sometimes it can be as simple, and as petty, as "I called you last" or "Why didn't you call me first?"

A fifty-nine-year-old white day-care provider with an older and a younger sister told us this story about why she and her older sister did not speak for years.

> Well, my sister was supposed to come over for our Christmas Eve dinner where we do our Italian Feast of Seven Fishes. I'd talked to her earlier that day and she said she was coming, but when dinner came she never showed up, which I didn't think anything of because she showed up only about half the time she said she would, anyway. So I left her a voicemail the next day asking if she was going to come over for Christmas dinner, and no reply. Called her later that evening. Again no reply. I didn't hear from her until the next day when she called and said [in a whiny voice] "How come you didn't call me that night when I didn't show up for dinner; you didn't think it was strange that I didn't show up? You don't even care about me." Well, I didn't apologize because I didn't do anything wrong, and we haven't talked since then.

It also could be a single comment at a sensitive time that causes a rift. A seemingly off-hand comment can lead to a cutoff if it brings to light a previously unknown and significantly different perception that existed in the family. For example, two siblings learned they had vastly opposing perceptions of their recently deceased father when one sibling wondered how their father was doing in heaven and the other replied that she assumed he was in hell. So upset was the first sibling by the remark that they did not speak for two years.

MAYBE IT'S ME

While most of the examples of reasons for strained relationships center on the sibling we interviewed, indicating that the other sibling's behavior is the cause, some siblings do consider that it may be their own behavior that started the distancing. Because of their actions, their siblings are keeping away from them. But they do not necessarily forgive their siblings and often resent being excluded.

One forty-seven-year-old white garage mechanic, the middle of four, said on his questionnaire that he wanted more support from his siblings. Describing himself as an ex-offender, he believed that his relationships changed in adulthood, particularly that with his youngest sibling, because of his incarceration. "When I got locked up, she wrote me off." He has no relationship with her now and a marginal one with another brother.

A sixty-nine-year-old white female, Suzanne, the oldest of five, struggled for many years with her relationship with her siblings. For most of her life since she left the convent, they have taken care of her. This could be similar to other relationships in which the siblings get together to take care of another sibling but resent having to do it.

> I am not good at relationships—part of it is the ADD and part of it is growing up in the family that I did. I am really good only at intense, sharing relationships, and we're not a family that breeds those. I have friends that I see maybe four times a year, and when we meet up, we don't do small talk, we talk about what's happened with us, and I live for those.
>
> A factor in my relationship with my siblings is that my financial situation is incredibly different than theirs. My sister, Jan, who is three years younger than me, sends me a check for $100 to $200 five or six times a year. She never talks about it, just does it. And my financial situation was fine with them as long as I was a Catholic nun. But now they don't approve of all the decisions that I've made, and I am a horrible financial manager. I think they are afraid that they are going to wind up supporting me when I get older. That is a real fear because I don't want that to happen, but I don't know how to avoid it, except to get on a bus with a bag and disappear.

Suzanne talked about wanting to vanish to avoid becoming a burden to her siblings, from whom she received financial support. She knew she was excluded from their socializing. Even though she accepted help from them, she also resented their overstepping the bounds and trying to run her life, thereby placing the siblings in a no-win situation.

> The other thing that I carry around is a strong sense of guilt about my youngest sister, Fran. We are not close. We are very isolated. I think that when I left

home when she was three years old, that was an abandonment thing for her. I don't think she ever got over it. She did not marry until her early thirties and, before that, had a series of failed relationships. Every time she broke up with someone, I blamed myself. I thought she couldn't trust. She has also chosen not to have children, and I blame myself for that. She and Jan have reconnected. They all have symphony tickets, and Jan and her husband will come down, and the four of them will go to dinner and the symphony together. They also vacation together. I wouldn't expect to be invited because I don't have the money for it.

There is a lot of contact, but a lot of friction. We don't talk things out. Last year, when it became obvious that my house was beyond repair, I got a letter from Jan. She had researched senior places and cheap places. This is typically her way of dealing with things, of dealing with her kids. She is a manager, a "solution-er." I also heard from Sam. He talked to me about it; the two of them had talked about it; and I blew up. I'm not going to have them run my life.

Suzanne is in a one-down position in relation to the others, the family's "black sheep." This position is similar to those into which others have been placed by their siblings when they have struggled with mental health or substance abuse issues or have lifestyle or personality differences with the other sibling or siblings. It can be a difficult position from which to escape.

CONCLUSION

Among the 20 percent of the relationships that are strained, the most common are those in which contact occurs *infrequently*, usually only at family events like annual holidays, vacations, weddings, and funerals. About three-quarters of those with strained relationships described their relationship with at least one sibling in this way. At the farthest end of these relationships are those that are nonexistent, although the siblings know how to contact one another in case of an emergency. In rare instances, a sibling has completely withdrawn from the family, and his or her whereabouts are unknown.

Severely strained relationships in which contact is *frequent* are not characteristic of most of the strained relationships in our research. These can be the most troubling for siblings, though, as the tension connected with the contact is unrelenting and often unavoidable. Such relationships endure in families who live near one another and have to interact a great deal because of caregiving of parents or shared family business responsibilities. When there is strain and little contact, it might be because siblings have moved away from one another, possibly to avoid too much interaction. But people also relocate for work or a partnership and the sibling relationship is not the reason for the move, though it may make the move easier or even more attractive.

We should note that we are aware of research describing sisters as working harder than brothers to stay in contact.[11] But when we explored this, we did not find such a pattern in our analysis of our qualitative interviews.

Returning to Agllias's work on parent-adult child estrangement, we see that, like intergenerational cutoffs, these sibling cutoffs also run afoul of societal expectations that siblings will get along throughout their lives. The loss that accompanies many of these breaks is great for many of those highlighted here and leaves them with ambivalence.[12] The lack of a relationship comes with a personal cost, as it leaves siblings sad, angry, and unsure how to proceed. Siblings often wish for more closeness, but they learn to accept circumstances they do not think they can change and settle for what they have. Some keep open their spigot of emotions and hope for a trickle or even a stream of inclusion, while others believe that not even a drop is probable; they adjust their expectations accordingly, albeit reluctantly. Sometimes siblings, like estranged parents and children, are uncertain what happened between them and why they became a persona non grata to their brother or sister. At other times they are certain of the origin of the break. Whether or not they know the reason, an element of fear may underpin some of our respondents' reactions. If they have concluded that their relationship with their sibling is over, they will have one less person for companionship and, perhaps, caretaking in old age.[13]

It is important to emphasize that even though the cutoffs happened in the present, the roots could also be found not just in the parents' treatment but also in patterns handed down through generations. For the cases we examined in depth in this chapter, only about one-third of the mothers and fewer than one in ten of the fathers were described as being very close to their siblings (the respondents' aunts and uncles). This is a much smaller number than in the larger sample, in which half the mothers and one-third of the fathers in the study were described as being very close.[14] We do not know whether the siblings we interviewed whose parents were not close to their own siblings saw their parents involved in conflictual situations or grew up with parents who just were never particularly close to their own siblings. If they grew up amid conflict between parents and aunts and uncles, they may be repeating the conflict or distancing behavior in their generation. If they grew up believing that siblings do not have to be particularly close, they may not have put a great deal of effort into trying to reconcile with the sibling from whom they are cut off.

Some cutoffs become less strained with time. People weary of being distant from one another decide to forgive or forget or to use a significant family event as an opportunity to reconnect. The relationships we described here have the longest road to travel and, in many cases, will most likely never be free of stress or even reconnected on any meaningful level. Even though the separation will cause great sorrow and anger to some, the lack of contact will provide a modicum of relief to others.

CHAPTER 6

Adult Sibling Relationships with Step- and Half Siblings

BARACK OBAMA HAS SEVEN OR more, Sigmund Freud had two, and Bill Clinton has one. Oprah Winfrey has one, Eleanor Roosevelt had one, and one of the authors of this book has three. Half siblings have been an integral part of families throughout history. Kings and pharaohs had concubines or harems and fathered many children by different mothers. In the mid-nineteenth century, King Mongkut of Siam, on whom the musical the *King and I* was based, purportedly had more than fifty children, most of whom were half siblings. In early times in America, parents frequently died young from workplace accidents, wars, disease, childbirth, or inclement weather while traveling across the country. Surviving spouses remarried, sometimes adding a new set of stepsiblings to the family and then often conceiving more half siblings. With advances in workplace safety and health care, the risks of such adult deaths have diminished. But the uptick in divorce in the last third of the twentieth century offered an opportunity for a new but different pattern of blended families. Women and men in the United States are increasingly choosing to delay or not to marry, paralleling the increase in parents having children without being married.[1] These changing and expanding family patterns have led to more children growing up in blended families, with the resulting increase in step- and half siblings.

In this chapter we examine some of the complicated relationships involving half siblings and stepsiblings of people forty years old and older. We combine stepsiblings and half siblings in our discussion for two reasons: first, stepsiblings and half siblings often appear in the same family, and second, other trackers of blended families, including the U.S. Bureau of the Census and the Pew Research Center, group them together. Because of the complexity and nature of these relationships, we decided to give them their own chapter, separate from that for full siblings.

Almost one-fifth of those we interviewed for this book reported having either a half sibling or a stepsibling, with half siblings being more prevalent. A handful of those interviewed also talked about their relationships with their adoptive siblings, who sometimes coexisted in families with step- and half siblings.

This blended family type has become quite common in the United States. Consider this statement from a Pew Research Center report: "Today, more than four-in-ten American adults have at least one step relative in their family—either a stepparent, a step or half sibling or a stepchild."[2] Moreover, of those with a steprelative, three in ten say it is a step- or half sibling, the focus of this chapter. The Pew report goes on to link the rise in out-of-wedlock births and the increase in divorce to this trend. Of those that Pew surveyed, the older that someone is, the less likely he is to have a step- or half sibling. In addition, more education and higher income are associated with fewer step- and half siblings. The younger that someone is, the more likely she is to have grown up without two once-married parents in the home. While 36 percent of those eighteen to twenty-nine years-old grew up without two married parents in the home, only 10 percent of those over fifty did; 23 percent of those between fifty and sixty-four have a stepsibling, and 16 percent of those over sixty-five have a step- or half sibling. Clearly, if this book dealt with only younger adults and children, the prevalence of steprelatives would be far greater, as the percentage of married Americans has fallen while the divorce rate has risen over the last fifty years and the number of children living with one parent has gone up precipitously.

Of great interest to therapists will be the Pew Center report's conclusion: "Most adults who have step relatives feel a stronger sense of obligation to their biological family members than they do to their step kin." For example, when asked about their sense of obligation to family members who might need caregiving or financial assistance, six out of seven respondents would help their biological parents, but only slightly more than half said they would help a stepparent. Two out of three would help a full sibling, and two out of five would help a step- or half sibling. By comparison, two out of five also said they would help a best friend. People feel closer to full siblings than to their other siblings, a fact that influences how such relationships are understood and maintained.

We are referring to full siblings as those respondents who report having no half, adopted, or stepsiblings. Some of our respondents have full as well as step- and half siblings. They are included in the blended families. What usually differentiates step- or blended families from a two-parent family with full siblings is the shift in a parental relationship that has resulted in the addition of a step- or half sibling relationship somewhere in the family's history. Because just as many of these families are formed by addition after subtraction, we note that loss, or any great change in family status, often is accompanied by tension between parents (if there is a breakup rather than a death) that can strain both parent-child and sibling relationships in the original family. A new stepmother or stepfather, who may come with a new brother or sister, is then added to relationships that already may be struggling with losses and unwanted changes. Steprelationships may be added slowly if there is a long courtship, or they may be added instantaneously if families come together quickly. Or a blended family may begin with other children, that is, stepsiblings living elsewhere but still "related." However the stepfamily begins, and it can have positive results, it differs from families with full siblings who have not undergone such seismic shifts.

In our research, a few respondents learned in adulthood that there was another half sibling. These "additions" to the family, which often were long-held family secrets, force family relationships to realign and shift the children's view of their parents. In one family, the father cheated on his wife, the children's mother, and as adults, the children learned they had a half sister they never knew. This is a prime example of a new relationship with this previously unknown sister being entangled with a loss, the loss of the children's vision of the father as loyal and faithful. In another case, the mother had had a child before marrying the children's father and did not reveal this to her younger children until they were in their forties.

Lyle is fifty and was born in Senegal. He and his family came to the United States almost thirty years ago. His father had three wives in succession, each younger than the previous one. His mother was the third wife and was with Lyle's father when he died. Lyle has two full siblings, an older brother and a younger sister, and several half siblings. While growing up, he and his siblings received favored treatment from his father in comparison to that of his half siblings, who were tied to his father's ex-wives. Resentment between families continues today, even twenty years after their father's death. Clearly, their father's differential treatment of the three different sibling sets affected the adult relationships within that web of full and half siblings.

Our interviews helped us understand how people view these complicated, often lifelong relationships formed in the crucible of the blended family or, in Lyle's case, in the crucible of three families. Because they are so complicated, we decided that the best way to offer insight into these families is to provide some of the stories and themes that we heard from adults with stepsiblings, half siblings, and adopted siblings. Some, like Leon, have non–blood siblings who get along well; others have half and stepsiblings with whom they never lived or saw rarely; and a few of those with blended families that have dissolved even have ex-stepsiblings with whom they may still have contact.[3] The range is as diverse and complex as the nature of these families.

A NOTE ON THE LITERATURE

If there still is any question, blood is definitely thicker than water. Using data from 1,389 respondents with a half or stepsibling who participated in the National Survey of Families, sociologists Lynn White and Agnes Riedmann found that siblings are more apt to stay in touch with full siblings than with their half or stepsiblings. At the same time, having no full siblings encourages contact with half and stepsiblings.[4] Furthermore, and confirming other research, sisters are more likely to maintain their relationships with half, step-, or full siblings than brothers are. African Americans place a higher value on their sibling relationships than do whites, and they also make fewer distinctions regarding blood and non-blood ties than whites do. For example, Leon, a forty-one-year-old African American professor we interviewed who has three living stepsiblings and one adopted sister, considers them all full family members. White and Riedmann also reported that stepsiblings are more apt to leave home earlier than full siblings are and do not get along as well with each other. Eight percent of those with only full siblings said they did not get along with one of them;

11 percent of those with one or more half and stepsiblings said they did not get along with someone in the family; and 14 percent of those with two or more half and stepsiblings reported not getting along.

Because of the instability of some of these relationships, maintaining contact with half and stepsiblings in adulthood is likely to feel more voluntary than obligatory, according to White and Riedmann. Staying in touch may also be a distressing reminder of a traumatic event that led to the formation of the stepfamily in the first place. One Dutch study found that negative events in a family, like a divorce, psychological problems, addiction problems, or abuse, often resulted in siblings being less close.[5] Seeing a step- or half brother, depending on the circumstances, could be a reminder that one's father had an affair with the stepbrother's mother.

Tom Pollet, a British psychologist interested in evolutionary theory, posited that stepsiblings and half siblings are less close than full siblings because they have less social investment in each other; that is, they have spent less time together and care about each other less because they are not as biologically related as full siblings are.[6] Other research has shown that in adulthood, social relationships tend to fray even more if age gaps caused the social separation in childhood, if there are gender differences, and if geographic distances preclude frequent contact.

Such variations in full siblings' relationships with step- or half siblings have been observed by therapists who have written about clinical work with blended families. For example, Emily Visher and John Visher,[7] a psychologist and a psychiatrist, respectively, who founded the Step Family Association of America, provided guidelines for therapists in assisting these relationships with families with children. The key issues are (1) stepparents slowly rather than quickly trying to parent stepchildren, (2) carefully approaching the boundaries between family members in blended families, (3) avoiding assumptions based on past family roles, (4) helping clients be patient in accepting new members, (5) recognizing that family members have experienced the loss of other members, and (6) recognizing that issues of power and loyalty complicate all family relationships and need to be openly addressed.

As we mentioned earlier, stepfamilies are often formed following a conflictual divorce. In social worker Elinor Rosenberg's review of the literature, children entering a stepfamily must acknowledge the loss of the old family, accept that it no longer exists, and look for future relationships. These families are forced to confront complex financial, personal, and legal impediments with shifting family loyalties. For a child or teenager, moving or changing schools, leaving friends and beloved activities, can be traumatic Boundaries must be redrawn to include new parent figures and stepsiblings, regardless of the age of those involved.[8] Whereas the Vishers and Rosenberg focus on children's and parents' adaptation, we focus on adults who often experienced many of these disruptions.

WEAVING THE THREADS

Among our sample of step- or half siblings, most encountered one another in childhood or adolescence. The impact of the new family relationships thirty, forty, and even sixty years later still was great. In our sample of 262, thirty-seven had half siblings, fifteen had stepsiblings, and five had adopted siblings, with some reporting more than one type of blended sibling relationship. Our respondents were between forty and seventy-four years old, slightly younger than the average age of the full siblings; approximately half were white; one-third were African American; and one-fifth were Latino/a; and the rest were "other."[9] The median number of siblings of all types in these families was four, in a range of two to eleven. Almost half were families in which the age gap between at least two half or stepsiblings was ten or more years.

We asked those we interviewed about their level of satisfaction with the support they received from their siblings. Approximately half said they were very satisfied, and the rest said they were somewhat satisfied or wanted more support. Among the full siblings we surveyed, two-thirds said they were very satisfied.[10] These differences, while not statistically significant, reflect what we learned in the literature review: that in regard to all their sibling relationships, those with step-, half, and adopted siblings *tended* to be less satisfying than those with full siblings.

Statistically significant differences did appear between the blended-family siblings and the full siblings. Our respondents perceived much more favoritism was shown by parents when they were young and also when they became adults. For example, 50 percent of siblings in blended families perceived favoritism when young, compared with 24 percent of full siblings. In adulthood, 42 percent of blended-family siblings perceived favoritism was shown by one or both parents, compared with 21 percent of full siblings. Stark contrasts also appeared with feelings of jealousy and competition: In childhood, 29 percent of blended-family siblings felt jealousy toward a step-, full, or half sibling, compared with 13 percent of the full siblings, and in adulthood, 17 percent of blended-family siblings felt jealousy, compared with only 4 percent of the full siblings. Twenty-five percent of the blended siblings reported feeling competitive with their siblings during childhood, compared with 18 percent of the full siblings; and 14 percent of the blended siblings still felt competitive during adulthood, compared with 5 percent of the full siblings.

ISSUES IN HALF AND STEPSIBLING RELATIONSHIPS THAT EMERGED FROM THE INTERVIEWS

As we present these themes for therapists to consider raising in treatment, remember that these relationships usually were formed in at least one of three life stages: the childhood years, during late adolescence or early adulthood, or in later life. Those formed in childhood clearly could have had a significant impact on development, whereas those formed in later life—for example, if one's widowed mother at sixty-five married a widower with children—were likely to have less impact. In addition, some of the issues cited here are universal ones among all siblings, but when applied to blended families, they seem different given how these families were formed and maintained.

Exclusion/Inclusion

The feeling of being included or excluded is one of a family member's most powerful experiences. This process is related to the amount of closeness and distance that is maintained in family relationships, and it may be entangled with favoritism, two issues we discuss next. How half and stepsiblings cope with being excluded or included in the family's dynamics can be a bellwether for other family interactions. It is related to our earlier discussion about boundaries and the ways that family members in previous generations dealt with half and stepsiblings in sharing information, getting people together to celebrate, and caring for aging parents. Sometimes such siblings are actively excluded, and at other times they all are included.

Clark, a forty-nine-year-old African American who is the manager of a store and the married father of five, actively excludes his half sister from his life. He is eleven years younger than Cleo. When Clark was born, Cleo was living at home with their mother. They have different fathers. Whereas Cleo took care of Clark physically when they were young, at one point he began to take care of her emotionally.

> Our relationship has been tough because of the choices she's made with her life. It is important, but the family I have now is more important. She'll always be my sister, but we have just been very different in our life choices. We've never been that close, but despite the age difference, I think I was the mature one in the family as far as choices I made.

Even though Clark described them as not close at the beginning of the interview, he shifted a bit when asked to be more specific.

> She had to drag me along with her friends and stuff, and I tried to be a good son so I told on her sometimes to my mom [laughs]. She took me to be with her boyfriend and I would play with his brothers and sisters, so we had a close relationship when we were younger. She's always looked out for me, always been protective of me. I had a lot of support from her but she was always around the wrong crowd. So our relationship was flattering, but she was always getting into trouble.

What is noteworthy in his description is that while Cleo may have been protective, at some point Clark stopped feeling protected. He recalled the seminal event when he dropped the curtain on their relationship. He was in high school and their mother had gone to Jamaica and left him with the car, which he needed to get to work. "One day my sister asked if she could use the car to run some errands. I hesitated but I felt bad denying her so I said she could have it if she picked me up after work." She never showed up.

> I was embarrassed in front of my boss, who had to drive me home. It didn't look good and was out of his way. When I got home, I got a friend to take me to her place and I waited there for her all night. When she finally came home, I grabbed the keys, said a few things, and drove off. The tank was on

empty, and the car was full of liquor bottles. That was a turning point for me. I thought to myself, Never again will I trust her.

They have grown further apart in the last ten years. "I haven't seen her. She moved down here in the late 1990s. I saw her a few times but not since. This has been the longest time since we have had contact."

We asked to what extent having a different father played a part in his sister's exclusion from family.

My father left my mom when I was three. He had been a military man, and we had something of a relationship. We'd do school shopping and he would give me money from time to time, though nothing pertaining to manhood or life lessons. Cleo's father was laid back, got high, kind of a hippie dude. They indulged in the same crazy lifestyle. But at one point he dropped her because she would take things from him. She was into living wild. I had a relationship with both dads and she burned my father once, and he wouldn't have anything to do with her after that. She would say having different dads played a part [in her relationship with her mother and Clark] because she always blamed others. But she is not blameless.

Ellis, a white, forty-six-year-old newspaper man with two younger sisters, is trying to be more inclusive of a newfound half sibling. Although his relationship with his sisters is important, he has other people, his friends, in his life whom he would call before he would call his sisters for help. Two years ago, the three of them learned they had an older half brother.

My mom had a baby before she met my dad. She was under twenty-one and gave him up for adoption. This guy was adopted by a judge and his wife, and when he reached his late forties, he began looking for his birth mother. His adoptive father had died, and his mother and sister were estranged from him. He found my mom and she was like, "Ah, I wondered when this would happen." She had never said a word to anyone, except my dad knew and her older sister who helped hide the belly. Now he is suddenly in our life, and my mom went crazy. She was like, "I don't know what I am going to say to my kids." She didn't want to tell us. It took her six weeks to get up the courage. "Mom, come on. This is fine," we told her.

So he comes into our life, this guy we had never met, and he looks just like us. It turns out he hung out with people we knew, a group of ne'er-do-wells who have rock bands and motorcycles. Coincidentally, before our brother knew my mother, he knew her cousin who was a prison guard and he was in prison. He was involved in a bank holdup and had a heroin problem. And he knew some of the same people my sister knew. We had a fiftieth birthday party for him with bands and bikers and everyone invited. So you have this new person in the family who we are very excited about, and then slowly you learn they are just like anybody else. They have problems and issues and do things that you don't always like. We have all learned that about each other. I have spent a total of an hour with my half brother. If I had to characterize the relationship, he would be someone I would feel I *have* to give a hand to. I feel he would give that to me.

Ellis believed they had a congenial relationship and wondered while he was talking whether he had communicated enough with his half brother. "I feel he could call me [if he needed me]. But I probably have not made that as clear to him as I could."

Whereas Ellis's family has reached out to their newfound half brother and long to include him in more family events, Frederika and her half sisters have a longer tradition of inclusion, which came to the fore in taking care of their father. Anyone who wanted to participate in his caregiving could help. A forty-four-year-old African American schoolteacher, Frederika is married with one small child and has one full sibling and four half siblings, all in their fifties. They all have the same father, who has been married several times.

I was not raised with my older siblings, so we spent very little time together except on vacations. My younger sister and I are full siblings and spent our whole childhood together. Now I am close to my eldest sister and younger sister, my brothers not so much, and my second older sister is a mess.

Though not very close when young, they have grown closer with the help of Frederika's mother.

My mom is the center. Everyone talks to her, and she spreads the information. We are comfortable with her dealing with the whole family. But the sisters speak with each other pretty often, and my younger sister and I text all the time. Since having kids, we have become closer. And we stopped depending on our parents to organize things and made more of an effort.

Issues that could have arisen with a father with different wives have sorted themselves out.

I feel like we were caught between my stepmothers and my dad when he was sick. Part of that was how fast he became ill. It was like we were all in panic mode. We took over his nursing care, the sisters at least. We did all the hospice stuff. It was exhausting and went on for weeks.

It was the caregiving for the same father that ultimately helped bridge whatever gaps existed, and it was a cultural imperative that helped facilitate their actions, according to Frederika.

It unified the women in the family, even the stepmoms. It made us a unit. It was very traditional, like what black families have always done, take care of their own. It was terrible and exhausting and had to be done. My father was determined to die at home [Frederika starts crying]. I hated taking care of him. He had been so mean his whole life to us, yet we were the ones bathing him, and cleaning and caring for him. He wanted his children to do it, so we did.

Frederika sees herself as both an older sister, which she was in her household, and the next to youngest when taking into account her half siblings. They are not a particularly affectionate family, and holidays can be stressful when everyone gets together. But for the important work and for their identity as the family, all the sisters pulled together, even though they were not especially close.

Favoritism

As we pointed out in earlier chapters, favoritism shown by parents can be a powerful force in sibling relationships even decades later. Favoritism was more likely to be perceived in step- and half sibling families. Favoritism was described in three different contexts: (1) when several siblings were perceived as favorites, as in Lyle's immediate family, in which his mother was the favored wife; (2) when a sibling was told or perceived that he was favored by a sibling or a parent; and (3) when a sibling thought that another sibling was favored.

Clark is an example of the second situation. "Cleo always let me know she thought I was the favorite," Clark noted. "I had made this decision as a young man that my mom was trying as hard as she could as a single mother and that I was going to try to be a good kid in order to make her life a little easier." While growing up, Clark always sided with his mother, trying to protect her. Cleo made things "messy both physically and emotionally" when she visited after she had moved out. Being the favorite when Clark's and Cleo's behavior was so different might even have been expected, especially because their relationships with their fathers were so different. Clark acknowledged that because he and his sister had different fathers and he worked hard to please his mother, he may indeed have been her favorite.

Leon, the professor whom we introduced earlier, heard specifically from his father that he was the favorite. In addition to his adopted sister, he has a number of step- and half siblings by both parents.

> My dad started paying a lot of attention to me when I went to college, as opposed to my brothers and stepbrothers, and he even said to me, "I love all my children but you are my favorite," which [Leon laughs] is actually crazy. I took him to task about it. I asked, "Why are you saying this? What is this about?" And I told him I felt uncomfortable with that. He charged it with, "Well I have always been that way since you were born." And I am like, "Well, you know, that is crap." But he left me everything in terms of being in charge of his affairs, and I had to be the administrator of his estate. He left no directive. It was only "I want you to handle everything." I think he would have wanted an even distribution, which is what I did.

Luckily for Leon, his siblings, many of whom were older than him and male, did not resent this favoritism. They remain very close, and he is the one who is also in charge of his mother's estate.

We also heard about the other side of favoritism, when someone believes that another sibling is the favored one. Alice, a white, seventy-four-year-old widow who is retired from government work, has a sixty-seven-year-old half sister and a seventy-year-old stepsister. Her father died when she was a baby, and five years later her mother married a widower with a then two-year-old daughter who was being raised by her maternal grandmother. Alice's half sister was born when she was seven, so she grew up with a half sister in the home and a stepsister who lived nearby. When Alice was sixteen, her stepsister (then twelve) moved in with them. Alice left soon afterward to marry and subsequently had four children. "I didn't play with my half sister growing up because of the seven-year age difference, but we loved each other and we have a good relationship now. When she married, she moved two doors away from me. When we had our kids, they were really close."

The early years, however, were not easy for Alice.

> I was jealous of her. She was very pretty. I always thought Mom loved her more than me. I feel like Mom pushed me out when she came along. When my stepdad came, I felt like he stole Mom, and then my half sister came and stole mom's attention. I was jealous of her until I got married.

Although Clark has not been able to work through his differences with Cleo, Alice has with her half sister. One reason they became closer was that her half sister struggled in her marriage and turned to Alice for support, and that redressed a perceived imbalance in the relationship. "When she separated, her children were grown, and she moved in with me for a while. We have had some fun times together now."

Although Alice moved past conflict with and resentment of her half sister, her relationship with her stepsister is more problematic.

> My stepsister was always mentally unbalanced but was able to take care of herself at some points. She's been back and forth between a nursing home and mental ward for twenty-five years now. In the past year, I have seen her three times—she has good weeks and bad weeks.

Some relationships among multiple siblings are easier to balance. There never was much closeness to the stepsister. They grew up separately, and then mental illness intervened. With the half sister with whom Alice lived, she struggled when young with jealousy issues that can arise when a mother remarries and wants to build a new life with her husband and their child. In this case, Alice's mother set aside both her former life and her daughter to make room for the new marriage. Alice then had to separate from the family through marriage at a young age to find happiness. Over time, she built a better relationship with her half sister, and she now chooses to focus on the positive side of the relationship, for example, the fun vacations they take together. Most important, she wants a relationship with her half sister, even though she acknowledged that it is not as close as she would like it to be.

Emotional Distance Versus Closeness

With all relationships the question arises of how close to become and how much distance to maintain. Similar to the exclusion/inclusion issue, this issue covers how close or distant step- and half siblings feel. Usually, but not always, they feel less close. *Exclusion* and *inclusion* refer to the structure of the relationships. Specifically, people can be included in family gatherings but may not feel close to anyone. That would be an inclusive but distant relationship. The goal of many families is to have an inclusive and close relationship, even though they may settle for an inclusive and somewhat distant relationship. Many blended families have come to peace with the relationship and accept their siblings for who they are, without great hope of changing them. Frederika's family was not close, yet they all were included in caring for the father. Hers is an example of an inclusive but distant relationship and shows how some families balance structure and process.

Abe, a fifty-eight-year-old, white, married schoolteacher, told us about his five brothers, plus a half brother who appears to be fully integrated into the family. Abe was the third oldest of four boys and was three when his father died. Their mother remarried, and Pete, four years younger than the youngest of the full siblings, was born soon afterward. The family is spread around the country, and Abe longs for more closeness.

We don't see each other much at all except for when my mother and stepfather died, that's when we reconnected. When my mother died, we were together.

And since my dad died, we tried to get together. That lasted for about two years [Abe laughs]. So when we get together, not all the brothers come.

Abe's relationship with each brother is different, but it would be difficult to label his relationship with his half brother as unique. Pete was the "tag-along" brother when they were young and still living in the home. The relationships have waxed and waned since then. Abe feels he has a solid relationship with Pete and one other brother, a closer one with one of his middle brothers, and a more distant one with the other two, placing Pete in the middle of Abe's sibling relationships. There is a ten-year age gap between Abe and his oldest brother, so he actually spent more time in the home with Pete and subsequently feels closer to him. This is an example of how being a half brother did not influence the feelings of closeness that evolved as much as age differences did.

This new family with Pete as a half brother formed when Abe was young, but stepsiblings that blend at Abe's age may not always have the same sense of togetherness.

Carole is a fifty-one-year-old, white, married social worker. She was ten years old when she acquired a stepsister, in addition to her three younger full siblings. She encapsulated in her opening description what can happen with a stepsibling, even if they spend most of their childhood with one another.

> I'm close with my youngest sister [age forty-five], and we are best friends. My brother who is next oldest to her [age forty-seven] lives in Oregon. He and I are pretty close. He confides in me the most. My brother who lives far away and is next oldest [age forty-nine], we know we can depend on each other but I don't care for his wife or their parenting, so I don't see him except for holidays and family events. My sister who is two years older than me [age fifty-three] is actually a stepsister, but we grew up together. We were closest when we were younger, but now we aren't as close because she lives far away, and we don't really have that much in common.

We asked whether Carole and her stepsister would be closer if they lived near each other, and she responded, "Not at this point because I am not as bonded to her as I am to my younger sister." The shared history with the stepsister that started at age ten was not enough to have them feel close.

Later during the interview, Carole was asked to describe her closeness to her siblings. Systematically and in great detail, she talked about falling out and coming back together with one sibling, always being close to another sibling, and maintaining the bonds with the four full siblings. She mentioned her stepsister only in passing.

Carole's mother died when they were young, and Carole, the oldest, took care of the younger siblings until her father remarried and a stepsister joined the family. It was her raising the youngest children for a few years that formed an attachment that may have made it difficult for a new stepsibling to break into. Right after describing her early rearing of her siblings, Carole added, "If there is ever an issue, we pretty much come together as a family." That being said, they are not extremely close.

> We generally enjoy spending time with each other, on a short-term basis. We are not the type of family that goes away on a cruise together, but we do enjoy being together for the holidays. We are not a very affectionate family. My sister and I only recently began to hug each other.

This description speaks to the quality of their closeness. Closeness of any form may seem too intense for one sibling but not close enough for the next. With stepsiblings and half siblings, we found the level of support is not as high and the expectation for closeness is not as great. With stepsiblings and sometimes with half siblings, exclusion and distancing were the basis of how the family was formed. Although expressing closeness and trying to be inclusive can be an attempt to redress past instances of distancing and exclusion, it may not be enough if the frame within which it occurs is not agreed on.

For example, Clark's situation poses the interesting question: When do therapists help set boundaries, and how should they be set? When would distancing in a relationship be more helpful than pushing for reconciliation? Clark's and Cleo's parents are deceased, so they are not pushing for greater closeness. Clark seems to need to be ready when and if his sister comes back into his life. *Braced* seems to describe best his overall orientation to his half sister. This is certainly not ideal, but therapists should be careful when deciding to build a better relationship, as disrupting the current homeostatic pattern may not lead to a better situation for someone like Clark.

Entering a Closed Family System

To extend our application of systems thinking, and related to the three previous issues, how stepsiblings enter each other's family can be linked to future relationships. Some families have established roles and ways of interacting that its members are not willing to relinquish. The children probably have different-sized sibling sets and may move into an already established home in which the newbies may be "intruding" on the resident siblings' space. An only child joining a family with two or more other siblings may have a particularly hard time if that sibling system is not open. When children are not of the same age, assumptions about hierarchy may come into play, as may the assignment of household chores based on age and gender. In addition, siblings may be very angry at the new stepsibling if they tie her or him to their own parents' divorce.

Carole described taking care of her younger siblings for many years following her mother's death and forming a very strong bond with them. It would be difficult for an older stepsister to enter a family system like hers, given the cohesiveness of the sibling set. The stepsister's age could have played a part, too, as she could have replaced Carole symbolically as the oldest sibling. But Carole was not eager to give up that role, so it was difficult for them to accommodate the stepsister. Of course, we don't know much about the stepsister trying to enter a closed system. Maybe she felt comfortable keeping distant from the others and "floating outside" with her own peer group.

Ellis struggled with how much to reach out to his newly discovered fifty-year-old half brother. Although this family's system seems open, many years have passed, and the half brother's life, which includes prison time, clearly does not fit in neatly with the rest of the family.

OTHER ISSUES THAT EMERGED IN STEP- AND HALF SIBLING FAMILIES

Family Culture Driving the Relationship

Frederika told us how African Americans take care of their own. Even though she was angry at her father for some of his behavior, she tried to put those feelings aside and thus align with her half siblings. Although these feelings of responsibility and connectedness are not unique to African Americans (and do not apply to all African Americans), it is important to note that our interviews revealed a strong sense of kinship bonds between step- and half siblings in the families of color. Because of trends in intermarriage and partnerships, step- and half siblings from different backgrounds will be increasingly called on to work together in taking care of parents. An awareness of cultural differences on the part of therapists may be especially important when working with such families because, for example, the family members' views of familial responsibility may not be the same.

Impact of Stepparents and Parents

Relationships are not driven only by the stepsiblings, even in the later years; parents play a part, too. Frederika disliked her father yet had to take care of him. Leon was the favorite and was given executive responsibilities for his parents. Luckily, his siblings accepted him in this role. Ellis learned that his mother had kept a huge secret almost her whole life. Each of these exemplifies that in middle and later adulthood, parents still can influence how these relationships evolve.

The Third and Future Generations

While we have focused on the adult siblings and their parents, children and cousins may also play a part in these relationships. Clark believes he has become a better father with a greater understanding of boundaries because of his struggles with Cleo. In his parental judgment, he is unwilling to have his children interact with her.

This younger generation, holding the family's future, needs to be considered when issues arise in blended families. The relationships formed and maintained between step- and half siblings send a message to the next generation about who is considered in the family and under what circumstances, how families incorporate such differences, and how and whether family members can work together to become closer.

Stepsibling Problems as Metaphors for Other Problems

Sometimes step- and half sibling relationships need to be managed and not drastically reworked. Initially, a problem with a stepsibling may be the presenting problem, as it is easier to talk about. The sibling may wonder how a therapist will approach what may be a more difficult issue. Deeper and more vexing issues for the sibling-client, though, may be struggles for a more meaningful relationship with a full sibling, parent, child, or partner. By exploring both horizontal and vertical relationships, the therapist can help the siblings see the interconnectedness of the relationships.

WORKING TOWARD CHANGE

In chapter 12 we look at changing sibling relationships by using education, insight, and action. Here we focus first on insight into the family and then the action to take. Education is best gained by reading about blended families.

Therapy considerations with these families are similar to those for full siblings, but they are often characterized by, paradoxically, a weaker connection but a greater intensity when issues arise, and, in turn, are complicated by entanglement with parallel losses. We say "intensity" because when, for instance, aging parents have health care issues, concern about inclusion and exclusion will come up if the boundaries are not clear. With full siblings, everyone has a "right" to be at the table, but it is less clear to what extent half siblings and stepsiblings are or should be there. Issues of inclusion often may be metaphors for past issues with which family members have struggled, issues that may not be resolved.

Often, a family is coping with more than one of the issues we discussed in this chapter. To work with these issues, some overarching theories should be considered. Approaches are shaped basically by whether the sibling seeking help is in the position of including others or is being excluded by other family members. Approaches also are shaped by the impetus for greater closeness. For example, it is often a family crisis (e.g., a dying parent) that brings to the fore issues among siblings. That is, the family members being under stress is the impetus. At other times, siblings come to a point that they want to resolve past relationships and become closer.

When issues of exclusion are at the forefront, it is helpful to determine whether a step- or a half sibling should be included, by looking backward and forward at the family through both a Bowen systems lens and a structural family therapy lens. First, the family's history in relation to inclusion and exclusion for other full, step-, and half siblings should be explored. Patterns have a way of repeating themselves in families. If all the grandmother's siblings (full, step-, and half) banded together to take care of the great-grandmother and if all the mother's siblings banded together to take care of the grandmother, then a precedent has been set for the siblings to take care of their mother. But if step- or half siblings are new in this generation, there is no map and family members may not feel the same level of loyalty to all the siblings as the previous generations did. And if the family has never shared responsibility for caregiving, even with full siblings, establishing a new tradition will be harder. Drawing a genogram to find out about the past can be helpful in getting this information.

The longer that the family members have been together, the greater the expectation will be of including everyone in caregiving decisions. Ellis and his sisters, who just met their half brother, would feel less pressure to include him than would Abe, whose adopted brother grew up with the family. Ellis and his sisters could decide that if they were going to include their half brother in some way, his input would not have as much weight in the decision making. By contrast, full siblings are usually given more equal decision-making power.

The sibling seeking therapy either may be in the position to include other siblings or may be the sibling historically excluded. The sibling in the first position, the gatekeeper, is more powerful than the one in the second position, so he or she should be encouraged to look forward after having looked backward. Looking forward, how does the family want to redraw the boundaries for future generations? What messages do they want to send to their children about inclusion in the family business? They can be asked to draw a family map using structural family therapy theory (a map is different from a genogram) for the current boundaries and then a map of what they wish the family boundaries would be in the future. These tools can be helpful in visualizing the past, present, and future.

Perceptions of siblings who are excluded are often fairly set at this age, as in Clark's case with his sister, Cleo. If greater connection is desired, then the sibling in the room can be asked to consider, first, whether change will ever be possible and, second, whether it is possible to include the sibling but keep emotional boundaries on the relationship. This is related to our earlier discussion of structure versus process in relationships. Clark could decide that it is important for his children to have some contact with their aunt yet keep the boundaries by controlling the amount of time together, where the contact takes place (e.g., at his house or at a restaurant), and what is discussed when the family is together. While similar on one level to what all siblings would attempt, with a half sibling the emotional pull on Clark and Cleo to reconcile may not be as great, thus making a boundaried relationship more possible.

The excluded sibling, with less power, has fewer options and may never be able to work into a closer family position. Keeping lines of communication open and asking for inclusion without accusations or blame is a first step. Hoping for change in the future and maintaining clear and positive communication may be the best hope if the other half or stepsiblings are adamant about their position.

Favoritism is a common theme that step- and half siblings raise. The first step is to have the sibling talk about his or her experiences of being favored or not favored, with an eye to the stage of development the family was in at the time of the favoritism. For example, the Vishers describe the favoritism of the biological over the stepchild, so the members of families whose loyalties shift after divorce and remarriage frequently feel discarded. Accordingly, Alice felt abandoned when her new sister came along. If the favoritism occurred in childhood, helping the sibling gain an adult perspective on his or her own reaction as a child—by understanding where the family and parents were in their own development—can help in taking a more cognitive view of the favoritism. Determining the nature of the favoritism and the context of the parent showing the favoritism is important. Was he or she repeating a pattern from the past? From that parent's perspective, was there a reason for the favoritism? Unless the situation of the individual showing the favoritism can be placed in the context of the family at that time, an opportunity will be missed.

One way to deal with favoritism, whether it pertains to being the more favored, as in Leon's case, or the less favored, as in Alice's case, is to make sure that closeness is the desired goal. While this is true for all siblings, the sibling relationships we examined in this chapter do not have the same breadth of shared history (inside jokes, nonverbal cues, common memories, etc.). Full siblings often know what the others mean without its being explained, but this is not true for these siblings who have to work harder to communicate clearly.

Virginia Satir's work is particularly helpful in learning how to be a clear communicator. As we explained in chapter 1, common roles of dysfunctional communication include those of the blamer and the placator. If family members wish to become closer, they must put aside past events. That includes not blaming the other sibling and not accepting blame (the role of the placator). The leveler is the model in which one sibling can speak directly to another about the hopes and fears of becoming closer and the reasons for wanting to do so.

This approach can be combined with the other approaches already presented that focus on family history and boundaries. Here a direct and present-oriented approach is used. Saying to a stepsister "I know we weren't very close growing up because of the way our families were formed. I know there was favoritism shown. But I would like to be closer to you now, as I would value having more meaningful contact with you in the future" could offer an opportunity for a new relationship. This way also does not blame the other sibling yet acknowledges the history between them.

Closeness is more easily achieved when systems have been open and inclusive and little favoritism has been shown. When families are blended, their understanding of, and history with, closeness varies, as does the way that they handle loss. When conducting family therapy, we often ask parents to describe how they view their roles in relation to each other and what types of parent-child relationships they want to have. The same applies here to asking step- and half siblings what type of relationship they are seeking. Knowing the level of openness when the blended family was formed can be helpful in predicting where the family can go in its evolution.

Naturally, the cultural appropriateness of these approaches, the role the parent plays as the family's matriarch or patriarch, and the degree to which future generations should be included all must be considered. A fractured relationship, such as with a stepsibling, must be considered as an indication of fractures in other relationships. Working in one realm may help the other.

Finally, regardless of the approach, the sibling seeking repair must be comfortable with taking risks, weighing the benefits of pursuing a relationship, and living with ambiguity. We mention these themes here and repeat them in chapter 12, on intervention. No growth is possible without some risk taking. Where, when, and how this looks in regard to relationships will differ. But any attempt to consider our recommendations for genogram drawing, structural mapping, or direct communication is linked to risk taking. In weighing the benefits of pursuing a relationship, the sibling must consider how much he or she is being affected by the pursuit. When is it no longer beneficial to keep pushing family members for resolution? Finally, living with ambiguity, not understanding why some things happen, is necessary when trying to improve relationships. Strained relationships are rarely resolved in a way that puts them into a neat package. Instead, being comfortable with dynamic relationships that are never completely resolved but are more satisfying must be the goal.

Sometimes family problems cannot be fixed, and it is the wise clinician who helps the client accept this. Stepsiblings may not, as Tom Pollet argued and Carole stated, have enough in common. Sometimes people (either the sibling in the room or the sibling being approached) want to maintain their distance, hold on to their anger, or are uncomfortable for myriad reasons and do not want to be closer. Mental health issues, addictions, and family injustices all can make reconnections impossible. We therapists can address only what people bring us and work with whatever they are motivated to change. But if we know what to ask, we are more likely to open the right doors with them.

* * *

Our research found that throughout the life span, blended-family relationships were fraught with more competition and jealousy as well as more perceived parental favoritism. What, then, is the model for adult sibling relationships in these blended families? We do know that full siblings' roles and expectations should become increasingly and more equitably shared as birth order and gender differences wash away with age. Clear models for blended families are harder to find, because loyalties between parents and siblings are much more complex and often of shorter duration, as they usually did not start at birth. We described common themes that emerged from our interviews and recommended that these themes be considered as topics of discussion when members of blended families want to grow closer.

PART 3

Case Studies

CHAPTER | 7

When Siblings Cut Off Contact

MANY OF THE PEOPLE WE interviewed for this book have wonderful and fulfilling relationships with their brothers and their sisters. Others we interviewed struggle with their relationships with one or all of their siblings. Some even face the difficult reality of having cut off relations with some or all of their siblings, as we talked about in chapter 5. At its worst, that struggle can lead to a closing off of the self, preventing the formation of other intimate adult relationships. That does not, however, have to be the case, as we will see in this chapter. Ron, whose family situation is described here, has no relationship with either his sister or his brother, but he does have strong, close relationships with his friends, parents, and son. Ron's story illustrates how someone adapts to having no relationship with two siblings because of their unusually difficult behavior. His story also shows that ambiguity can be useful in characterizing an entire family, much of whose history Ron does not understand.

Stephen Bank, who has written about sibling estrangement, described a woman tearfully recounting being ignored by an older brother who had not called in five years and acted as if she did not exist. The woman had been physically abused by him when they were young. She kept this from their parents, however, who, she thought, would not believe that their "perfect" son was capable of such behavior. When considering such a case in therapy, Bank cautioned the woman not to blame herself. "Sibling conflicts, when extreme, bitter, and prolonged are a significant outgrowth of a disturbing family situation which could not, originally, have been the children's 'fault.'"[1] He advises therapists to consider what part parents played in "weaving the fabric" of their siblings' relationship problems. How families become estranged varies greatly and is often, but not always, the result of disturbing family situations related to the parents and not the children, according to Bank.

Some adults are aware of their parents' explicit and implicit roles in shaping their relationships with their siblings, so it is easy for them to pinpoint where their sibling struggles and eventual estrangement originated. For many, however, the family stew is mixed in a murkier, more ambiguous way. Sometimes genetic factors are involved, making family members more vulnerable to the typical stresses of life. Or deeply ingrained, multigenerational patterns are perpetuated. In well-functioning families, the parent or parents can help mitigate some of those challenges, preventing damaging reverberations in sibling relationships. In less well-functioning families, the stew sometimes comes to an uncontrollable boil, blowing the lid off sibling relationships and scalding everyone.

For each individual, for each family system, decisions about how—or whether—to maintain relationships with siblings are complex. The nexus of the family of origin and the family of orientation would suggest that at some point, adults must make decisions about lost or troubled relationships. When does a sibling let go of what happened in childhood with another sibling in order to try to build a new relationship? And when does a sibling close himself off and decide to focus more on his family of orientation and no longer pursue a relationship with a sibling who may be reasonable and may even be harmful?

Some siblings are selectively estranged and juggle different relationships with parents and/or siblings. For example, Olympic skier Lindsey Vonn has not spoken to her father for years yet is close to her mother and siblings. Actress Angelina Jolie did not see her father, actor Jon Voight, for eight years before they restarted their relationship,[2] but she remained close to her brother during that period.

Bowen would say that such cutoffs from family members come with a price, that a relationship within the family must be established when possible and that cutoffs resulting from escalating conflict or a serious emotional episode should not be allowed to continue. Rather, in order for cutoffs not to hold the family members psychologically hostage, they should come only after thoughtful and rational consideration and attempts to reconcile have failed. In other words, sometimes a relationship with a sibling may, in fact, be more damaging or toxic than a complete cutoff. Still, for some siblings, a cutoff could be a reflection of other difficulties they have in establishing intimate relationships. This is when considering and attempting a reconnection becomes a topic of discussion in therapy. Given the emotional and often visceral nature of such cutoffs, this clearly seems to be an issue to which a therapist's support, encouragement, and guidance may be crucial.

WHEN TWO SIBLINGS WITHDRAW

Ron, a sixty-year-old white man living outside Wilmington, Delaware, and raising a young son as a single father, lives with the fairly rare situation of estrangement of all three siblings, compounded by several family members' serious psychological problems. Ron's older brother (by six years) and older sister (by three years) are no longer in touch with him, with each other, or with their parents, with the exception that the sister receives financial aid from their parents. The parents, both now in their nineties, are in an assisted living facility, with only Ron to care for them. His relationship with his brother was always difficult, a sign of early psychological problems in the brother, whom Ron's mother once described as "never feeling comfortable in his own skin." His sister's struggles started in late adolescence, a typical time for some serious mental illnesses to develop. The early years in the role that the parents played in weaving the fabric that Bank refers to are left unexplained, ambiguous, an entangled combination of a genetic lens and an intergenerational transmission of family patterns. But unlike the experience of the woman to whom Bank introduced us, Ron's parents tried to protect him and his sister when they were young from an abusive oldest brother. It is unclear how their efforts affected the trajectory of their relationships into adulthood.

THE INTERVIEW WITH RON

Our interview took place in Ron's study during a sunny afternoon while his son was in school. The family dog was running in and out as we talked. Ron, now divorced from his son's mother, has a master's degree and is a business consultant. With the economy slowly rebounding from the Great Recession of 2008, his consulting income is better than it was in the previous four years, although concerns about the future still loom. Financial independence is a theme that emerged during the interview in relation to both of his siblings. The division of property after his parents' deaths is anticipated to be a sticking point with his sister, but not with his brother.

To our opening question about the importance of sibling relationships, Ron's response showed how he had compartmentalized his feelings about them based on their years of interaction. Not only were the siblings never emotionally close, but he had not seen his brother for nearly ten years, and he had had no contact with him for eight years and none with his sister for sixteen years. His siblings had cut themselves off, and as a result, Ron had stopped pursuing them, though he is definitely open to other relationships. His family of orientation and his friends are very important to him, and he is a loving father to his son.

> I would say that they [sibling relationships] aren't important because I have not had a relationship with my siblings for well over forty years. My sister left the house when she was eighteen and I was fifteen. She had gotten into an Ivy League school but did not go. My brother was already out of college [he dropped out but finished twenty years later] and was gone, so the contact has been very sporadic. Totally no contact for years.

His tone and affect as he states this profound information were more matter-of-fact than sad or angry.

When intervening therapeutically in sibling relationships, it is important to understand when they ran aground and how. Ron learned early on that he needed to avoid his brother because he was terrorizing both him and his sister. So Ron's eventual adult cutoff seems to have begun very early and may have been predetermined by how his older brother treated him and his sister in childhood.

> I felt like an only child from a fairly young age, maybe as young as twelve, because my sister was not around much, and it was never a close relationship. In fact, it was a pretty difficult relationship. My older brother had a very troubled life emotionally from the day he was born. I am not aware of the dynamics that happened between when he was born and when he was six years old and I was born, but I understand, from what my mother has told me, he was a difficult child, a child today who would have had special education for behavioral issues. He was a small but very angry child. I don't have any memories of him at all until I was six or seven, at which point he was very physically abusive to both my sister and me. That was the way he let out anger. So my memories of my brother were of being abused in the truest

sense of the word, hurt. When I was nine years old, he threw a football at me. He was fifteen and it broke my arm. And there were other instances. My parents became so concerned that they kept a vigilant approach toward my brother. He couldn't be in the same room as my sister and me. It was a pretty bad situation, as you would think of an abusive situation.

Again, Ron relayed this with a matter-of-fact affect that reflected how long and to what extent he had had to deal with an older sibling with serious psychological problems.

Physically threatened by his brother and never being close to his sister, he felt like an only child. Ron's parents were consistently involved in the siblings' interactions, which, our research suggests, can be one of the family characteristics leading to troubled adult sibling relationships. For this family, however, it was a *protective* role that seems to have been born out of necessity. Ron has moved beyond what Bank suggests could happen in therapy—that the parents shoulder some of the blame for the later sibling conflict. To Ron, they acted appropriately under the circumstances.

> I think my parents were as protective of me as they could be at the younger ages and got more protective when I was nine or ten because of the injuries I suffered, which weren't insignificant at that point. My brother was threatening, and it was a very fearful situation being around him. We are talking fifty years ago, and my parents did what they knew to do and could have done at that point in time.

The Adult Years: Differences Between the Older Brother and Sister

The legacy of those early years, as expected, continues today. Ron's parents were protective of him and his sister when they were children, and the protection continued, albeit in a different and dysfunctional way, in their children's adulthood. Parents' influence on sibling relations, as we know, can continue into adulthood, even when all the siblings are out of the house.

> My relationship with my brother and sister does not exist now. The last time I talked to my sister was 1998. She left home, lived a very alternative life. I think of her as a grifter [a person who cons people out of money and pos-

sessions]. My father enabled her and supported her. She has three children by three different men, never had a full-time job or went to college. And emotionally, once I became an adult and much more aware of the situation, I realized she was almost like a second wife to my father in terms of the way he supported her and enabled her to live the life she lived. My feelings and memories of her since my early twenties are of someone who is always taking money. She gets and does not give.

This is where the estranged relationships with his brother and sister veer further apart. We cannot assume that estrangement, even within the same family, takes only one form. In this case, even though Ron's sister may have been regarded as a victim of the older brother (as was Ron), she, as an adult, has taken as much from others as she can. The brother, in contrast, separated himself from the family voluntarily, continuing to this day. Both siblings came from the same family, and even though one distanced himself as soon as he could, the other tethered herself financially to the family and found her father willing to support her. Having lost contact with his oldest son, Ron's father may have thought he should repair that wound by going out of his way to support the next child when she asked for help.

My brother actually left the family. Probably from the age of twenty-one, there was a period when he became estranged from the family. We did not see him for twelve years and didn't know where he was. He traveled the world. [This was in the late 1960s when many young people went on personal journeys.] I did not see him until I was thirty-six [twenty years later]. We didn't think he was a missing person because he would send us postcards from time to time, but there was no real contact. Because of how difficult it was with him around, I think there was actually a sense of relief in the family that he was not around. His absence did not cause heartache and pain because of the relief that he wasn't there.

It is hard not to wonder how Ron's older brother felt when he decided to leave his family behind. Was he feeling out of place, "uncomfortable in his own skin," as his mother declared, or as if he were a burden on the family? Whatever it was, some of his reactions years later might make it seem as if he were the victim and the one who had been mistreated, even though what exactly happened is not clear. He finally resumed contact with the family, but it was very contentious.

Ron visited him on a road trip that he took in his mid-thirties to Colorado, to try to figure out if reestablishing a relationship was possible.

I went out to see him when I was driving across country, but it was not very comfortable being around him. I was not afraid of any physical harm, but I was afraid of the way he drove. He was a very difficult person to be around. He could not conduct a normal conversation from his end. He was full of rage. There was a period when I tried to call him every two weeks. That started when I was in my thirties. But the calls were always so difficult because he was filled with such anger towards the family. It was so primal that it was difficult to have a give-and-take conversation. I think that my mother, who was a counselor, would say he suffered from paranoia and was a borderline personality. Talking to him when I visited him many years ago, he was always a contrarian. He could not say, "I am sorry about my life and the way things have turned out." He didn't have any self-reflection other than to say how much he hates the family and hates Wilmington.

Dropping Out Again

Although Ron's brother remained in sporadic contact, his acrimony did not abate. He moved ahead with his own life. He finished college in his forties, earned a teaching certificate, and started working in a big-city elementary school, not the kind of position one would have envisioned given his nature and the social and interactional demands of such a job. From descriptions of him as a youth, we might hypothesize that succeeding at such a position would be difficult given the dynamics of the family and the sibling struggles. Perhaps it was his professional daily contact with children at work that caused him to reach out to the family one more time.

My brother made an attempt to reconnect about ten years ago, [Ron recalled.] He came to visit a few times and was at my second wedding in an attempt to try and form a relationship with my parents. He gave me a toast and said some nice things. But he was never comfortable. He tried to be around people in his way, but you could see he was physically uncomfortable. My brother was very envious of my accomplishments in work and sports. He was also very proud. It did not make me feel a lot better about him when he told me he was proud, because there was so much other stuff that his telling me he was proud of me did not overcome those issues.

The brother's ambivalence toward the family is quite evident here, and it seems to add to Ron's own ambivalence about him. Clearly, at that point, so many painful things had transpired between them that Ron rejected even his brother's genuine attempts to be caring and supportive. This is the position that many siblings are in after they have built up a lifelong catalog of pain at the hands of another sibling.

After my son was born, it might have stirred up a lot for my brother. . . . He came to visit, and I think it was hard for him seeing me with a wife and baby. I think he spent so many years being estranged and building up a narrative about the family that I don't know how sustainable his relationships with us could have been anyway. By about eight years ago, when he had given up trying to be part of the family, he made it clear to me by phone that he was never coming back to Wilmington.

Ron told us that there was no contact now. "He stopped sending letters four to five years ago, and even those letters were very irregular. He wouldn't even answer the phone. I know my father, until a few years ago when he became demented, gave up trying to correspond with him prior to that." Ron's brother has made it clear that he is not interested in any inheritance and does not plan to come to their parents' funerals.

As Bowen would note, the brother always returns to wanting a total cut-off from the family. This leaves Ron unable to establish a relationship with him even if he decided he wanted to. As far as Ron knows, his brother has no compensating relationship, no one to meet his social needs. "He does not have a partner, never been married and, to the best of my knowledge, has no friends."

Ron's Sister: Still Attached

Compare the brother's approach to the family with what Ron described his sister doing. She turned down college admission and became pregnant as a single woman soon afterward, something that was not socially acceptable in Ron's family. She moved out of the country and did little with her life, according to Ron. He resents her.

> My sister's contact with my parents has always been around asking for money. She has never supported herself. They have not seen her for fourteen years and have not spoken with her for almost ten years, yet they still send her money every month. My brother has never asked for a dime and is the complete opposite in terms of dependency.

Bowen might regard the dependence of one sibling and the rejection/independence of the other as representing equally low levels of differentiation. Despite the estrangement from his sister, Ron is in contact with her second child, who was recently married. He attended the wedding, but his sister (who is estranged from her daughter), who was invited, did not come. Thinking intergenerationally, his sister and his niece could be seen as continuing the parent-child cutoff that his sister had with her parents.

When all of one's siblings have stopped contact with their parents, all the weight of caregiving falls on one person. Ron described his experience with that situation. "I have been the only child for my parents. My brother didn't want any money and my sister's only connection was for money." He also was left to deal with his parents' disappointment with the two very different family roles that his siblings have assumed. Yes, they both have dropped out, but one is still taking while the other has renouncing everything connected with the family.

Ron's relationship with his sister was never warm, and he was even more critical of her than of his brother.

> I am angrier at her than at my brother because of what she was doing to my father. She never was a good mother to her children, and all three are being raised by their fathers. I have deliberately cut relations off with my sister. She, in many ways, may be more emotionally ill than my brother, who is an independent, functioning adult. My sister never turned her life around.

The pain of losing a relationship with a sister can be greater than that of losing a relationship with a brother, according to Victor Cicirelli. "The perception of a close bond to sisters by either men or women appears to be uniquely important to the older person's well-being."[3]

Putting Pieces Together

How does a family get to the point that two of the three children drop out of contact with each other and with the rest of the family? Were there issues before the children were born? Bank talked about the importance of family history. Even though Ron's mother had always been close to her sisters, she was physically abused as a child by her mother. Ron's father had strained relations with his siblings. "On my father's side, there is some craziness in those siblings," Ron told us. "His oldest sibling, a sister, lived across the street when I was growing up, and we saw them only at family functions. She was difficult. When she became sixty, she broke off relationships with many people in the family, including my father." Multigenerational patterns of cutoffs between siblings in adulthood are common.

Ron's father had a geographically close but emotionally distant relationship with his sister, and eventually she cut him off. First his sister and then his children refused to have contact with him. Ron did not describe him as an abusive man and maintains a relationship with him. Now the pattern of cutoffs is being repeated in the next two generations—Ron's father, Ron's sister, Ron's brother, Ron, and Ron's niece all are cut off from their siblings or parents.

Although the issue of familial connection has been a topic of conversation between Ron and his parents, given their own history the parents never encouraged their talking about it.

> My parents and I have talked about the fact that we are not close and really do not have a family unit of brothers and sisters. They did not emphasize to us that we should be close as siblings because it just wasn't possible. My brother and sister were emotionally ill for a long time.

Some parents would insist on contact with a child to whom they were providing financial support. We believe that most parents would end such support without any contact, but that was not the case here. When asked about the relationship between his father and sister and why he gave her financial support despite the lack of contact, Ron was not specific but offered a hint. "I think there were some uncomfortable oedipal issues going on between father and daughter that I don't think were very healthy." He left it at that without specifically saying there was sexual abuse. Guilt, if the father was guilty, can be a very powerful force in a decision to provide support, as can great affection. Or as we mentioned earlier, he may have continued his support because after having lost contact with one child, Ron's father could not emotionally cope with losing contact with another, and maybe the once-a-month check feels to him like contact.

Ron wondered what happened before he was born.

I wish I could have been a fly on the wall in those early years to see what happened between my parents and my siblings. When I was four and my brother ten, those were difficult times for my parents and him, so it is hard for me to understand what happened. I imagine it was a combination of that generation of people getting married after the war, my mother coming from a very abusive family, beat by her mother. They both brought a lot of trauma into their marriage, but they are still married almost seventy years later. I think there is a huge biological and genetic component of anxiety and depression from both sides that got passed on. Back then, there wasn't the type of therapy available for families and children, so I don't think it was very easy.

NO ADVICE FOR OTHERS

While success in sibling relationships may translate into advice for others, we wondered whether estranged relationships could also show how relationships could be strengthened. Ron disagreed, not because he did not have an opinion, but because he has come to see himself as not having siblings. Being the youngest and believing that his sibling and family relationship patterns were set before he was born, Ron does not seem to feel that he had any influence or even much meaningful participation in how his adult sibling relationships evolved. In short, all this feels like it just happened *to* him.

How a therapist using a multigenerational family conceptual framework could have been helpful at different points in the past, or even now, is difficult to answer, but one thing seems clear—it would have taken a great deal of motivation and hard work for Ron to have changed the trajectory of his adult sibling relationships. His reluctance to give advice may reflect his realization how hard it would have been, and would be, to change the dynamics.

> For me it is hard [to offer advice] because I really felt like a single child from twelve on, and there was so much trauma in the family around my older brother and sister. I don't have any advice because it has been almost fifty years since I have had a relationship with them. My cousin became like a big sister to me when I reached my twenties, but that was as close as I can come to knowing what it is like to have a sibling.

Ron's self-identification as an only child appears to be a kind of adaptive denial allowing him to feel all right about how things are with his siblings so he can move on and ignore the pain of how things have evolved; that is, he can let go of the need to change them.

Ron reflected on his situation and raised some points about the advantages of his parents' financial stability and about how he felt having his own child be an actual only child. Underlying his comments is the theme of how loved ones, of any generation, are taken care of.

> I am lucky that my parents can be in assisted living because if I had to take care of them alone, I would have no support from my siblings in doing that. I wish I had been younger when my son came along so my parents could help me out more with him. But he is an only child and I am a single dad, and he will be raised in a much safer, more loving environment as an only child [than Ron had as one of three siblings].

For most of us, especially those who had difficult childhoods, our main goal as a parent is to provide a better childhood than the one we had. Ron is working on that.

Ron turned philosophical at the end of our interview. He is a man who is deeply committed to his parents, his son, and his friends. He loves socializing and entertaining. Nonetheless, he has let go of his sibling relationships. Out of necessity, he has closed himself off, if only to them. "I don't reflect any more on the deep impact on the early relationship with my siblings in terms of the violence that happened. I don't think about it anymore. I rarely reflect about my brother and sister—they are not a part of my life." For Ron, moving on was the healthiest choice.

CONCLUSION

Each parent brings the dynamics of their family of origin to the marriage (or partnership), and the parents' relationship can set the tone for the family's emotional life and for the family's response to child-generated conflicts. The personality of a particular child might be such that some children (e.g., Ron's brother) are simply born more troubled than others. Parents can sometimes, though not always, help resolve these troubles. But even the best-functioning parents would have struggled with Ron's brother. In any case, parents treat children with more difficult tempera-ments more harshly,[4] and the family history of Ron's mother and father suggests that Ron's brother might have been difficult for them to handle. The parents' history also would have affected the climate in the family— the mother was treated harshly as a child, and the father's sister eventually divorced herself from the family. Such a history influences what they bring to parenting and their relationships with all their children, so pointing to a single event or person is risky. The family can be a stew, and it is impossible to know what went into it first and when the other ingredients were added and how much.

In Ron's family, his parents intervened to protect him and his sister from his older brother's outbursts. Was this playing favorites or correctly protecting the younger children? It is hard to know how the oldest per-ceived it, but the violence stopped when he left home at eighteen, and life, at least on the surface, was less stressful for the remaining family members. We say "on the surface" because we do not know exactly the nature of the father-sister relationship. The sister followed her older brother out the door when she reached early adulthood. Even though she clearly was pro-tected from her older brother, she still withdrew and behaved in ways that were not socially acceptable to the family's culture: no college after private school, several unwed pregnancies, lifelong underachievement, pathologi-cal dependence on others, and estrangement. When parents intervene to protect their children (as they should have done here), the children may not learn how to resolve conflict by themselves or manage relationships as well. Also, the parents' actions may have left the oldest son, as a young child, with developmentally inappropriate power in the family, exacer-bating whatever his underlying pathology may have been. As a result, the brother's withdrawing from the family in which relationships may seem unsafe, was a reasonable option, and this may have been what happened in Ron's family.

In working with families with similar issues, Bank saw a strong parental connection to the next generation's relationship problems, but he did not advise his clients to blame their parents. Rather, he encouraged his clients working on rebuilding positive sibling relationships to join with one another in their loss of what a good relationship could have been. In essence, Bank might say that both have lost something and they can mourn this together as they form a new relationship. If we apply this advice to Ron's situation, he and his siblings would have to begin communicating and then try to accept that their parents were doing the best they could in the 1960s, mourn what they had lost from their sibling relationship over the years, and decide whether they wished to move forward and possibly form a new relationship based on the present. They would have to become comfortable with the ambiguity and ambivalence of their history. Ron was not optimistic that such an approach would be possible, given his siblings' nature. But he may be more open to trying this after his parents have died, as currently he is protecting his parents, just as they tried to protect him many years ago.

CHAPTER 8

Coping with the Death of a Sister (a Twin) and Other Losses

GOOD PARENTING SET THE STAGE for Penny, Carrie, and April to build a lifelong sister relationship that has nurtured and sustained them through the loss of their mother thirty-three years ago, their father nineteen years ago, and Penny's twin sister, Maggie, nine months before our interview, after a multiyear battle with cancer. They are being interviewed together, sitting around a wooden dining room table in Carrie's suburban stone house outside Boston on a summer day. The street is quiet at two in the afternoon, and the house is comfortable, well constructed, and elegant, similar to the relationships of the three women. Penny, the oldest, and Carrie, the second of the three, are in their early sixties; April is twelve years Penny's junior. All are married and have children in various stages of adolescence and adulthood. Penny, married to a man ten years her senior, recently placed him in a nursing home because of his advancing Alzheimer's disease. Although it has been an unusually difficult year for the family, it seems to have strengthened these sisters' bonds. The twins' relationship was a loving one throughout their life, as is typical of twins, according to research psychologist Tony Vernon. Vernon, who was interviewed by Jeffrey Kluger, explained that "when a twin dies, the bereavement the survivor feels can be worse than for all other family members."[1] April acknowledged during our interview that this particular loss had been the most painful for Penny. The pain is still palpable.

As sociologist Melanie Mauthner wrote in her book about sisters,

> Rarely do sisters experience continuity in all aspects of their relationships from their teenage to their adult years. The way that "sistering" changes at the micro-level from closeness to distance, or dependence to independence, reflects other transitions in girls' and women's lives which are linked to key events such as moving home or to school, making or losing girlfriends and boyfriends, starting work, leaving home, motherhood, divorce, and bereavement.[2]

We touched on many of these issues during the interview, especially in reference to the age gap between the oldest and the youngest sisters, how they grieved their growing up and moving out of the home, Penny's temporary return home in her mid-twenties, and, now, how they mourn Maggie's death. We highlight here the special bond among the sisters even while they are struggling with one another. Alliant University psychology professor Sue Kuba pointed out in her book, *The Role of Sisters in Women's Development*, that in the past, sisters' relationships did not receive the attention they should have. Modern feminism has drawn interest to the topic, she wrote, as has the greater participation of women theorists who often were using their own experiences as a guide.[3] As Victor Cicirelli's research showed more than thirty years ago and as more recent research has confirmed, sisters have the strongest sibling bonds.[4] In this family, those bonds were put to a number of tests and survived each one.

THE INTERVIEW

After administering our questionnaire, our interviews typically start with the general question "How important is your relationship?" April answered first.

> I was thinking about this on the way over here today. If I don't see Maggie [referring to her photograph, which is prominently displayed], Carrie, and Penny every day, they are in my mind. I wonder about them and I stay in touch, thanks to electronic devices with Facebook or e-mail—the devices are not a substitute for this [she points to the two of them]—or through walks and shopping. The question about best friends on the

questionnaire—I don't think about you as best friends, but in a way you are my best friends. I think when something is deeply troubling me, *you* are the first people I turn to.[5]

After a pause, Penny starts to tear up. She immediately refers to the loss of Maggie, their fourth sister and Penny's twin, and the "loss" of her husband with his needing nursing home care.

> This is very emotional to me. Especially because it's so raw. When we moved back here [from the Midwest three years ago] because of my husband's disability, we lost a lot. I lost my friends, my support system out there, my work identity, and faith community. I came back here and, even though so much of my support system was lost and it takes time to get that here, it never once felt, in the most primal sense, like the wrong thing to do. I couldn't get the kind of support there, and I could not have stayed that far away while she was dying. I would have cracked up. I need Kleenex.

All of Penny's sisters live within thirty minutes of one another, and Penny and her husband moved nearby.

Carrie chimed in.

> It was essential for us to be together because we share the essence of the family stuff all the way in our daily lives. These relationships are primal. I was ten when April was born so, in many ways, there are like two separate families. When I went off to college, she was seven and we were in one set of relationships and now [forty-four years later], she is a mother, so we are adults and whatever the years were [they] do not have meaning, they begin to shrink.

Clearly, the separations based on differences in developmental stages when these sisters were young have faded away, replaced by an adult bond. When there is a ten-year difference between siblings, the experiences growing up in the home can be so different that they could be two families. In a well-functioning family, as these adult bonds develop, the sibling hierarchy flattens, and as adults, siblings take on the roles they are most capable of assuming, not those dictated by age gaps, gender, or sibling position.

April described what the shift in their relationship meant to her.

The transition from baby sister to peer sister began to happen with each of my sisters at different times. I have very strong memories of when Penny moved back home and I was still little. [She starts to tear up.] It was really one of the highlights of my horrifying middle school years. Those years were horrifying because of family stuff. When I was little, it was always Maggie and Penny, the twins, but when Penny moved back home for various chunks of time, I got to know her as an individual because Maggie was married at that point. And then we hung out. And then Maggie, in her second marriage, came back around when Mom was ill. When I got older, I had my time with Carrie. I felt like I got to know each of my sisters alone and at a different stage, and so I stopped being the little sister. I feel like the relationship has evolved and deepened. I know some of my friends have grown apart from their siblings as they have gotten older. For me, I feel like I have gotten much closer. There never was a time that we weren't close. We have just grown closer. It has been enhanced, and I rely on them as a woman.

This is one illustration of how a "baby sister" builds new, more adult relationships with each of her sisters, impelled in part by their common concern for an ill parent.

Penny added her perspective on what happened when she returned home in her twenties to find work as an actress. The time together provided an opportunity for the sisters' connection, but their mother, who was emotionally devastated by having had three of her four daughters move away, wanted Penny to stay. When she left again, Penny worried that she no longer would be able to be a buffer between April and their mother's intense desire to parent. "I had come home and was working locally. That was one of the nice things about having April around. When I got an acting job in Chicago, Mom was not happy that I was leaving. I felt like I left you," Peggy said turning to April.

While Penny felt this exquisitely, April saw it differently at fourteen and maybe saw Penny as a role model for growing up. "I was in my self-absorbed stage so I never felt like you left me [she laughs]. I felt like, at your age, you were supposed to go."

"I was so glad you had developed this wonderful social network of friends because you needed to get away," Penny responded. "Our mother was so unhappy to have us leave because she was a mother and there wasn't anyone left to take care of. Our father worked very long hours and was not there a lot." Four years later, their mother became ill and died. Penny and Maggie were thirty, Carrie was twenty-eight, and April was eighteen. Fortunately, from the perspective of the need for children to grow up and move on, they do not believe that her illness was in any way related to the loss of her mothering role.

The Twins and Their Relationship

In Carrie's and April's eyes, Maggie and Penny were always unusually close because they were twins. Although some twins take time to bond and although Penny believes Maggie competed with her when they were in their teens, Penny never felt any distance.[6] As teens, they were perceived by both their younger sisters as a unit and as each other's best friends.

"Being twins, you guys shared the stage of the family for the first couple of years of your lives," Carrie remembered.

> They would come home from school and go upstairs together and laugh their heads off, and I knew I was never going to get in on that—and it seemed like so much fun. Hilarity up there. They would laugh for hours, and I would listen and say to myself, "That is so cool." I felt envy but I never felt they were being mean to me [by exclusion].

Unlike what we have heard from many other siblings in this book, there was also no triangulation. Neither Maggie nor Penny tried to form an alliance with Carrie, the next oldest, in order to gain power or a competitive edge within the family.

"The twins were like a force that made more of an impact than any one of us," Carrie observed. April agreed. "They were one word when I was little—no space between 'MaggieandPenny.' In my mind, they were one. It was not until they both went away that I got to know them individually." It seems a reasonable hypothesis to see the twins' bond as the foundation for the close bonds among all the four sisters. Had the twins not gotten along, a cascade of troubled relationships might have beset the family.

As Penny recounted, "When Maggie and I left for college, it was a huge chunk away from the table, and that is when April and Carrie got close [despite their nearly ten-year age gap]. And our mother was in mourning."

Their mother worked to make them two words instead of one. "Mom insisted we go to different colleges. I think that was a good thing, but Maggie hated college and got married years sooner than me to escape college. That marriage did not work out." It was not until many years later, after marriages, children, and ultimately Maggie's illness and Penny's husband's illness that they began living close together again. As we have heard so often from other siblings, a health crisis, involving either a sibling or a parent, can bring family members close together.

SUSTAINED BY THEIR PARENTS' EARLY INFLUENCE

Throughout this book, we have noted that messages from parents can influence siblings' closeness. Helgola Ross and Joel Milgram, family researchers at the University of Cincinnati, believe that the key factor in building feelings of closeness among adult siblings is the family of origin: "The sense of belonging to the family . . . was, for most siblings, permanently affected by experiences shared in childhood."[7] Here we heard specifically how a positive parenting approach paid off for these sisters after their mother's death and their father's remarriage.

Carrie painted the picture of their early family life first.

One of the things our parents did very well was to give a sense of family. It is a very powerful thread going on among and between all of us. We were raised by people in the 1950s and no feminism and with those values and a very smart and strong mother with bumps in her road growing up. Her whole fulfillment was being a mom and having this family she loved but, in the end, "What was the point?" We were all going to grow up and leave her, and she got sick and died. So there was all this core strength we had and these problems that pulled us together. There was a core of affection and love between all of us and we tried to slog through the problems together as her cancer came along. And then there was this next problem. Our father married this difficult person [laughter from all the sisters], and that was very tough. We all had different relationships with her. She was contentious and controlling and played us off against each other.

We wondered whether their new stepmother's approach made them less close as sisters. "She tried to play us off against each other, but it didn't work," Penny answered and then explained their upbringing.

Our family had something that she did not have a clue about: togetherness and trust. Our parents' greatest achievement was never playing each other off against each other or holding one of us up for the other. They never said, "Look at how good so and so is doing and why can't you do that well?" We were all supposed to celebrate each other's triumphs and support each other with our struggles.

We asked how this was conveyed to them.
"A doctor once said to our mother," Penny recalled,

"Remember three words: acceptance, affection, and approval. If you remember those three things, you will be fine when dealing with your children." I know even my own daughter got that from me. She knows she is loved, and all our children know they are loved, and our stepmother's children do not know that and are struggling and moving as far away from her as they can.

Penny then told a story about their stepmother, who was blocking their access to their father. They believed that she wanted to exclude them from caring for him by providing little information about his health and that she was trying to turn them against one another.

When Dad had his stroke, I came to Boston to see him, and he was having a difficult time. I walked into the room and our stepmother came in, and she started screaming at me about my sisters: "They won't tell you this and that," and I just started crying. I don't fight back, and she wanted a fight. We were raised to avoid conflict and here it was. I just started crying.

Visions of the archetypal evil stepmother made famous in fairy tales come to mind here. But as adults, the sisters were able to fend her off better than the children in those tales could.

Talking about their stepmother triggered remembrances of their mother and how different she was. "Our mom was kind of wounded in her upbringing, and one of the things she would do, as a result, was to let us be who we wanted to be," Carrie explained.

> The downside of that is that she never made us try harder. She could have done a bit more of that but, all things considered, she let us be. She made us feel those three things—acceptance, affection, and approval. Yes, she heard it from the pediatrician, but she knew it anyway.

"She was also incredibly proud of each of us," April continued.

> We are very tied together but very different. Mom and Dad would talk lovingly about each of the sisters, but I never heard them criticize any of you or the choices you made. I think later I heard they weren't happy with some of the choices, but they never said it to us. I felt loved.

April offered a concrete example of how love was shown and how she now shows love to her daughter.

> Mom would send me little notes and put them on my pillow; a sorry note if we had a fight. I have kept them all in a box and have done the same with my daughter. It stopped after my junior year when she got ill, but that was very powerful. I felt loved and admired. At school, I was another sister, the last of four, but my parents never said that to me. They loved us.

When parents express their love of their children, it is often an outgrowth of the parents' love for each other. But it can also be the unhealthy manifestation of a fragile spousal relationship and a parent seeking affection from children that he or she is not getting from the other parent. We asked if their parents loved each other.

Penny gives a partial answer after a thoughtful pause.

> Yes, in a complicated way. He was a workaholic and loved his work. We always had dinner together, regardless of the time—7:30 or 8 at night. And it was a surprise to me when I met fathers who did not like their work because he loved his, and he always encouraged us to do what we wanted. So when I wanted to go into acting, there was no problem with it.

We wanted to get a clearer sense of how the sisters' closeness developed and tried to summarize what they said. "So your closeness comes from the love your parents felt for each other and the way they raised you." They all nodded in agreement. "And your stepmother's behavior helped unite you further."

"We had to begin to be clear with each other," Penny explained.

Dad raised us to not be confrontational and not to make waves. And you swallow your icky and angry feelings. And then he married this harridan who loves anger, and we had to learn how to express our feelings to her and step up to the plate. I had to have this flat-footed discussion with my father where I confronted him and said to him, "The reason I don't call here is because of her." And he said, "I totally understand."

Their father's approval was important to these sisters and was always forthcoming. Approval of all the children is not always perceived, as is the case if parents are too active or too withholding and leave a gap.[8] The three sisters we interviewed never had to struggle with that.

DEALING WITH FAMILY COMMUNICATION

Communication and shared values have been found to be good predictors of siblings' closeness.[9] We wondered how this successfully functioning family of sisters had dealt with any communication mishaps in their lives. As might be expected, they handle things honestly and openly, even though they may have to go through an extra step to get there. They communicate by means of "checks and balances." By this we mean that they check with one another about what the third sister may be saying before approaching one another directly. Confrontation can be difficult for some of them. Despite this pattern of indirect communication at times, it is carried on in a context of love in which eventually everything is clarified and without triangulation.

"We don't edit ourselves," Penny offered.

When there is a misunderstanding, I will talk to one about what is going on with the other and the first one might say, "I don't know what you're talking about." *Then* I will ask the other directly. Life is short and we can't play that game with each other. I do it enough in the real world.

"I think this is the biggest chink in the family," Carrie observed.

> We were not raised to deal with any communication unless it was positive. Everything was "I love you and you are wonderful." I did not have a toolbox for expressing my feelings unless they were positive, which I can do well . . . I make everyone feel good but I can't say, "It really hurts me." I don't think April could say, as someone in another family might be able to say, "You guys are leaving me out of the loop." That is our family's biggest, weakest link. I work at my relationships at work and in my marriage to say what is bothering me. For me, if there is anything left in my development, it is honing those skills. So I love that we are doing so well that there aren't any awful things between us. But there was a time [around Maggie's illness and death] when the communication was messed up. But no one was ever trying not to communicate.

Events were rapidly being shaped around taking care of Maggie. The change came coincidentally when one or two of the sisters were with Maggie and it was hard to keep the other up-to-date. As Carrie pointed out, there was never an attempt *not* to communicate; it just might not happen fast enough. First April, and then Penny, described the complexity of the communication and how Maggie's husband may have contributed to complicating it.

> Every fourth e-mail, it was "What did I miss? What are they talking about and why did they not tell me?" And because of the nature of Maggie's disease and what was happening with her care, things would happen and one of us would ask of the other, "Didn't her husband tell you?" But I never felt slighted, just out of it.
>
> We were all grieving and because of that, we dropped the ball [on communicating well].

As we showed in earlier chapters, communication is the foundation for success, though the means and types of communication may vary greatly from one family to another. Some may be emotionally and physically expressive; others may prefer email or Facebook communication. Sisters generally are more capable of, and comfortable with, more frequent communication and more depth in the content in that communication than brothers are. For these three sisters, such a foundation had been in place for years, and it helped them enormously.

Carrie explained how this developed in reaction to Maggie's illness.

First of all, the ten-year difference in age initially made a difference in how we talked to each other. We had to make sure in the sibling relationship we were all speaking to each other about everything in a clearer way than in the past. Every family has that: "Well, you didn't tell me this and so it happened that way." That started to happen. April had little kids at home still when Maggie first got ill, so she could not go out to Maggie's house as much. Penny and I had to tag-team going out there, and we live close by. And then we would fail to close the communication circle with April, though we did improve with time as this horrible illness went on. We said to each other, "We aren't doing a good enough job of communication—let's do better." That bumped this thing [our relationship] up a notch.

Carrie returned to the issue of communication with a person "outside" their circle. Because they had been excluded from taking care of their father, they relived being prevented from taking care of their sister Maggie when there were disagreements about medical versus holistic treatments.

The communication thing became an issue again with Maggie's husband, who was managing her care, and whether we agreed with that or not. We were talking to each other about what our role should be and if we disagreed with his approach. Communicating with a man can be hard for us. We are already on solid ground with each other because we are female and loving sisters, but I can say, for me, that is where I need to get better. Because the problems with communication became more explicit with Maggie's illness, I now think we can do this better. Dealing with Maggie's husband, a man, was difficult but we learned to speak up because it was Maggie. I could do it for her because it was for her and not me. In the old days, I couldn't have even done it for a sister; but now I could. All of that should play out in our future relationships.

Penny continued.

There is the role of the husband but also the role of the sisters with a capital S. The Sisters are trying to force this even as he was expecting us to shoulder much of the work of this. This was going on even as the real issue was that Maggie was dying, which was linking us.

Carrie added, "And we had the responsibility. April would come one day, and I would come another day, and Penny another, as Maggie got really severe. It was so hard and so many hours and miles and so much anguish."

Dealing with the Loss of a Sister and a Twin

These sisters had to navigate the tragic illness and death of their sister Maggie, which could have pulled them in different directions. It is one thing to get along when not faced with adversity. It is quite another to confront a long, drawn-out crisis such as what they faced over the past several years.

Penny brought up the broader notion that we examined in the first chapter, that siblings are relations for life (the sisters with a capital S), which is all the truer for a twin because of their parallel developmental trajectories and genetic similarities. Penny also confirmed that the way they survived the loss was to do it together.

Who wants to talk across the line in your family about mortality? You expect to lose your parents, which we did, but you do not expect to lose your sibling this young. I was never going to lose my twin—it was not in my understandings about the way the rest of my life was going to go. We still have open wounds. It has been horrible and it is still horrible, and I just put my husband in a facility last week, so "OK, how many more tests will I have?" What am I supposed to do with all of this? And that is where they [she indicates her sisters] come in. I don't know what to do with it any more than they do, but at least we are in it together. We have each other. It definitely has brought us together because one thing mortality shows you is you never know what is going to happen. Even though Maggie would ask, "What did I do to deserve this?" we begin to ask the same thing. And then I think, "It is just not in your hands. It is what it is."

Carrie and then April added their thoughts on mortality and how their relationship sustained them: "We lost our parents young; we lost a sister and Penny's husband—it is enough already."

A few years ago I had a lump show up. It was biopsied, and I had to wait ten awful days to get the results. And we had a mother who had died of cancer.

Well, the way to think about it was, "We cannot lose a sister." The only way that would happen was like [the movie] *Thelma and Louise*. We would all go over the cliff together. That's how I always felt about all of us. But then Maggie died and we did not go over together. It wasn't supposed to happen because we were all supposed to grow old and funny together, and Maggie's death really messed with my worldview. I am still trying to figure out what that is. Obviously, I am a wife and a mother and teacher, and they bring me great joy, but that hole is there and things are different. It is as if a lot of color has gone out of the world. I have made a vow to myself that I am going to look for that color. She is not here, but she is here somewhere. Maybe she is in that beautiful flower. And I also look at my children and think about how she was a fairy godmother. And I am watching them deal with it, as it is their first loss. So I am trying to deal with this new universe, as both a mom and a sister. I have had a pretty healthy dose of loss in my life, but they haven't.

ADVICE FOR OTHER SIBLINGS

Penny offered the following advice:

Don't judge each other; hold each other for what you are to each other. Don't compare yourself with each other. Be there for each other. I don't know how you do that. If there is a first-aid kit for that, it would be great. If you can center down and quiet yourself instead of letting all those wild thoughts about growing up and competition come up, get quiet. Find a quiet place and don't take the bait when you are getting challenged, and see if you can get your sibling to a quiet place with you.

While offering specific advice consistent with having both a constant awareness of self and actively changing behavior, she also inserted a more pessimistic view of the possibilities for change: "I don't know about people with bad relationships. I have never seen them get worked out. I just see them get further and further apart, like my stepmother's kids."

Penny also mentioned the role a therapist could play. "Having a third party there to be the objective person would be helpful."

Carrie agreed about taking specific steps to improve communication through insight.

If you don't have a good basis for connection and you want it, you need to say to each other, "What happened to us in our family that makes this connection hard for us now?" Everyone will have a slightly different story on it, and maybe [you need to say] "I never heard what you felt." Those are the things that siblings need to go back through to work out. One of my dear friends has no siblings and she makes it clear all the time how lucky we are, no matter what. What she carried as the only child was a lot.

April commented on the temporal nature of healthy relationships—that each person may need to be there for the other during a crisis. In her account, the loss of a twin and a husband to Alzheimer's has made this an especially difficult time for Penny.

Like any relationship, it requires effort and sustenance and the benefit of having a close relationship. With the exception of the biggies, like the loss of Maggie and Dad and Penny's husband, each of us is needy at different times, and this is Penny's time. With my daughter going off to college, and that is a biggie, they are both there for me and have gone through that. I know they have both experienced loss at different times. Like any relationship, I can't just take from them for me. I can give to them too, and I can't expect they will always be there for me if I am not there for them.

Acceptance, affection, and approval are the hallmarks of these three sisters' relationship. Their acceptance style was evident during our interview, as they never disagreed substantially with one another—they would say "and" and not "but" and build on what the other was saying without arguing their point. As Penny would say, they are quiet with one another and show their affection and approval in this way. To different degrees, they recognized that their "chink"—their indirect style of communication—may or may not always be effective for them, but it is conveyed in the language of acceptance. Like the brothers in the next chapter, they have learned to frame their communication in the best possible light.

They have been buffeted by forces beyond their control—a double loss [Maggie and Penny's husband] for the family. Yet they demonstrated that making sibling relationships work over the long term requires recognizing when one sister might need and, subsequently, to get more of something than another might, and they are willing to do this for one another.

CHAPTER | 9

Three Brothers
Who Get It Right

AS WE HAVE MENTIONED THROUGHOUT this book, the bonds between sisters are, according to a variety of sources, stronger and more affectionate than those between brothers. Sisters are often the glue keeping siblings communicating, coordinating care of parents, and sending birthday cards. But this does not mean that brothers are not able to cherish and nurture their relationships with one another. We interviewed three brothers who are extremely close, as are their spouses, and offer them as a model of how brothers can sustain one another across the life span.

Reporter Jeffrey Kluger's look at his brother-centric family in *The Sibling Effect* offers a different view of fraternal relationships. He is one of four brothers who grew up in a noisy household. Two stepsiblings joined the family when he was ten years old, and his relationship with his father deteriorated over time. When looking at photos from his early childhood, when his parents were still married, he was struck by how physically close he and his brothers were, as if they were physically holding on to one another for dear life as their parents' relationship faltered. Unlike some families in which the parents are divorced, the brothers were not emotionally divided. Kluger enumerated the benefits of age for sibling relationships: "Steve, Gary, Bruce, and I never had much conflict to overcome, so things have admittedly been easier for us. But the mellowing that comes with years has still helped us move beyond those things that did cause divisions."[1] Even though they don't communicate verbally every day, e-mail allows frequent contact that is tinged with everything from the serious to the frivolous. To this extent, they probably communicate more than most brothers.

In their review of research on brothers, psychologists Victoria Hilkevitch Bedford and Paula Smith Avioli noted that even if brothers do not feel particularly close, they believe they can rely on one another in a crisis. In their own research, they initially found that brothers who were born during the baby boom period, compared with those who were born earlier, originally appeared to have closer relationships. But on closer examination and after a second wave of interviews, the researchers decided that the younger cohort of men may have better relationship skills when dealing with men but may not necessarily be any closer. Bedford and Avioli wondered whether they mistakenly had used the lens for sisters and their intimacy to examine men's behavior.[2]

In Ezekiel Emanuel's book, *Brothers Emanuel: A Memoir of an American Family*, about his relationship with his brothers, Rahm (the mayor of Chicago and one-time chief of staff for President Barack Obama) and Ari (a movie producer), he portrays a noisy early childhood with two loving parents in the home. Such an environment does not always equip one for adulthood, though.

> When it comes to feelings, matters were a bit more complicated. We could show love and flashes of other emotions, like envy, jealousy, pride, dejection, or remorse. But as I realized later in life, when problems arose, we did not have many ways to discuss them deeply. The emotional vocabulary in our family was limited. We were never encouraged to articulate our deeper feelings. Indeed, discussion of how we felt tended to be brief, if not monosyllabic.[3]

Even though the Emanuel family also has an adopted daughter, it was the brothers who ran the, apparently rather loud, show.

Was it the parents in the Emanuel family who set the tone? It is unclear, but they described their mother as enforcing a few rules consistently and asking them to kiss and hug to make up after a physical altercation. She would swat them when they were bad and could be moody and withdrawn for days. Yet perhaps because of her moodiness, the boys were also given a great deal of encouragement and freedom to both pursue their interests and manage their relationships while their father, a pediatrician, worked long hours. They described their father as understanding the importance of physicality to the healthy development of children, and so he believed in hugging and kissing them. Physical contact was thus their form of communication, and emotions were shelved in this family of highly verbal sons. Their own high level of energy is credited to their father, who had remarkable stamina himself and worked fourteen-hour days. Accordingly, their parents, albeit in different ways, set the tone for the three Emanuel sons. For the three brothers we interviewed, now in their late fifties and mid-sixties, the situation is very much the same. The three brothers always ran the show with the full participation of their father while their sister grew up on the periphery.

The three brothers, like the sisters in the previous chapter, show a great deal of affection, which men sometimes express as teasing and self-deprecating humor.[4] These brothers feel comfortable expressing affection as well as occasionally teasing one another and punctuating their conversation with self-deprecating humor. According to much of the research, the bonds between sisters are the strongest, but you would not know that from talking to these three brothers, all of whom are married. Their wives also are very close, and the six of them love spending time together.

THE BROTHERS' BACKGROUND

Charlie, the oldest at sixty-five, has six children from two different marriages. He works as a mechanical engineer and is interested in the innovative design of ergonomic chairs. He plays the guitar and sings in an oldies trio, which we heard perform live. As the group's centerpiece and only instrumentalist, his voice melds perfectly with those of the two other men, one older and one younger than he. Comfortable around men, his singing partners could also be considered professional brothers. Mick, at sixty-three, has four children and is a retired college instructor. Also a musician, he plays the guitar and sings with various groups in his area. Bill, fifty-eight years old, has no children and is also a musician. He reached great career heights as a sought-after studio engineer in Nashville before retiring and working in construction. Marianne, married and also without children, has a successful career as a nurse.

The interview took place with all three brothers and their wives present as they were preparing to play music at a fund-raiser for a local small-town theater that Charlie supports.[5] Coincidentally, their mother had died nine days before our prearranged interview. She had been ill for years. Their father had died eighteen months earlier, also after a lengthy illness precipitated by a stroke. He died surrounded by his family with the sons playing the music they had enjoyed their whole life. Though it is never easy, his death was a celebration of the family's life together. They sang, laughed, told stories, and drank a lot of wine together in the hours immediately afterward. Faith has a part in their lives, and they felt uplifted by what they shared at that time. Their experiences with their father also provided a good model for when their mother died, which made her demise easier to assimilate.

While interviewing the brothers with their wives present, it became evident that the boundary that therapists may assume exists between the family of origin (the brothers) and the family of orientation (the wives) did not obtain here. In classic family therapy theory, the brothers might consult their wives and then discuss issues related to their parents. But in this family, it appears that the wives have an equal voice; the divide is less clear. Assumptions that a therapist might make about the way a family *should* operate would not apply. This family has created a more egalitarian system that works beautifully for them.

The brothers revel in their closeness. They cannot believe their good fortune in having one another. This does not mean that they have not had hard times in their relationships with one another and in their personal lives. They have a sister who is sixty years old and does not blend in as easily. To the brothers' chagrin, she is both emotionally and physically distant. Charlie, the oldest, struggled for many of his early adult years with his relationship with his father. But they found a way to accept and love each other and eventually stitched their relationship back together.

THE INTERVIEW

We began the interview by expressing our condolences to the family on the death of their mother. They appreciated the thought, and after a serious moment, they began bantering as they took turns talking. In fact, the bantering, much of which cannot be adequately captured in the text, is an ongoing communication pattern with the brothers. Sometimes sotto voce, it is teasing in nature, meant to be funny and occasionally sarcastic, but never hitting below the belt. Humor is an important communication and coping mechanism for these brothers. It is often self-deprecatory and is used to lighten the conversation. This "keeping the conversation light" is consistent with what the brothers hope to achieve in their relationship with one another. With the help of their wives, they also can strike a serious note, but they would prefer to keep it light. Because men generally tend to not engage in serious, face-to-face communication but, rather, in activities, this pattern is typical. Here, much of their interaction entails sports and music.

Beginning by reflecting on their mother's death, Bill tells us, "It was a real tough two years, and fortunately Charlie and I were around and close, and Mick kept driving in from Ohio. He was there the Monday before she died." "His timing was, as always, impeccable," Charlie noted with a grin.

"And the three of us have three incredible wives, and we're a good team," Mick added.

This was an opening to learn specifically how they had handled their mother's illness and death. "When you say 'you are a good team,' what do you mean?"

"Well, go ahead there, Mick, leader of the pack," Charlie invited.

We really admire and respect and delight in one another. We are each other's biggest fans, and we each bring a unique blend of things to the table. It is not like we all bring the same things, but there is enough of an overlap that we can really appreciate what the other guy brings whatever we are doing, and we have a lot of fun. We have always been able to get together for whatever reasons and whatever harebrained project one of us has dumped us into, and it has always just been a lot of fun.

Yeah, I think the key to our relationship, [Charlie continues,] is that we all have a great sense of humor and we feed each other. I was thinking about this this morning. In every relationship you get to a point where you can say something negative to a person or you can say something positive to a person. These two guys, without fail, always say something positive and because of that, I always say something positive and therefore ending up dissolving in giggles. We have a lot of fun.

"I am better at saying something stupid," Mick joked.
"That's true," Charlie agreed, to general laughter.

"Positive, negative, stupid," Mick added, to further laughter.

Bill, who had been smiling while watching all this, jumped in.

I am the dumb guy in this trio, and the fact of the matter is that when I say something stupid, I will get called on it but not aggressively. I will get straightened away by two guys that I have a lot of respect for, and I think that is key. And the fact that when we screw up, and we all screw up, especially me, and I can be cranky, these guys will put up with me. I don't know how they do it. And I can be a handful. That is a wonderful spot to be in when you have the family around. They have you covered. They are never going to dump on you. No matter how bad it is, and we all know it can be bad, when push comes to shove . . .

"That's true," Mick interjected before Bill continued.

"We can rely on our wives, and I can rely on these guys all the time."

And I think that is really important, [Charlie emphasizes.] To be able to rely on your wife, to be able to rely on your kids, and your parents. . . . But to be able to rely on your siblings, that is a rare commodity. It is wonderful. It is great. We always laugh about it. Did you play the lottery today? Nope, *I already won.*

This conversation captures the essence of what makes their relationship work. They believe they are lucky and fortunate to have their relationships. They always try to be positive. They have worked together on the potentially difficult issues of coping with their parents' deaths. They have supportive and loving wives. They have one another's back. And they have fun together.

Growing Up in a Household with Three Boys and a Sister

Because we are interviewers, we sometimes ask clumsy questions. Here, in trying to get a sense of whether they saw themselves as especially close for men, we asked what it was like growing up male and how different they thought it would have been if they were female. Mick gave a joke response but then used the opportunity to talk about their relationship with their father.

I remember when we were female . . . [We all laugh.] Seriously, being male was good in our house because we had a house that was really built around our dad. A very athletic guy, he wasn't like a "*Field and Stream* go-out-and-hunt guy," but he was a terrific athlete. He liked having sons who could play games. He liked anyone who could play games. In our house, it was a terrific advantage being guys because it was easier for him to load us into his fun.

In some homes, such fathers become the magnets for other boys in the friendship sphere. This was not the case in this home, according to the two older brothers. But Bill, the youngest, had a different impression about the role their father played in other males' lives. Bill and his sister were home during their high school years while Mick and Charlie were at boarding school.

I went to day school [and was home]. There was a guy in my class who lived next door to us whose father died [when he, his son, was twelve], and we were close. Yes, you can get the picture of our father from us, but you can get the minutia from Greg. Dad kind of opened up and brought him along. He didn't come along and play, but he was definitely influenced by my dad.

We found that when our parents died, all these wonderful people came flying out of the woodwork and said how much they enjoyed our parents. Lots of guys, Tim and Dean, told us that our dad was a father figure to them.

When Bill finished this description, Charlie burnished their father's identity and included his role as husband.

He was an outstanding model, a great model for a young man growing up. He was tough and he was tender and he could be a pain in the rear end, but he loved my mother ferociously. It was an unbelievable love. These were all good traits as a young guy growing up. He loved to have fun. The four of us would go out and play tennis or golf or bridge or horseshoes and just fall down laughing. We would go out to the golf course and easily be the foursome that was having the most fun.

"And we were the worst golfers," Mick added.

Bill picked up on Charlie's mention of their father's love for their mother. "When you talk to any siblings, you should explore the parental side, because I will guarantee you the relationship that develops between the mother and father and then gets dropped down to the kids is vital. This is where we come from."

We asked for a further reflection on their parents' relationship and how that affected the brothers. Bill answered first.

I never saw them fight. I would occasionally see them get into their car and leave. I can remember them rolling out of the driveway and stopping and you knew the shit had hit the fan. But that never happened in front of us, and we never saw them getting snappy with each other. Always respect.

Our father was a very physical guy. He was old school, [Charlie explains,] and if you got out of line, he would whack you. If you did good, he would give you a pat on the head. It was real easy because we knew where we stood. Mick and I, when we were in our teens, didn't even need to ask. We knew if we were going to step out of line, we didn't even need to ask. We would have to figure out how to keep the old man in the dark. We knew exactly where he stood and we knew exactly where Mom stood, and we also knew that the two of them would back each other up. Right or wrong, they would always back each other up.

Their Sister

In most families, it is the sister who keeps the family together. She might be coordinating the care of aging parents, keeping information flowing, and working to maintain the emotional contacts. We asked the brothers where their sister, Marianne, fit into the picture. We heard all of them groan. Mick spoke first.

My wife and I have this feeling that there is one person on a different page of the book in a family, for multiple or whatever reasons. I think it was very tough for my sister to be the one girl in that family. It was a very male-oriented family.

There is no getting around it, it just was, [Charlie agrees.] Dad was as sweet and nice to Marianne as he possibly could be, but there was a point past which it was very hard for him to get because it was, "Let's go play tennis," and the three of us would get in the car like three little puppy dogs and Marianne loathed tennis so . . .

The brothers took an empathic, nonjudgmental, approach to the struggles they had had trying to create a relationship with their sister and made it more a matter of "fit" between the atmosphere in the home and being female. This was consistent also with their "avoid the negativity rule."

"It was hard for her, and I think it was tough for you, too," Mick says to Bill. "In the beginning, it was the two of us [the two older brothers] and we were 'the boys' or 'the bigs' and then there were Marianne and Bill, and they were 'the littles.' That had to suck."

Age gaps that appear large—recall there is a five-year difference between Mick and Bill—tend to diminish in adulthood. Bill's response to what it must have been like when he was "little" was consistent with how the family moved forward and did not dwell on the past.

"Yeah, it is all good in the end, and by the time I got to be eighteen, it was a whole different animal."

"But I am awash in guilt over how we made it tough on this guy" [Mick pointed to Bill].

"Do you feel guilty about Marianne?" Bill asked Mick.

"No."

"I do," Charlie replied, entering the discussion.

"Don't feel guilty about me, man," Bill offered. "I am the winner. I made out like a bandit. I feel guilty about her."

We asked specifically what the issue was with their sister. Bill responded first.

"She met someone who we have a hard time getting along with. Their relationship is very strange, and that is really uncomfortable for me."

"For all of us," Charlie interjected before Bill continued.

Yes, and so we pull away from that. She lives in a distant state. And every time we talk to her, she says everything is great and her husband is wonderful. I can't jump in there and say you're doing it wrong. She is happy there so, OK. Her relationship for us is a little odd, just as our relationship for her is a little odd.

We wondered if the feelings of guilt were engendered by anything the brothers thought they had done.

Bill explained, "I can't do anything about it now, so the question is if we had been more inclusive and gotten her to play with us more and gotten her to play more tennis . . ." Mick and Charlie shook their heads no, indicating that there was nothing they could have done, and that stopped Bill. "I got nothing, man, I can't tell you."

Mick hopped in with a joke. "If Mom and Dad had given her a Johnny Red cannon for Christmas . . ."

"There you go," Bill added, to laughter. "We were wild Indians," Bill said, bringing the discussion back to what it must have been like for Marianne.

This reference to their level of activity in childhood caused Mick to enter the conversation and try to shift it from Marianne.

> And God love my mother. She would put up with anything. We did some of the most creative things, and she would put up with it. One time we collected used cups from under the stadium at a tennis match. We brought hundreds of these disgusting things home. They were encrusted with soda and cigarette burns, and we built a fort out of them in our bedroom, set up soldiers on them, and knocked them over with tennis balls. Mom accepted all of that and just told us to clean it up before Dad came home. That woman was a saint to put up with that craziness, and we felt free to do that kind of creative wackiness wherever we were.

Because their father had attempted but failed to engage Marianne in sports, we wondered whether their mother had a special bond with her, as sometimes happens in families in which the minority gender spends time together. A father-son or a mother-daughter might have their own cocoon if they are the only males or females in the home. But their mother had a parenting style that did not specifically allow for this. It was a common parenting style—a sincere attempt to treat everyone equally. But in that attempt, a child that is left out of a lot of child-focused activities does not get anything compensatory. Mick explained:

> Mom was really anal about everything being fair to everyone. I swear that woman kept track of every calorie of energy she spent on each child, so it would be equally spread out. She was really obsessed with this, and I think either she must have seen something when she was a child that made her sensitive to this, but she was just went way over with it. You know, none of us ever kept score or cared. There was never this, "he got more than me." So whatever she did for Marianne, and she did lots of stuff, she did that for everyone, too. But she may have done more for us in a lot of ways because we

were more aggressively involved in things. She was very quiet. We got into music big time, so Mom was the one that took us to all the gigs and bought the instruments for everyone.

This last comment about being "aggressively involved" is an interesting insight for therapists into what happens in a family with more than one child. It is not just the "squeaky wheel that gets the grease." It is the children who are the most actively engaged on their own who receive the most resources and time from their parents. A passive child is not as demanding. It turns out that Marianne did not engage either parent that much in the last few years. First Mick spoke about Marianne and their father, and then Bill segued into Marianne and their mother. Both were puzzled by her behavior.

"By the time he died, you couldn't tell where she was with that."

"I was surprised that she wasn't around. We tried to get her to come out to visit Mom because we all knew she was going to die."

Marianne came for their father's funeral and plans to come for a memorial service for their mother to be held in a month. She has not traveled the two thousand miles for a visit since their mother died. The sense from the brothers is that she made only a token visit to their parents in the last years of their lives.

Taking Care of Their Father and Mother and the Role of the Wives

Because Marianne was not engaged, the way that the brothers took charge of their parents' caregiving gave insight into their teamwork. We wanted to know whether they actively discussed their roles. Charlie provided his view as Bill further explained his motivation:

"I made a decision a long time ago to stay fairly close to Mom and Dad because I was the oldest, and we had talked a long time ago about my being the executor. Then, by the grace of God, Bill and his wife moved closer."

"Dad had a stroke, and I wanted to be near."

"That was huge [Bill's moving close]. Instead of us [Charlie and his wife] hauling down to see Mom and Dad every week, we are hauling down there every other week."

Mick, who was living four hundred miles away, used the opportunity to praise his brothers and their wives. "And these guys were amazing because they would go down and spend the whole weekend with them and do all kinds of things for them."

Charlie returned the compliment. "And then Mick and Bianca got into the groove where they were coming in once a month, which evened it even further, but really, by the end of the day, it was a group effort."

The brothers did not forget the roles that the wives played in the caregiving. Mick explained, "It was a group effort of the six of us [pointing to their wives]. If there is one thing the three of us do really well, is follow their lead." And they credited both their parents with their choosing such great wives, their father with encouraging them to marry someone like their mother and their mother for being such a supportive parent.

"Dad always said, 'If you are lucky, you will marry someone as smart and wonderful as your mother.' And he said that over and over again," Bill recounted.

Mick agreed. "He said that for decades. He pounded that into you."

"What were the great things about Mom? Smart, proactive, empathetic, incredibly aware. And we have all been really lucky," Bill explained, returning to the opening theme of the interview about how fortunate they have been.

While it seems as if the brothers have had many good years together, we ask if there was a time when they were not on the same page. Here the issue of the age gap came up for Bill, as did the fighting that went on when the two older brothers were home from boarding school.

"When these guys went to private school, I was left in the dust. And I was fairly clueless until I was thirty."

"That makes you a guy," Charlie reassured Bill.

"For me, the relationship did not blossom until I got to be somewhat of a more normal person," Bill countered, meaning that getting older helped them grow closer.

"When Mick and I were teenagers, we had some pretty good tiffs. We shared a room."

Mick agreed with Charlie. "We got into a fight in a tree once, and I knocked him out of the tree and jumped out of the tree to go after him. And then he locked me out of the room once, and I broke the door down."

This is not atypical of other brothers we have interviewed who could get into some significant scrapes yet still also pull together to enjoy each other's company. In fact, this is typical of males, especially boys, who tend to resolve conflict physically, whereas girls tend to engage in "relational aggression."

In the descriptions of both the Emanuel and the Kluger homes, fighting was a frequent component. Kluger noted that one researcher advised him that as long as fighting does not get too dangerous or abusive, it can teach siblings to push limits further than might be possible outside the family.[6] Other researchers have also found sibling conflict can help with social and emotional development.[7]

The discussion about teenage fighting led Charlie to speak about an emotional and physical cutoff that began between him and his father that was not resolved for more than twenty years. It appears to have been a classic oldest son–father struggle in which both have distinct and strong personalities. Because it was resolved, it also shows that relationships can be patched together after years of strain. But the conversation also revealed, later in the interview, the role that another child, in this case the second oldest, can play in the family in breaking the tension:

When I was a teen, I started to really buck Dad. Hard, on a visceral level. I was done. When I got out of the house, it was good-bye. And we fought like cats and dogs. And I moved out of the house and that kept up until I was like forty-five and I got divorced. He really liked Susan [his current, second wife] and not my silly first wife. And I think Bill and Mick had worn him down a little bit and that mellowed him a bit. And then I started my own business, and he would come up and help out with the books. So it got better. I think the really great thing was doing the sports together. He was like the quintessential straight man. When you have a straight man in the group, it is great. You could just goof on him like the end of the world. And all of us would just goof on him.

As Charlie described the struggle with their father, we asked how their parents treated them.

Charlie answered immediately with a twinkle in his eye. "Mick was their favorite."

After the laughter died down, Mick embellished.

I think that was a little simplistic. You had the toughest job because you went first. It is always difficult for the first. They had ridiculously high expectations for you that they never dumped on me. So then Bill comes along, and he was the cute, youngest baby. And the youngest always gets the special stuff.

Bill agrees. "I got the great ride. And after I got married, the four of us got really close. And then we'd get together as a family and it was always loud."

"One time we went back to a restaurant a year later after having been there, and they remembered us and immediately put us in our own back room [laughter]. And we had so much fun," Mick remembered. He then cited one of the reasons they became closer; the realization that Bill was now a competent adult, another sign of a vanishing five-year age gap.

I remember when you had started your job in Nashville and were twenty-five, and I went for a visit and got to see him in his natural habitat and that makes all the difference, when you see someone in his milieu. To see him around music, I got the impression that everyone in town knew him.

Being Humorous and Being Serious

The brothers banter both on and off stage. Teasing can also be a way for men to have contact with one another in a fun way. Here the teasing was never unfair or "too mean." They do feel that they have certain roles in both contexts that are played out. Charlie identified himself as a straight man at one point, even though he clearly, as was demonstrated throughout the interview, operated with a dry wit. Mick occupied a distinct role in the trio. He recalled how he was drawn into the conflict between Charlie and their father and how that role, honed after many years, is one that he still sometimes feels compelled to play.

I believe everyone has different roles that everyone gets stuck with. I got to be the entertainer, and I think my mother encouraged me to be very verbal and to entertain by whatever stupid things came out of my mouth. Bill would have had that role because he was so cute, but I already had that role, and that has been a factor my whole life. As a teacher, I am entertaining. I think I deflect tension with humor. I would use humor in the family when things were getting tense. When Charlie was about to go postal with dad, I would be compelled to do anything I could to get that to lighten up. Even now, if things are happening [motioning to his brothers and the three wives], I am biting my tongue to not say something because I feel that that is what I have to do.

Bill then added that it was easier to be lighter because he thinks both Mick and Charlie were funnier than they used to be.

"It is not that we are funnier, it is because your sense of humor matured," Charlie quipped.

One of the ways the brothers have fun is through music. Charlie believes that he and Bill are more into the music for its own sake and that Mick, the entertainer on and off stage and, consistent with the role he has just described for himself, is more interested in providing a show that people will enjoy. He sees Mick as the consummate front man and he and Bill as the backbeat. As Charlie said about their relationship with music as brothers and one reason that Marianne felt excluded, "It was huge from the jump."

The fun side is balanced by the wives they married. They are substantial women who are capable of going with the humorous side as well as the serious side. Charlie offered his view.

"We married smart women. We like smart. If you were at a party, would you want to be the smartest, the middle, or the dumbest in the room? I would want to be the dumbest. First, because anyone smarter than me is a genius."

"And we are good at being the dumbest," Mick added to general laughter.

"When you climb into bed with someone at the end of the day, I want smart and light, which goes a real long way. Smart is really important," Charlie confirmed.

"Like Mom," Bill chimed in.

"Like Mom. Yeah, like Dad said," Charlie agreed, harking back to the early discussion about the importance of marrying a woman like their mother. We have to agree that it does look like all three have done so.

ADVICE FOR OTHER SIBLINGS

Charlie was the first to respond when we asked for advice for other siblings about how to maintain their relationship.

Have a sense of humor. Lighten up. Life is short. If there is one thing I have learned in the last year is that life is short, it sneaks up on you. One day you are eighteen, and the next day you are thirty-five with a bunch of kids, and then you are fifty and the kids have left, and then you are sixty and whoa.

Bill has this great line. Our birthdays are a day apart, and each year he calls me and asks, "Did you find it yet?" and what he is referring to is the pause button in the sky that you hit and everything stops. Wouldn't that be great? But it never does. We were at the viewing for my mom the other day, and at the back of the room was a grandfather's clock ticking away, not real fast and not real loud, but it never stops. So what I would say to other siblings is, "Lighten up." Have some fun, enjoy them. If they give you a shot, rather than giving them a shot back, say OK, roll with it. If you do that a couple of times, maybe they won't give you a shot next time when they have a chance. And there will be a chance. These guys get chances all the time, and they never give me a shot. Lighten up. You wake up one day, and they have moved away. You wake up another day, and your children have moved to the other coast. We went out to Ohio a few years ago, and we all spent time together. A guy who stopped by and hung out with us said, "I want to be part of your family." This is a win. It is very unusual. It is a gift. It is a huge win.

As the interview wound down, a few other points were made about the brothers' relationship. First, their wives get along extremely well. That fact makes their relationship go more smoothly. Siblings are not pitted against one another by their loyalty to their spouse. As one of them pointed out, we are not just relatives, we are friends. Bianca chimed in, "I would rather be with this group of six than almost anyone else." Second, their friendship works in part because they work at it. Mick offered this advice: "You have to be deliberate about it [getting along]. You have to set up situations where people can get together and have success together. If that is not going to happen, it won't happen." Third, while they were never especially comfortable having what one wife characterized as deep conversations, that changed with age and when they married women who were comfortable with that level of interaction.

CONCLUSION

Always moving forward is the hallmark of these three brothers' relationship. They consciously make choices about how to respond to one another. They believe they have won the lottery when it comes to their relationships and that they admire, accept, and genuinely enjoy being together. They were eager for us to interview them, to play music with them, to tell us about their parents, and to see their own relationship in action. And they handled it all with humor. They are three highly verbal, expressive men who unflinchingly love and praise their wives. Their wives' relationships are key to their sibling relationships. With more time, it would have been interesting to pursue their wives' relationship with their own siblings to see how their husbands' relationship paralleled their own.

Each of the brothers brings something different to the table, but they also overlap in important areas and share core values. The way they seamlessly handled their parents' deaths is one example of their teamwork.

Their parents clearly laid the foundation for who they are. That upbringing may not have worked as well for their sister, according to them, but they are open to the view that their style of operating might be as foreign to her as her style is to them. She had to grow up in a home full of music, sports, and physicality. Sometimes mother and daughter would bond under those conditions, but in this family the mother was dedicated to balancing her time and affection so no one would receive more than anyone else. It is hard to know if, by nature, the sister was comfortable in that home. The more people in any family, the more likely it is that someone will not fit in as well with the others.

These brothers clearly share interests such as sports and music. More important, they trust one another, love one another, count on one another, and give one another the benefit of the doubt in all situations. How do they keep this going after so many decades and the unavoidable struggles of family and life? We suggest their motto could be, as Charlie advised, "Keep it light" and recognize and appreciate when you have a winning relationship with your siblings.

PART 4

Therapy Approaches

CHAPTER 10

Working with Siblings When Aging Parents Need Care

▸ *BARBARA KANE AND LINDA HILL*

OVER THE LAST THREE DECADES, we have helped thousands of adult sisters and brothers contend with one another as they care for their aging parents. We do this through Aging Network Services, our geriatric clinical social work practice in Bethesda, Maryland. We often work with adult siblings when they are reengaging with one another in very intense circumstances, often after decades of being focused more on their own families than on their family of origin. The stakes are usually high, as can be the associated emotions and opinions about how to best help their parents. As they sit in our office, sometimes with one or two siblings on a conference call, they may silently wonder whether they are even going to continue a sibling relationship once this last parent dies. The process is never easy, but once we have a plan of care in place, siblings frequently look at one another with a rush of gratitude and maybe even a new respect.

Coordinating care for aging and ill parents is difficult for many adult siblings and frequently reawakens old wounds and conflicts. The presenting problem is not the sibling relationship; it is the effective care of the aging parents. Still, working to resolve issues related to taking care of their parents may offer siblings a fresh opportunity to resolve past conflicts.

Despite the charged and complex nature of such situations, we have found that therapeutic progress can be made within a sibling group in even one or two consultations. Rather than focus directly on old wounds,

The authors are director and associate director of Aging Network Services, Bethesda, Maryland.

rivalries, or favoritisms, we zero in on the needs of their parents. It is our job to help them operate objectively so that their sometimes decades-long conflicts do not get in the way of meeting those immediate and consequential needs. Quite often, siblings repair their relationships in unpredictable ways. Indeed, this may be the first opportunity for them to work constructively as a team as adults.

Some adult siblings get together only for weddings, funerals, births, or holidays, and a few do not get together even for those infrequent occasions. In fact, a parent is often the center around which the adult children orbit, sometimes out of obligation. When the parent is ailing, the orbit becomes unstable, so it is up to the adult children to recalibrate, if possible, their family constellation. That recalibration may be unanticipated but urgently needed in the midst of a crisis with a parent.

The demands of siblings' earlier get-togethers do not compare with their negotiations in the face of sudden health emergencies or rapid declines in their parents' functioning. In the past, the siblings may not have cooperated on anything more than a Thanksgiving menu. But on issues like these, they sometimes cannot even agree on what the problem is or even whether a problem exists. We see many daughters and sons who overreact or underreact to events involving a parent. As a result, our work usually begins with trying to get the sibling group on the same page.

Our initial aims for siblings who come for consultation are twofold:

1. To help siblings gain awareness of themselves and one another and the circumstances with regard to the parent in need.
2. To develop a plan in the best interest of the parent(s).

We also see siblings individually for longer-term psychotherapy. Part of the therapeutic work may be understanding their role in the family and coping with their siblings in the here and now with regard to care for the ailing parent. This deeper work, which can be quite rich, usually includes revisiting their life in their family of origin.

To illustrate this work, we introduce three different sibling sets from our practice. The first set is Ralph and Mary, who differ on the next steps for their mother's care. The second is Judy and her disabled brother Bob, with whom Judy is infuriated because they share caregiving responsibility for their mother. The last set is Rita and Sally, who survived in a metaphorical lifeboat together until Sally decided to reunite with their physically abusive mother, thus rocking that lifeboat. We are using the plural for our voice, although sometimes only one of us (i.e., the therapist) was in the room. Names and other identifying information have been changed to protect identities.

WHEN SIBLINGS DIFFER ON MOTHER'S CARE

"Sis, you can't continue to visit Mom three times a day to give her pills and meals. And she has fallen so many times lately. We need to come up with a better plan. I think we should move Mom to assisted living."

"Ralph, stop telling me what to do. You may be older but not wiser. Mom and I are doing OK."

"But you look so worn . . . I'm more worried about you than Mom."

"OK, I admit I'm tired these days. But it's not just Mom, it's my kids . . . just the stress of my life. Just come down here more often and give me more breaks. That's all that needs to change."

This conversation between Ralph and Mary is typical of siblings we treat. Siblings often have to engage in such negotiations regarding the care of one or both of their aging parents. Mary, fifty-nine years old, unemployed and divorced with two adult sons, lives five minutes away from her eighty-five-year-old mother, Dorothy. Ralph, sixty-three years old, is a successful CEO and married father of two daughters. He lives two hundred miles away from Mary and Dorothy. We became involved with the family after an initial call from Ralph. He said he lived out of town and was concerned about his sister and mother. Their mother had fallen four times in the last month and was getting more forgetful. Mary was visiting three times a day to assist with meal preparation and a medication regimen. Ralph was coming to visit and wanted him and his sister to meet with someone who could help plan the next steps.

The Initial Session with Ralph and Mary

Ralph is well dressed and businesslike and walks in as if eager to get started. Mary is thin and worn looking, dressed casually in jeans and tennis shoes. They sit on opposite ends of the couch, with a bit of tension in between.

We wanted to start by talking with Mary so we don't lose her. We suspect that she was talked into coming by her brother, as she does not see a need for a big change in her mother's care. Accordingly, we needed to form an alliance with her early on in the session so she will feel heard and not drowned out by Ralph (who has more of an agenda for this meeting). We are guessing that this is not the first time that Ralph has been worried about his younger sister. In fact, just being with her for a few minutes made us concerned as well. Ralph's efforts at demonstrating empathy for Mary are irritating her. We are also guessing that she needs him to look out for her at times but that right now he may seem overprotective.

THERAPIST (*to Mary*): How do you see your mother?

MARY: Mom marches to her own drummer. She has been a widow for so long that she doesn't have a regular schedule for eating or sleeping. She kind of grazes all day, eating her favorite sweets and TV dinners. As for sleep, she takes a couple of naps during the day, does seem to be sleeping more and more. Then she is up all night. That has been for the last three months, but it is just an extension of her poor life habits.

I think all we have to do is move Mom's bedroom furniture around so she doesn't stumble into her nightstand at night, and then she won't fall. I'm there every morning to set up her pills, and then I stop by midday and then around eight to check on her. She's usually napping these days. Her mind isn't as sharp anymore, but she sure knows me. All of this slowing down and napping more is part of old age. I'll just make sure I go every day and not skip any days. Mom would hate having a helper in her house and certainly would not hear of moving out of her home. I know Ralph thinks we should get more help, but he is not here to see her up close like I do.

THERAPIST (*to Ralph*): How do you see your mother?

RALPH: I have seen a real decline in Mom over the last few months. She is repeating herself more and gets very anxious when I tell her I am going to visit. She calls me about eight times a day, asking me over and over again, what day and time I am coming. I think her mind is going to mush because she is alone all day, so one day melts into the next day.

Mary, you mean well, but you have seemed more tired and irritable lately. I think you are taking on too much. I know how close you are to Mom and want everything to be the same. But Mom is changing. She is eighty-five and slowing down. I agree she would hate having a helper, so I think we should look at an assisted living [facility] near you. I can only come down four times a year. These falls she has are a real symptom that things are not right.

From first glance, it seems that Ralph has emotionally separated more from his mother than Mary has, and from that less emotionally charged place, he is showing more perspective by his recognition that something has to change. This emotional separation might be expected, given the geographic distance between them and the typical pattern we have seen of daughters being more likely than sons to remain emotionally close and be involved in the physical care of mothers. Mary seems more enmeshed with their mother. Even though it seems like an unsustainable sacrifice to care for her three times a day, Mary feels that she can continue on this path. But we doubt that Mary can weather long-term caregiving at this pace without risking her own physical and mental health and the efficacy of the care she provides. If Dorothy has dementia, for which we see a number of signs, she will progress to the point that Mary will have to supervise her mother all day, which is not a sustainable plan. Mary wants to take care of Dorothy, and Ralph wants to take care of Mary, but his approach is not working with her, which may be a pattern in this sibling relationship that goes back decades. The stress of their mother's being ill has exacerbated these problematic patterns. We suspect their mother's problems are due to a more serious underlying health issue than either of them realizes.

CLARIFYING A DEMENTIA ASSESSMENT

We decided to ask both Ralph and Mary some assessment questions to see whether a dementia work-up by a medical doctor is in order. Neither of them is thinking along these lines. Mary thinks that her mom is merely getting old; Ralph thinks their mother's mind is declining because of her isolation.

The following are some of the questions we asked:

1. When was the last time you were *not* worried about your mother? Tell us about her lifestyle, her social support system, her typical day, and her typical mood.
2. When did you notice a change in your mother's mental capacity/cognitive changes? Can you recall an event that worried you?

3. When did she stop driving, and why? How did you and she handle it?

4. Tell us about her medications and any recent changes. Does she go to the doctor regularly? What is her relationship with her doctors? Is she compliant?

5. What do her doctors say to you about her memory? Are they encouraging further testing?

6. Is your mother aware of her memory losses? What is her reaction? What is her reaction to her falls?

7. What are her health problems and treatment for them? Does she allow you to go to her doctors with her?

8. You say she does not eat regularly and forgets to take her medication. How long has this been happening for each of these? You also say she is sleeping more. Tell us more about all this.

9. Ralph, you say she calls you eight times a day asking when you are coming to visit. Mary, do you also regularly see this kind of anxious behavior?

Quite often, because such change are so gradual, siblings like Ralph and Mary have difficulty distinguishing old patterns of behaviors from problematic recent behavior that is symptomatic of a more serious health issue. They can easily describe Dorothy as having poor eating and sleeping habits since widowhood. But her recent falls, forgetting, and anxiety seem to them like a continuation of old behaviors rather than new symptoms. Through our questioning, we learn that there have been significant changes over the past six months. Ralph and Mary gain insight as they answer these questions out loud. Because all these changes may be indicative of cognitive changes in their mother's brain, we recommended an assessment by a neurologist.

A diagnosis of their mother's cognitive condition by a neurologist would offer further objectivity that they need to cooperate in short- and long-range planning. A diagnosis also would give them an opportunity to agree on what their mother needs. If the diagnosis is a vitamin B_{12} deficiency, her cognitive problems can be reversed. If the diagnosis is possible Alzheimer's disease, her cognitive problems will worsen over time, and a different care plan needs to be initiated immediately. If the diagnosis is mild cognitive impairment, she will have a greater chance of progressing into a type of dementia. In addition, a diagnosis may help Dorothy (as well as Mary and Ralph) accept more care from a non–family member. Although this is not always the case, some individuals in the early stage of memory loss are able to face the reality of this diagnosis and the need for care.

SIBLINGS' REACTIONS TO DIAGNOSIS OF ALZHEIMER'S DISEASE

Ralph and Mary returned to our office for a second consultation after their mother had received a diagnosis of possible Alzheimer's disease. They were told that her anxiety is common with this diagnosis and should be followed by a geriatric psychiatrist. Furthermore, she will need twenty-four-hour supervision in either her home or a facility. The neurologist emphasized that she should not be left alone, due to her falling at night and her anxiety.

Such a diagnosis requires siblings to work together to move forward carefully. The old patterns between siblings may continue to drive the conversation until they work through their initial reaction to the diagnosis. The therapist should anticipate such behaviors and help the siblings work through their expectations about what the next few months or years might look like.

RALPH: I knew Mother's mind was going. After all, she stared at the TV all day.

MARY: Oh, it's so sad. I can't believe that she has Alzheimer's. She still knows who I am and calls her dog by his name. I always thought doctors can't tell it's that disease until autopsy.

THERAPIST: Actually, both of you are a little off the mark. Ralph, you think that idleness leads to the disease. And Mary, you have talked about her forgetfulness being a normal part of aging. Your mother had a PET scan where the neurologist saw plaque and tangles in her brain, the hallmark sign of Alzheimer's disease.

This information touched off some unresolved issues between the siblings. Apparently Ralph, the more distant sibling, believed that Mary was not competently fulfilling her role as a caregiver. This may be consistent with his lifelong view of her.

MARY: See, Ralph (*she replied with fire in her eyes*), you are wrong about Mom and the TV and her mind. You have been blaming me for not keeping Mom more active. That just isn't fair.

This is where we believe our role is to intervene and clarify communication.

THERAPIST: Mary, do you feel Ralph is blaming you for your mother getting this disease?

MARY: Yes, sort of.

THERAPIST: Ralph, are you blaming Mary?

RALPH: I'm not blaming Mary. I guess I'm just frustrated with how long it has taken Mother to get help with all of this.

We try to reframe their situation as normal reactions to a difficult situation. We tell them that, in our experience, it takes most families a while to recognize a problem and take action. But now that there is a diagnosis, we ask whether they feel ready to move on, and Ralph and Mary both agree they are ready.

Division of Roles

We often find that discussing roles and responsibilities is an opportunity to coach siblings on how they can work together more effectively. We may interrupt them to show healthier ways of communicating, both listening and talking. With these siblings, we point out that each has different temperaments. Ralph tries to use rational argument, while Mary tends to show emotion. We work to help them acknowledge and respect these complementary differences and the strengths of both.

After a diagnosis, we suggest that they regard care-planning discussions as business meetings and recommend that they have monthly meetings by phone to check in. They like this idea. It is the first time we have seen them calm down and feel less tense with each other. We give them a checklist to use at their monthly business meetings. The list is specifically geared toward getting siblings to work together to deal with the inevitable changes they and their mother will experience. Note that all these questions are oriented to the present. We often do not have time, nor are we asked, to delve into their past relationship. We may surmise certain things about the past based on the present, but usually siblings want to move forward and are not seeking a corrective experience for past perceived injustices.

SIBLINGS' BUSINESS MEETING WORKSHEET

1. Do you feel that I have been doing enough?
2. Do you feel that I have been doing too much?
3. Is there anything that I have said or emailed over the last month that bothered you?
4. Do you feel that I have asked you for approval for big care decisions during last month?
5. Do we need to revise our division of labor?
6. Do you feel I have been respectful of you in tone and action?
7. Have we communicated enough over the last month?
8. Are any old wounds festering?
9. Overall, how do you feel we are doing as a team?

Points of Interventions

We saw three turning points during our two sessions with Ralph and Mary: (1) moving them to get an assessment and diagnosis of their mother, (2) clearing the air about the causes or possible blame for their mother getting this disease, and (3) suggesting monthly business meetings with a list of questions. We felt positive about these sessions and Ralph and Mary's ability to move forward with coordinating the care of their mother. They now have tools to use with each other for their mother's care. However, as Dorothy declines and if the siblings' tension reemerges, we made it clear to both of them that we would be available to help them.

WHEN ONE SIBLING HAS A DISABILITY

Judy is furious with her brother Bob, who is doing a "less than adequate job" taking care of their father, who suffers from dementia. She has asked for several therapy sessions to help her not be so angry with him all the time. Judy works full time for the city government as a planner. She is forty-two, has a husband and two school-aged children, one of whom has a learning disability. Her brother Bob, aged forty-eight, does not work but is paid by their mother to live in her home and take care of both parents. Bob has been diagnosed with ADHD and a tendency to hoard. He has never held a job for more than six months.

The following exchange occurred during Judy's third therapy session with us. An incident with Bob and their mother was foremost on her mind:

JUDY: I can't believe what happened yesterday. It's all about Dad's infected toe. Dad complained all morning about his big toe, as it was red and inflamed. Bob looked at it and told Dad that he needed to take him to the doctor right away. Dad refused to go and said that although it hurt, it would get better on its own. So Bob dropped the ball and didn't take him.

THERAPIST: You mean, Bob did not try harder to convince your father to go to the doctor?

JUDY: Yes. Now his toe is twice its normal size, and I had to take him to the emergency room last night. In fact, it is broken.

THERAPIST: So you ended up doing what you wanted your brother to take care of. Does that happen a lot?

JUDY: All the time, and that's why I end up furious with him. I have to clean up his messes.

THERAPIST: What do you mean?

JUDY: Back in elementary school, he was supposed to bring home his homework assignments, but he always left them in his locker. Mom and Dad would ask me to go back and get them, as they knew I would find them. As I think about it, our parents would praise me when I got all As. All Bob would have to do to get praise would be to get a good attendance record. They always expected more from me. It felt like they favored him and would lower the standards for him.

THERAPIST: [It] did not feel fair, did it? What was his diagnosis? Sounds like he has a learning or mental health problem.

JUDY: He has ADHD and he hoards. You should see his room and the kitchen.

THERAPIST: How were his grades?

JUDY: He would get Cs and Ds.

We wanted to explore with Judy whether there was a parallel process with her own children's uneven abilities, as one of them also has a learning disability.

THERAPIST: Didn't you say that your daughter has a learning disability? How do her grades compare with her brother's?

JUDY: My daughter gets As and Bs, but she works real hard for them. My son gets As and Bs but doesn't have to work hard at all.

THERAPIST: Do you praise them both equally for the As?

JUDY (*she laughs*): Of course not. I give my daughter extra praise.

THERAPIST: How does your son feel about that?

JUDY: I never asked him. I just assume he knows why I praise her so much.

THERAPIST: You may see where we are going with this. Do you see a similarity of how you treat your children's different capacities and how your parents treated you and Bob? In families in which one sibling struggles, it is quite common for the other to feel resentful. And when siblings are young, they do not have the capacity to analyze the situation. They just feel that their parents are unfair.

However, now that you are an adult, is it possible to reframe the differences between you and Bob? It sounds like he does not have the capacity to function nearly as well as you can. Are there advantages in being more competent?

JUDY: When you put it that way, I guess I have always felt good about getting all As and in getting into a great college and having so many close friends. Life has been good to me, in that way.

THERAPIST: Do you mean, you have achieved a standing for yourself that Bob can never achieve?

JUDY: Yes, I guess you can put it like that. But how do I get over his messy habits and ineffectual care of Dad?

THERAPIST: I wonder whether you need to lower your expectations of Bob and feel that he is coping the best he can. You may have to do more for your father. That is the reality.

JUDY: OK, I'm going over to Dad's right now. I'll try to think about Bob doing the best he can and lucky that I'm not in his position. But I don't know if it takes care of all my resentment. We need to talk about this more.

Reaching Resolution

During the next session, Judy realized that she had to make peace with the fact that her brother would not be as assertive with their father, would not follow up adequately with her father's physicians, and would continue to have a messy house. Her anger with her brother began to dissipate. In therapy, the "lightbulb" moment for Judy came when she reflected on her love for both her children, despite her uneven treatment of them. She quickly connected to her parents doing the same thing with her and her brother. She could then make an emotional shift to accepting that her brother could not help being a less than perfect caregiver. During her last session, she reported that she and her brother went out for a meal, and for the first time in a long time, her feelings toward him were improving. The core of our work here was looking for a vehicle for Judy to gain perspective and insight and, ultimately, empathy for her brother's limitations. These steps allowed her to appreciate Bob's efforts.

WHEN SIBLINGS ARE TOO CLOSE

Rita, fifty-five years old, came to our practice because she was upset about changes in her relationship with her younger sister, Sally. They had been very close until recently, drawn together as allies during childhood in response to their mother's emotional and physical abuse. Keeping that abuse secret further united them.

RITA: My sister and I used to say we are in a lifeboat together. We are like peas in a pod. We would try to protect each other from Mom's rages and would comfort each other after the beatings. We couldn't wait to grow up and get as far away from Mom, which we both did as soon as we turned eighteen.

Keeping in mind that Rita had made it clear during intake she wanted to focus on the here and now and on the sibling relationship, we responded in the following way:

THERAPIST: What has your relationship with your sister been as adults?
RITA: It was great up until two months ago. Then my aunt called us both to say my mother's health was very bad. I don't wish my mother ill, but I have no interest in establishing contact with her. But my sister told me she was interested in contacting my mother.
THERAPIST: How did you feel about that?
RITA: I was surprised, taken aback. I strongly suggested Sally think about it more. After all, Mother is very toxic, and of the two of us, Sally has always been the weaker.
THERAPIST: Tell us more about Sally being weaker.
RITA: Well, Mother always got angrier with Sally than me. Sally took the worst of the physical abuse. Sometimes after those incidents, Sally would withdraw and I couldn't get her to talk or eat. Then, when she was sixteen, Sally tried to kill herself.
THERAPIST: Tell us about that.

RITA: She took a lot of pills. I found her on the bathroom floor. I didn't know what to do. Mom would go crazy if she found out. I was just paralyzed and crying, and suddenly Sally started to vomit. Fortunately she was OK.

THERAPIST: Did you or Sally ever tell anyone?

RITA: No, we had to keep it a secret, so we wouldn't get into trouble.

THERAPIST: So you and Sally kept two big secrets. The abuse and the suicide attempt. You two were like buddies in a foxhole during a horrific war.

RITA: Exactly.

THERAPIST (*getting back to the here and now*): So now Sally is contemplating reconnecting to Mother.

RITA: Yes. I can't believe it after all we have been through together.

THERAPIST: It sounds as if Sally establishing contact with your mother feels like a betrayal. Is that right?

RITA: Yes, I feel like Sally is deserting me. She is going over to the enemy.

THERAPIST: So Sally might be a traitor. Have you two ever had other times when you have disagreed about a course of action?

RITA: Not really. I didn't like a lot of guys she dated, but then she started going out with a good friend of mine and that has worked out.

THERAPIST: It is unusual for siblings to almost always agree. Why do you suppose you and Sally rarely disagree?

RITA: Like I said, we are two peas in a pod.

THERAPIST: Yes, that seemed like a great way for you two to cope under the duress of your childhood. Now that you two are older and in safer environments, do you still think you need your lifeboat mentality?

RITA: I guess not, but the decision to see Mother is huge.

THERAPIST: So without any practice of disagreeing, all of a sudden there is a huge difference of opinion. How does that make you feel?

RITA: Besides feeling betrayed, I feel very anxious about Sally's well-being if she sees Mother. I am afraid she will become depressed again.

THERAPIST: You sound like you are trying to protect Sally now as you did when you were younger. Is Sally still so fragile?

RITA: Actually, Sally has had a lot of therapy. She has a good job, some great friends, and the boyfriend I mentioned. She seems stable and happy.

THERAPIST: But even so, you think she needs your protection?

RITA: Only when it comes to seeing Mother. Do you think I'm overreacting?

THERAPIST: It's hard to say, especially since we've never met Sally.

RITA: How about if Sally and I come in together next session?

We discussed this and agreed to have Sally join us. During the second session, Rita expressed her concern to Sally about being able to maintain her hard-earned sense of well-being if she contacted their mother. Sally reassured Rita about her ability to remain stable while interacting with their mother. She also gently told Rita that she did not need her to be her protector any longer. Rita started to cry but said her tears were more about sorrow over their childhood and relief that both she and Sally were doing so well now. This seemed, at the time and retrospectively, like an important process. Sally has, it seems, grown beyond where Rita thought she was in regard to their mother, something Rita needed to see. Rita also needed to let go of taking care of Sally in order to experience new growth herself.

Sally did resume regular contact with their mother and took on some caregiving duties. Rita ultimately decided she did not want to see her mother at all. She did, however, support Sally as a caregiver by making dinner for Sally on the days that she took their mother for treatments. Making dinner helped Rita feel that she had a role in family events, and it partially helped ease her guilt regarding her decision not to see their mother. Rita accepted Sally's bridging the cutoff with their mother but stayed in her role as caretaker and protector of Sally. Sally could interact with their mother and then go back to the long and safe relationship with Rita. It would be easy to conclude that Rita needed to bridge the cutoff as well, but the new equilibrium allowed Rita to take care of Sally, Sally to take care of their mother, and both sisters to avoid being triangulated with their mother. As their mother grows weaker and Sally stronger, a new equilibrium among all three may emerge.

·   ·   ·

Besides knowledge of the theoretical perspectives informing the multigenerational and adult sibling dynamics, this work requires a solid understanding of the physical and emotional changes that accompany aging, plus a Rolodex of the services available in the community to assist with caregiving. We have found that some siblings simply want a brief problem-solving consultation focusing on the here and now; others seek more long-term and insight-oriented therapy that will allow them to explore how the past affects the present. Regardless of the services sought or the approaches taken, service providers should be aware of their own countertransference. Working with siblings and with chronically or critically ill parents can be like traversing a minefield—there are bombs, but it is not always evident where or when they might explode. Having trusted colleagues to consult on troublesome cases can help therapists avoid potential explosions and free them to be fully present to listen, support, and guide adult siblings during a very stressful and universal life stage.

CHAPTER 11

Dealing with Adult Siblings in an Emergency Health Crisis

▸ *ANNE P. HAHN*

AN EIGHTY-YEAR-OLD MAN SUSTAINED A flame burn over 50 percent of his body when he accidentally set himself on fire while fueling his lawn mower. The patient had multiple comorbidities and suffered from early dementia. Consequently, given his age and poor health, he was not likely to survive his injury. His wife told the social worker that she wished to bring him home to die, and at first their three adult children agreed. The family and the social worker then met with the rest of the medical team. During the discussion, two adult children argued against home hospice and comfort care in favor of aggressive intervention. The patient's wife and the third sibling remained silent, despite the earlier consensus on comfort care at home.

A seventy-eight-year-old man with a history of dementia and multiple medical problems was hospitalized for an infection, during which time his condition continued to deteriorate. A widower with three adult children, he lived with one of his daughters. He did not have an advance directive or an appointed surrogate decision maker. The medical team informed his children that his prognosis was poor. The daughter who lived with her father wanted aggressive care and blamed the hospital for his decline, but the other two children became less involved in their father's treatment.

Dr. Hahn is a clinical social worker at the Johns Hopkins Bayview Burn Center, Baltimore, Maryland.

THE CRISIS AND ITS BACKGROUND

Decisions and emotions at times of crisis in regard to aging parents and end-of-life issues are difficult under all circumstances. Ideally, those parents have advance directives conveying their preferences to their adult children, but even with a directive, the family may disagree on their parents' care. The conflict may arise from the developmental demands of middle-aged adults,[1] strained relationships with the ill parent and siblings,[2] reactivation of childhood conflicts and rivalries,[3] or the stress of an unexpected illness or injury coupled with intensive care.[4] Adult siblings' conflict can be compounded by an emergency and then the limited time to work through family-related issues. Clinicians may recognize that adult siblings are "stuck" and cannot manage the demands of making end-of-life decisions for a parent.[5] Unfortunately, though, there may not be enough time to process the family members' grief in order for them to relate to one another realistically in the present. Another complicating factor is the health system in which the adult siblings are often unprepared participants. Each member of the health team also brings his or her own perspective, customs, and values regarding end-of-life issues, which can further influence and complicate family conflict.

Medical, social and legal issues present challenges for adult siblings sets facing end-of-life decisions, particularly in a sudden crisis. Sometimes these adult siblings are helping another living parent make decisions, and sometimes they are making decisions about a sole surviving parent. People are living longer with chronic illnesses that are managed well with modern medicine. But when frail, elderly persons experience a sudden health crisis, their ability to tolerate vigorous medical treatment can be significantly compromised. As a result, they may be maintained in intensive care units for extended periods.[6] Families, and particularly adult siblings, may be either geographically or emotionally distant from one another, or both. One or more siblings thus may be participating in the end-of-life decisions only irregularly, during visits, by telephone, or through second-hand information. This complicates the therapeutic process that would be ideal for clinicians: working through emotions and arriving at resolutions and shared decision making. Legally, if there is no advance directive, the patient lacks capacity, and a competent spouse is not available who is able and willing to make decisions, all their children will have an equal say in decision making. The therapist's desired goal is to help the siblings gather the relevant information, listen to and support one another, and ultimately work together to arrive at a plan for end-of-life care.

THEORETICAL PERSPECTIVES AND CLINICAL TASKS

Given the long history and complexity of adult sibling relationships, how can health care social workers (and other involved clinicians) respond effectively to these challenges, particularly in emergency situations with a limited time frame? There is no one correct answer. A variety of perspectives on crisis and end-of-life care should be considered. The issue is not which perspective is correct but having a range of frameworks on hand. For example, synthesizing, developmental theories, biomedical viewpoints, mediation concepts, and end-of-life literature will provide ideas and tasks to guide clinicians.

Developmental Theories

To Erik Erikson, the concept of trust, the sense of feeling at ease and comfortable with another person, is the basic relationship task that must be mastered and internalized.[7] It is the cornerstone of all relationships. If a developmental stage is mastered in infancy/childhood, less conflict and ambivalence can be expected when entering new relationships. In any case, the clinician is faced with not only developing trust with a family in crisis but simultaneously assessing the trust among the adult siblings. Time constraints set by the crisis and the need to make decisions quickly can make this assessment difficult. If possible, the clinician may try to slow down the decision-making process to give the adult siblings a sense of comfort and calm from both one another and the health care providers. Families may need to hear that decisions can wait until everyone has time to absorb information and deal with his or her feelings. At the same time, the clinician may reassure the family that the health care team's first priority is good patient care, which includes not only the best technological approach but comfort and pain control as well. Adult siblings working together to make consequential decisions need to be reassured that concerns will be listened to and addressed in the same manner that infants learn to trust that their caretaker will meet their needs. In order to "set the stage" for trust, the clinician should meet with the family/siblings before a medical meeting. Trust in the health care providers accordingly becomes the "touchstone"[8] for all future interactions.

The developmental task of separation-individuation also comes into play when managing sibling relationships as a parent's death approaches. The task of losing one's parent, the real and symbolic caretaker, is first learned as a toddler, reactivated at other stages such as adolescence and young adulthood, and revisited at the anticipated final separation from the parent. An adult's image is closely tied to his or her relationship with parents and siblings, and the image of a competent, mature adult is tied to a person's image of himself or herself growing up in a family. Clinicians thus need to be aware that siblings may be grieving not only a dying parent but also their identification with that parent. The task for the social worker is helping them locate an image of themselves separate from the parent. This, however, requires the family's cooperation and flexibility, which may not be possible in a crisis. But if siblings can make these transitions, they may be able to relate to one another more realistically.

Even if the siblings do not have enough time now to grieve and renegotiate, the clinician could suggest that at some point they may want to have further counseling. The task for the clinician now is to establish trust with the family members/siblings, ensure good care of them, provide accurate information,[9] and explain the profound nature of grief and of anticipatory grief. It is confronting not only the loss of a parent but also the loss of an important part of one's identity and the need to establish a different image of oneself, siblings, and family without the parent.

Biomedical Literature

The biomedical literature[10] describes the tasks that the health care team, particularly the physicians, must negotiate. Physicians find it difficult to provide a prognosis, and they do so in only one-third of such visits.[11] Discussing a prognosis with patients and loved ones is problematic for several reasons: physicians are concerned about its accuracy, and different values influence physicians' and families' understanding of illness and recovery. Differences in interpretation also can lead to ambiguity and misunderstandings among and between siblings and the health care team.

The social worker's task is to help the physician and health care team address the need to discuss the prognosis with the family. To do this, the social worker, physician, and health care team could hold a "pre-family" meeting in which they decide on the goals of the meeting, discuss the social worker's assessment of the family members and their readiness to hear information, and address the patient's prognosis. The prognosis should include the likelihood of survival as well as a realistic picture of what the patient's life will be like if he recovers. The clinician also should support the physicians' skills in providing the prognosis. A prognosis is narrowly defined as an estimate of survival estimates. More broadly, though, it includes both the patient's chances of both a recovery and a functional recovery. That is, the patient may recover from the acute event only to be consigned to live in an extended care facility until death. The quality of life is generally more important to patients and families than the quantity of life. Although no physician can predict with certainty any one outcome, reasonable ideas of the life the patient will have after the acute event can be deduced from multiple factors, including age, comorbidities, functional status both before and after the acute event, laboratory results, and social factors such as family support and finances. The key question to be addressed in a prognosis is what a meaningful recovery is medically, emotionally and socially. These "pre-family" meetings can be difficult to both participate in and facilitate because they join two distinct systems, those of the family and the health care team, each with their own values, beliefs, and comfort levels. The social worker should regard these meetings as a process in consensus building, dissemination of information, and a coping mechanism for families and the health care team.

Mediation

The field of biomedical ethics offers a perspective on conflict resolution in which mediation is conceptualized as assisted negotiation.[12] The dialogue is the healer. Conflicted parties, such as adult siblings, arrive at a resolution by considering different viewpoints and accepting that sometimes opposite views cannot be easily reconciled. As Bergman pointed out, the origin of most family disputes are not ethical or philosophical principles but the result of poor communication, lack of information, cultural differences, or personality traits.

As the manager of the conflict resolution process, the clinician needs trustworthiness, empathy, insight, and creativity, characteristics that are ideally suited to social workers' or other health-based clinicians' training. Social workers should keep in mind that a true mediator is neutral. Social workers in hospitals are employees of the hospital and are responsible for carrying out the duties of their job, but these duties should not conflict with good patient care and ethical practice. The clinician must make it clear that the main concern for all parties is the patient's best interest.

Palliative medicine and research on end-of-life care offer additional perspectives on family conflict management. Scott and Coughlin[13] suggested that siblings may have difficulty discussing the end of life because of (1) fear of the dying process, (2) intense emotions, (3) loss of hope, and (4) the need to protect a loved one. These fears and emotions often keep siblings from discussing relevant issues such as palliative versus aggressive care, life-sustaining treatment, or the dying process. The task is often to keep the meeting focused by helping siblings understand these issues and acknowledge the emotional pain.

Quinn and colleagues[14] provided another perspective on siblings' behaviors regarding end-of-life issues. Their research describes family members' informal roles, which represent their various responses to the demands of a stressful situation. These roles are primary decision maker, family spokesperson, out-of-towner, patient's wishes expert, protector, vulnerable member of the family, and health care expert. The clinician's task is to determine who is playing what role, to understand that person's purpose for playing that role, describe what the siblings observe, and legitimize their roles as important. The clinician may then be able to guide the family through the decision-making process and reach a resolution.

All perspectives on families' conflict management at times of critical illness support the need for trust, honesty, and accuracy in answering questions and delivering potentially upsetting news.[15] Emotions are triggered in those siblings who have long and complex histories, and they can lead to conflict either among themselves or with staff. The clinician should recognize that the conflict may actually represent the family's internal struggle for control of their emotions and the situation.

Despite all the clinician's efforts to meet a family's needs, understand adult siblings' conflicted emotions, and assist with practical needs such as gathering information, the situation may not be resolved collectively.

Often, particularly when time is limited, families respond to the situation with a default mechanism. Rather than reach a consensus, siblings may gradually drift away, emotionally or geographically, and allow one person to make the decisions.

In the first case in this chapter, the siblings who objected to palliative care in favor of aggressive care faded from the picture. The patient's wife then decided to engage home hospice and bring her husband home to die. In the second case, the two less vocal siblings also became less involved and left the decision making to the sister who acted as a spokesperson and protector of the patient's wishes. The patient was transferred to another hospital for a second opinion and then was moved to hospice care. The team's intervention, spearheaded by the social worker, allowed the family members to step back and let the logical sibling make the decisions for the family members. The interventions also allowed the siblings to continue to stay in contact with one another, which facilitated future decision making.

Erik Erikson said that the personality is always engaged with the hazards of existence. There are few greater hazards than dealing with death, particularly in a technological age, when definitive answers to questions like the timing of or even the demarcation of life and death are elusive. Intensive care units can maintain patients in states of chronic acuity for long periods, leaving families in a state of ambiguity and confusion.[16] Paradoxically, life and death situations can be thrust on a family when a functional family member is suddenly stricken with an illness or injury. As clinicians, we can try to understand their emotions, translate difficult behaviors, and provide as accurate information as possible and facilitate communication. Negotiating conflicts within families requires not only skill and patience but also kindness, respect, and recognition of different perspectives. The primary tasks are to establish trust, help siblings recognize and better understand the grieving process, and support the medical staff in providing the best possible care.

Finally, unexpected family events are not only possible but likely. Social workers can prepare families and staff for meetings about end-of-life issues and their accompanying dynamics and emotions. Family meetings with distraught siblings who may not trust one another for unknown or reasons originating in the past can spiral out of control. There is no way to avoid this except to acknowledge the legitimacy of emotions and perspectives. Often it is useful after concluding the meeting to give the family time to address their emotions and renegotiate. The likely outcome is that the process will fall to one member to make the end-of-life decisions, as the siblings already may have lost their ability to engage with one another. Fixing that may not be possible in emergency and time-limited situations, and the clinician and health team should not feel they have failed. Skillfully facilitating a meeting in which adult siblings can hear the facts from the medical professionals, express their feelings, and have their opinions heard, without those meetings becoming a replay of earlier, unresolved sibling issues, may allow those who back off to do so sooner and with less conflict. Some interventions may have time-delayed effects. Helping an adult sibling set get through such an emotional family crisis without adding new toxic material offers the possibility of a change in the trajectory of those relationships. Still, the family's level of distrust and discomfort may be overwhelming for the family or at least for some of its members. Family members can be encouraged to follow up with grief counseling in the community, and some of them may even want to seek help together while grieving the loss of the same family member.

CHAPTER 12

Therapy with Sibling Issues

I think it's openness and sitting and talking. That's the most important. When there are any issues, sit and try to work it out. If you cannot work it out, go to family therapy. What happens in my relationship is, I think she is the big wrongdoer, and I'm sure she thinks I'm the big wrongdoer. So, it's like the Republicans and Democrats now, each one thinks it's the other's responsibility.

—Sixty-five-year-old white female (laughing), with one older sister

UNTIL THE LAST DECADE, CLINICIANS rarely treated adult sibling issues. Furthermore, adult sibling issues were not on the radar of researchers. Although excellent books cover siblings across the life span, they contain only a handful of chapters on older adult siblings.[1] With a few notable exceptions, then,[2] work focusing on the middle and later years has been scant. Interest in sibling therapy has always lagged behind interest in parent-child therapy; indeed, PsychINFO, a search engine for journal articles, displays more than ten times as many citations for the latter than the former.[3]

This chapter, on interventions with adult sibling relationships, begins with our own research on therapists and the extent to which sibling issues are raised in therapy. We then examine the therapeutic lenses that can be used with siblings and common problems that emerge when siblings' relationships are strained and how they can be approached. We close with advice for improving sibling relationships that was offered by those we interviewed.

OUR SURVEY OF THERAPISTS

We conducted an anonymous, online survey of two listserv groups for clinical social workers, one on the West Coast and one on the East Coast of the United States.[4] We received responses from 121 seasoned professionals with a median of twenty-two years of clinical experience, 85 percent of whom were employed full or part time in private practice.

To learn about how sibling relationships figured in adult clients' conversations in therapy, we asked these clinicians a series of questions. Their responses suggest that family relationships are centrally important to people who seek therapy and that half of the clients seen by the majority of therapists surveyed bring up sibling relationships (i.e., 60 percent of therapists said that 50 percent or more of their adult clients talked about their siblings).[5]

Other relationships also were important to clients. For instance, we asked, "About what proportion of your adult clients talk about their partner/spouse/dating in sessions?" As might be expected, 98 percent of the therapists said that 50 percent or more of their clients talked about romantic relationships in therapy. Parents were the second most frequently discussed in therapy, followed by children and then siblings. The therapists' own focus on parents and children may contribute to some of their clients' emphasis on those relationships. In our sample, 75 percent of the surveyed clinicians stated that they used psychodynamic and attachment theory as guiding work. We therefore suspect that they are less likely to ask clients about sibling relationships because those theories historically have focused on parent-child relationships, not family systems. Only a few clinicians said they relied mainly on family therapy theories, which would tend to lead them to ask about siblings as part of their assessment of new clients.

For more information about clients who discussed their adult siblings, we then asked, "Of your clients who talk about siblings, how often do they talk about them?" The answers show that for a minority of the whole sample, siblings are a frequent topic: 21 percent reported clients talking about their siblings in most of the sessions, and another 71 percent reported clients talking about them occasionally. By comparison, partner/spouse/dating was explored in most sessions by 91 percent of clients; children in most sessions by 69 percent; and parents in most sessions by 49 percent of clients.

Extrapolating from these responses, we surmised that nearly one-third of adults in therapy discuss their siblings at least occasionally. Their siblings are of greater concern to a minority of people than are most of their other relationships. What issues related to their siblings are clients bringing to these therapists? We asked our respondents to describe up to three different topics related to sibling issues that were commonly brought up in therapy. Most frequently raised were struggles with parental favoritism, disagreements about taking care of parents, sadness over a lack of closeness to a sibling, competition and rivalry between siblings, arguments over inheritance and money, and one sibling's physical or sexual abuse of another sibling.

Clients raised other, less acrimonious issues too. Concerns about another sibling's well-being, even among those not primarily responsible for taking care of the sibling,[6] also were brought up in treatment. A sibling may wonder how to help a sibling with a mental health or a substance abuse issue. Clients also described the positive process of bonding with a sibling to deal with a parent's dysfunction. Despite the range of concerns, in response to our final question, about the importance of maintaining adult sibling relationships to the therapists' clients, 29 percent of the whole sample said they were very important, and 63 percent said they were somewhat important.

These topics are similar to issues we found with the siblings in our research. They also are variations on themes presented by Barbara Kane, Linda Hill, and Anne Hahn in the two previous chapters. To explain working with these issues therapeutically, we use a variety of lenses and move from the broad to the specific.

A Cultural Lens

In our reading of the interviews as well as in our clinical experience, we came to believe strongly that families' experiences differ greatly for reasons including race, ethnicity, sexual orientation, country of origin, and religion. Some of those we interviewed for this book did bring up race and/or ethnicity, such as Leon in chapter 6, who described African American families' lack of distinction between blood and nonblood relatives. Being culturally responsive requires clinicians working within and across race to be aware of assumptions about family that may unconsciously interfere with treatment.

For example, Dr. Luz Lopez, a clinical associate professor at the Boston University School of Social Work who does research on Latino families, explained to us that Latinos typically stick together, even when one member immigrates to the United States and the rest stay in their country of origin. They still include that sibling in all their decisions about their aging parents. The collectivist nature of Latino culture also discourages competition among siblings, so it is easier for families to pull together for the benefit of its members. Working with a sibling group and assuming a priori that competition is a normal component of family life thus could drive the therapy in the wrong direction.[7]

We can expand the discussion of culture and consider age, gender, and religion. Again, women and men raised in the 1930s and 1940s grew up with different assumptions about the roles of brothers and sisters in the family. For them, therefore, responsibilities for taking care of parents also may be more bound to gender. They may be uncomfortable discussing certain topics, and, depending on their technological expertise, they may not be able to communicate by e-mail, Facebook, and the like. In addition, some religions expect women and men to spend their time differently. For example, Orthodox Jewish men spend more time praying outside the home than do Orthodox Jewish women, which could result in siblings assuming different roles in caring for their aging parents.

In sum, therapeutic work with siblings (as well as with all other client groups) must be guided by a cultural lens appropriate to both the family members in the room and those related to those in the room. In addition, as we become an increasingly diverse society and the range of family constellations expands, clinical practice with siblings is more likely to include adopted, step-, and half siblings from different cultural backgrounds, requiring the therapist to consider multiple perspectives when working with the same sibling group.

AFFECTION, AMBIVALENCE, AND AMBIGUITY AS FRAMEWORKS

We found enormous affection in the relationships of many of those we interviewed and believe that this powerful feeling should be nurtured when appropriate. Without some affection, siblings will have difficulty connecting in meaningful ways with one another.[8] We also saw ambivalence and ambiguity in those we interviewed and believe that when applied to sibling relationships, these two concepts can be helpful for therapists in shaping their interventions and for adult siblings in understanding the often complex and even contradictory experiences within those relationships. In short, sibling relationships are not easily classified. Even when siblings feel great affection for one another, their relationships are sometimes gray, complex, and perplexing. We began our work believing that we could construct, as others have, categories of sibling relationships. But given what we have learned, that is not possible. As our own research has taught us, these relationships rarely remain highly positive or highly negative over their life span. They are dynamic and often tinged with the mixed emotions of affection, anger, disappointment, comfort, and competition.

A majority of our sample (70 percent) indicated they had not always been close to their siblings. As we noted in the first chapter, ambivalence as a way of considering family relationships has come to the fore in the past decade. Writing twenty-five years ago, Victoria Hilkevitch Bedford noted that studies of siblings tend to be either positively or negatively skewed in their descriptions of closeness, and she raised the possibility of exploring siblings' ambivalent feelings for one another.[9] Her call for getting comfortable with ambivalence would be a good starting point for accepting the ups and downs of relationships as a normal part of adult life. After spending much time poring over our results, we have seen how relationships wax and wane over a lifetime and feelings between siblings are often mixed—indeed, that ambivalence characterizes siblings' relationship with and feelings for one another. Even those who told us their relationships were highly positive now often acknowledged that they were not always so. Clinicians and lay readers are better served to consider, become comfortable with, and help others with the gray of these relationships and the ambivalent feelings that naturally accompany them.

Besides accepting ambivalence, incorporating the concept of ambiguity is needed. People can have mixed—ambivalent—feelings about a sibling, and they also may be unclear about what has transpired in the relationship and whether their experiences of the same events match their siblings' experiences. Siblings may be left wondering: Why does the sibling act in a certain way? What is the sibling feeling? and What do they themselves want from the relationship? This leads to ambiguity in the relationship, which is different from ambivalence, in which a sibling might not be fully aware of his or her mixed *feelings*. Admitting that certain parts of the family history may never be understood and then figuring out what is wanted from the relationship is the starting point in gaining more clarity.

By definition, sibling conflicts are often linked to family issues, which lead us to the theories of Minuchin, Bowen, and Satir as guides from which to operate. Rather than viewing all presenting problems through one theoretical prism, we should use several theories to meet the needs of a range of clients. Using established family theory interventions, like marking boundaries, constructing genograms to understand the family's history, and clarifying communication among family members is key. The advantage of Satir's work, coupled with that of Bowen and Minuchin, is that siblings have the option in therapy of focusing on the present, the past, or both.

Other Approaches

Minuchin's, Bowen's, and Satir's theories and their key concepts can guide practice with and between adult siblings. Other theories can be helpful, too, and are used by therapists working with adults on sibling issues. In particular, clinicians often use attachment theory and feminist theory in regard to sisters' relationships.[10] Karen Gail Lewis, a therapist in Washington, DC, and the coeditor of a seminal book on siblings in therapy,[11] often has the whole sibling set spend a weekend intensively working on their relationships. She explains in detail the "frozen images" and the "crystallized roles" that siblings constructed for others in childhood and that have survived into adulthood.[12] "Frozen images" are the result of childhood interactions with siblings and parents and can be positive or negative. Lewis argued if a sibling were treated badly by another sibling during childhood, that experience would haunt their adult interactions. "Crystallized roles" are labels that people are given in childhood that are tough to shed. While such roles may be created by loving parents to help children avoid competition, they may result in stifling personal growth. A child may not achieve her potential if she is locked into or out of a role. For example, while he is growing up, a child may see himself as the family comedian but then as an adult feel he is never taken seriously by family members.

According to therapist Joyce Edward, the internalized representations of siblings shape how a person relates to others throughout life. In one case she recounted, a client always was late for sessions. When Edward confronted her about this behavior, the client revealed that she herself had often been made to wait for attention from her mother, who needed to take care of her brother. The therapist thus was the stand-in for the anger the client felt toward her mother and her brother.[13] By identifying these images and roles for siblings, Lewis and Edward hope that they will lead to opportunities for change.

Personal work and insight into the family of origin's sibling dynamics also help therapists working with sibling issues. Because therapists' training often spends little time on sibling relationships, an awareness of a therapist's own sibling history and cultural biases can alert him or her to issues that will arise in treatment and prevent countertransference from impeding the client's progress.

COMMON PROBLEMS AND HOW TO APPROACH THEM THERAPEUTICALLY

We next present from our interviews four common problems with which siblings struggle: parental favoritism, caretaking of aging and ill parents, sadness over not being closer, and cutoffs.[14] We first talk about how to approach favoritism and then use that approach as a model for the other three problems. We suggest a three-pronged model: the use of education, insight, and action. All of these can be used with just one sibling, the most common therapeutic scenario, and they can be adapted to a family if more than one sibling is present.

Parental Favoritism

In our research, 28 percent of the siblings said their parents "always played favorites" when the siblings were growing up, and 26 percent said their parents "always play favorites" now.[15] Dealing with the fallout from parental favoritism, whether one is the more or the less favored, is perhaps the most vexing therapeutic issue. It is also one of the most toxic to the sibling relationship. If being less favored is taken to the extreme, it can cut to the core of one's self-worth, and being more valued can result in guilt. It can harm the sibling relationship by sowing seeds of rivalry in childhood that can turn into conflict and distrust in adulthood. While some perceptions of occasional and mild forms of parental favoritism are to be expected, they usually are temporary and balanced by the sense that the less favored is still highly valued and loved and that the more favored is not placed on a pedestal.

The residue of favoritism can appear at any time in adulthood: when the parent is still alive and actively showing favoritism, when the parent is alive and is no longer showing favoritism yet showed it in the past, or after a parent has died and favoritism is revealed in the will, sometimes as a surprise. Using the three-pronged approach of education, insight, and action, the therapist can help the client work through any of these scenarios.

Using education, therapists can normalize the clients' experiences by instructing them about favoritism.[16] Favoritism has always existed in families and sometimes is unavoidable. The fact that in our sample of nonclinical respondents, approximately one-quarter was in a family in which favoritism had been shown by parents is information that can be used in therapy to help clients see favoritism as common in families. Still, favoritism takes many forms, from the largely benign to the highly destructive, depending on how it is shown and such factors as context, content, frequency, and intensity. It can also contain other problematic emotions such as jealousy or anger. In some cases, the issue may revolve around two siblings liking each other more and excluding or making a third sibling feel less liked, as with Jerome in chapter 5. Determining the form of favoritism requires a delicate therapeutic balancing act. It is the sibling's perceptions and the pain being felt that must be respected in treatment when education is provided. As we showed in earlier chapters, many siblings recognize it, perceive it as relatively benign, and disregard it, whereas others seem appropriately haunted by it. Determining the kind of favoritism (parental favoritism or sibling favoritism generated by parental involvement) indicates the type of education needed.

Offering readings about favoritism or case studies can help clients learn the different ways that favoritism is manifested and how it affects sibling relationships. For example, a client could read the following interview with Shari, a fifty-eight-year-old woman who struggled at one point with her relationship with her younger brother, in part because of her parents' favoritism. Her experience may be instructive for the ambivalent feelings that arise between siblings when one sibling draws more attention to himself through his accomplishments and lifestyle.

"It's so uncomfortable to acknowledge, but I was pretty jealous," Shari reported. "And because he was so good at stuff, he always got quite a bit of praise from my father. Even though he was the more rebellious of the two of us, I remember feeling especially jealous."

We asked Shari if her brother was the favorite because of all the attention he received.

> It's not like my parents never told me they were proud of me or praised me for a job well done. But maybe that was an issue for me looking back. Some of it could have been that my brother was a male and felt more connected to my father. My mom was even less obvious with her praise, but I recall them beaming during his piano performances. I don't know that jealousy continued to play a huge role as we got older. I think I matured and decided to not compare as much. We are very different, and I didn't want a fast-paced life. So in that way, I think things turned out the way they were supposed to. I'm at peace with it all. But as the years went by, and he moved away, my parents always talked about him in such a way you could see that they held him and his glamorous lifestyle in very high regard.

Eventually, as an adult, Shari has accepted that she and her brother have different talents and interests, though she still feels a slight tug regarding the attention he receives. When we asked if she ever talked about this with her parents, she gave this telling response, "No. That wasn't really how we operated." In other words, she knew that talking about it was not allowed and would not have helped. These words show the entry into both the insight and action that siblings/clients must consider in trying to understand and move forward.

To use insight, the siblings/clients first must understand their own parents' upbringing and the circumstances that led them to favor one of their children. For example, the parents might have been influenced by their own parents (the client's grandparents) showing favoritism to a particular child or by the family's always favoring older children. This is when applying a Bowenian perspective can be helpful. The therapist could ask whether Mom favored the girls and Dad favored the boys in their families of origin. Did the father who was a middle child favor his own middle child? Was there a high value placed on education or serving in the armed forces, so that children who succeeded in those areas received more attention and benefits than those who had other careers? Were the less favored siblings ignored, or were they loved and appreciated but not to the same extent? Was the favored sibling burdened with or freed from other family responsibilities? This is where an understanding of intergenerational patterns can be helpful.

Favoritism should also be examined in the context of what else is going on in the family with one or all of the siblings. Favoritism should not be confused with appropriate concern being shown by parents for a child with special needs who required more attention, energy, or resources. Such behavior could be as uncomplicated as loving parents who were trying to respond to events that had befallen a child.[17]

Alternatively, exploration leading to insight could include asking whether the favored sibling served a purpose in the parents' marriage. If she was the third side of a triangle that deflected tension in the marital relationship, the legacy may be especially powerful. As Michael Kerr, a protégé of Bowen's pointed out,

> Triangles are forever—at least in families. Once the emotional circuitry of a triangle is in place, it usually outlives the people who participated in it. If one member of the triangle dies, another person usually replaces him. The actors come and go, but the play lives on through the generations.[18]

A "favoritism-centric" genogram could be drawn that looks specifically at patterns across the generations. Regardless of the favoritism's origin, the sibling must explore why and how this is an issue today. Even though the favoritism may have occurred many years ago, we know from our research that for many of our adult respondents, at least one parent continues to show favoritism. Hence it may not be only a dormant issue that has to be "gotten over"; it may be an active issue that affects how love is shown, ongoing financial support, and potential inheritance.

Why and in what way the favoritism from the past or the present affects the current relationship must be appraised or reappraised.[19] Borrowing from Karen Gail Lewis, what frozen images are still operating? Do the siblings regress to their old roles when they are together? If parents are still actively stirring the pot, how are the siblings "choosing" to respond, and why are they choosing their responses? If a parent is no longer of "sound mind," how is that playing into the siblings' appraisal of the parent's remarks?

Is the client aware that each time a sibling acts in a certain way or repeats a phrase from their collective past, it triggers memories of favoritism? What else is going on in the client's life that may be making the strained relationship with a sibling more important and the favoritism upsetting? Is, for example, a failing relationship with a partner or spouse shedding new light on a number of relationships, including one with a sibling? If a marriage is ending, a sibling may need more from a sister or brother and may want to work on improving that relationship. This may lead to inequity in striving for closeness to siblings that can reignite issues concerning who was favored growing up.

Action is best considered after some insight has been gained and options weighed. In strategizing, therapists should decide what can be done given the personalities of the family members involved and the family's unspoken rules. Recall Shari's comment about whether she had talked openly with her family about her feelings about her parents' favoritism: "That wasn't really how we operated." Not all families are interested in direct communication or change, and not all siblings see a problem or want to work on relationships. That might leave a therapist with just one person wanting change: the client.

Kerr cited the following case as an example of working with one sibling. After their father's death, two (of four) adult married daughters who were not close and had separated from the family had a conversation that raised the specter of past injustices. The youngest, whom we will call Frieda, said to another sister, Ellen, with a great deal of emotion, "Why were you so nasty to me when we were kids?" Ellen responded in turn with a great deal of emotion and criticism, saying that Frieda was acting like a child. Kerr noted that in the past, exchanges like this had resulted in extended cut-offs from each other, with the mother trying to intercede. Frieda had been closely connected to their parents, but Ellen had been more distant. Ellen treated Frieda badly because Ellen was angry at being less favored when they were children. What their mother saw as sibling rivalry, Ellen saw as favoritism toward Frieda.

For Ellen, who also was struggling with issues with her husband, to change her long-standing patterns with Frieda, she had to recognize both the pattern and that her emotional life would have been better if she had received more attention from her parents. Ellen also needed to gain some control over her emotions, Kerr wrote, so that she could react more adaptively to future attempts by her mother or sister to triangulate. Ellen's commenting positively on how supportive Frieda and her mother were to each other could help highlight and demystify that relationship. This revealed the connections between the daughters and the mother.[20] Although Kerr does not tell us whether Frieda changed, Ellen's new approach helped her become less reactive with her family of origin, which in turn helped her avoid triangulation in her nuclear family.

We would add that even after their father dies, Ellen will always have to contend with a certain amount of ambiguity. She may not learn from Frieda what her experience was as the perceived more favored and, as a result, get used to not knowing.

A structural family therapy framework can also be helpful in dealing with a display of favoritism in the present that is affecting sibling relationships. With a focus on cross-generation (parent-child) and within-generation (sibling) boundaries, clients can deflect entreaties that they deem inappropriate. For example, if a parent starts to talk about a brother or sister in a demeaning way, the therapist can encourage the client to withdraw from the conversation by saying, "I do not want to listen to you saying bad things about my brother/sister." If the parent is showing favoritism to another sibling, the client can say, "You are very proud of (or close to) my brother/sister. I would also like to hear about what is going on in your life. How did you spend your day?" This accepts the situation but also redirects the conversation to a more comfortable area of discussion for the client.

Once the client understands the concept, boundaries can be drawn in similar ways with siblings. A forty-four-year-old counselor from India with an older and younger sister is struggling with her relationship with both of them. She first described how she came to be the favorite, a typical second-child tale that we have heard from others.

> My pain starts from a very long time ago with my elder sister. She always felt so threatened by me. As a second child I naturally figured out by watching her that the things she was doing and what my parents wanted or expected from us were very different. I molded myself according to what my parents expected. I realize that now, but at that time I didn't. I knew how to keep everyone happy.

Next we heard how she tried to avoid getting pulled into her older sister's histrionics. In essence, she took responsibility for herself and showed how individual therapy can work if no other sibling is in the room.

> When I was growing up, I held the belief that my family was very close. I held that belief because I thought that is how it was supposed to be. So I accepted and loved everybody and put up with the shouting and crying and blaming. I have even blamed myself for [my sister's] shortcomings. So I need to inspect this basic belief about close family. I feel the change has to be within me. It is about developing a sense of values and understanding that is not based on what I saw in the society or what was expected in my family but what works more for me. I have to temper that with the actual needs of other people. The path I'm working on right now in all aspects of my life is internal. I need to work on my relationship with myself by thinking and processing before I can start working on my relationship with my sister.

Building on the insight she gained, she is working to improve her sibling relationships by establishing a boundary between what she can and cannot do for her sister.

> Let's say that I do work that helps other people. So she would ask me to tell her what is going on with her husband. What she needs and wants is nonstop, constant, being available for healing every day. My sister also does hypnotherapy. She wants me to be available all the time so she can practice hypnosis on me for hours each day. She has no sense of boundaries. This doesn't work for me. She keeps trying to drag me into everything that goes on in her life.

By saying no to her sister, she is drawing a boundary that she hopes will protect and maintain her investment in the relationship. The realization that she must do this motivates her. How direct she should be must be based on what is consistent with expectations for women in her culture and whether she wants to adhere to those expectations. If she wants a direct approach, Virginia Satir would tell her to voice her feelings clearly and then deal with the consequences. Satir might then suggest that she say, "I feel as if I am being pulled into things in your life I do not want to be pulled into. I want to be close to you but not on those terms, as they do not work for me."

Finally, we encourage therapists to ask their clients how they want their relationship to work with their sibling after years of perceived favoritism. What would it look like if their current interactions did not remind the client of past favoritism? This helps lead to a better relationship and provides a road map for how to achieve it.

Conflict Over Caretaking of Aging and Ill Parents

Using the model of education, insight, and action, we next turn to another common source of strain for adult siblings, dealing with taking care of their aging parents. The two guest chapters, by Barbara Kane and Linda Hill of Aging Network Services and Anne Hahn of Johns Hopkins Bayview Burn Center, looked specifically at interventions that have been used with families struggling with both the emergency and the long-term care of parents, so we will discuss our approach to this topic only briefly.

In regard to education, a great deal of literature is available about the aging process and the impact that Alzheimer's and other diseases can have on parents and caregivers. Again, we turn to our own research as a new source of information about the extent to which siblings might agree on caregiving. When we asked our respondents about sources of their strain, slightly more than one-third (37 percent) cited a conflict dealing with one or both parents. Often this had to do with caretaking. More than half (57 percent) of siblings who said their parent(s) needed care told us that they shared the care with at least one other sibling. The remainder (43 percent) indicated that one sibling, sometimes themselves and sometimes another sibling, did the caregiving. When the family had both brothers and sisters and only one sibling was responsible for the caregiving, it was almost always a sister.[21] In the one exception, the siblings agreed that the parents would move close to the unmarried brother, who had the most time to spend with them.

As the two previous chapters stated, when adult children are taking care of aging parents, obtaining a clear diagnosis of the often comorbid illnesses of the aging parent(s) is an important first step. It also is important to note that a clear diagnosis does not guarantee a consensus on the prognosis for an aging parent's health, which can complicate the situation when siblings (and sometimes parents) are choosing a treatment. Education about the typical emotional reactions of both parents and children to the particular diagnosis can help clients accept their own and their families' reactions.

The ambivalence and ambiguity that accompany many conflicted sibling relationships would be the appropriate lens to use here. If the siblings never have been close or have unresolved issues with one another, expecting them to rally together would be unrealistic. Instead they should anticipate that this last stage of their parents' caregiving may be, normally, fraught with anxiety and sadness. Reassuring the siblings that they all do not have to respond in the same way to loss permits them to feel differently than other siblings do and can reduce the friction when they interact with one another.

Insight is necessary to begin processing the family members' reactions to one another in relation to caregiving. If there is sibling conflict, is it because a sibling is not sharing equally (or to his or her full capacity) in the physical and/or financial care of the parent? Is the conflict a repetitive pattern that began in childhood and is continuing, or is it a new conflict? Are in-laws or grandchildren pulled into the conflict? Is the ill parent asking one child for help and excluding the others? Does one child have an unresolved issue with a parent that is adding urgency or stress to the interactions?

Many questions are needed to get at the source of the conflict, which may be embedded in long-standing perceptions of favoritism, of privilege based on gender, age, or financial status, or whether a sibling is married, has children, and is less available. Siblings and parents also should consider whether philosophical, religious, and existential beliefs affect the extent to which medical intervention is necessary. The larger the family is, the more likely it is that at least one sibling will have convictions about life and death that differ from the others' beliefs.

Bowen's theory can lead to insight through the creation of a genogram to appreciate past patterns of intergenerational caregiving. Did one parent (or grandparent) die alone, and now the siblings are going out of their way to compensate? Have extraordinary measures always been taken to preserve life, and is that the pattern being followed now? Are the ill parent's wishes being honored as they were in previous generations? All families have dealt with death before, some with the death of siblings. How is the past informing the present?

If specific action is to be taken, structural family therapy with the parents could be helpful. For example, when a parent has dementia, the model of parents as the executives is reversed, and children become the executives. The siblings can be encouraged to work together to "parent" their parents and to try to prevent them from siding too much with one of the siblings.

This may be the first time the siblings have had to work together and requires understanding when their parents may be pitting them against one another. A sibling can be asked whether he has recently felt being pulled into an alliance with a parent that was disempowering the other sibling.

Siblings may also need to realign their own relationship and no longer necessarily follow the hierarchy in place when they were young when, most likely, the oldest was in charge. They must decide if they want to interact on a more equal basis according to ability, knowledge, areas of expertise, and desire to take responsibility.

If more specific interventions that are not connected to the parents' behavior are needed for the siblings to work as a team, they might agree to put aside their differences until the care of the parents is decided. An expert outside the family can be especially important here, either as a consultant to the family or, as some suggest, as the power of attorney for health care if problems with living wills or estate distribution are anticipated.[22]

Sadness Over a Lack of Closeness

Many of those we interviewed wished they had closer, more fulfilling relationships with their siblings. Some never were close and longed for contact; others had drifted away over the years. A few told us they were sad when they saw how close other siblings were because that was a reminder of what they were missing. Bill, a fifty-year-old discussing his relationship with his older sister, admitted this: "I feel I continue to give it my all, but I have had to lower my expectations." They were never particularly close because of the age gap and what he characterized, in a semijoking way, as "oedipal relationships" between his father and his sister and between his mother and himself. Bill felt that the history of alignments complicated the dynamics of him and his sister working together to care for their mother after their parents divorced and the father remarried.

> It was quite difficult to care for my mom, who lived out on the Jersey Shore and an hour and a half from my sister but farther from me. My mom was stuck and was mentally deteriorating. She had hoarding issues. One of the things that happened was, in my effort to be supportive and be there, even though I couldn't be there as frequently as my sister, we had lots of conversations about getting my mother into a place where she didn't have to care for

her home, which she wasn't capable of. I put it on the line with my sister and said, "I want to make Mom an offer to move down here to Richmond, and I will care for her. If she needs transitional living or whatever, I'll make sure it happens." My sister said, "If you do that, you can count on me not helping out at all." The reason that sticks in my head is, even though we've had lots of nasty conversations and arguments since, it was kind of like the fault line that began to fracture.

Working with Bill to improve his relationship with his sister required his learning that sibling relationships have normal ups and downs across the life span—70 percent of our sample reported this pattern—and that caring for a parent who does not live near either child is difficult to balance fairly. Both siblings seemed to take extreme positions: Bill wanting to move their mother closer to him and his sister threatening to withdraw totally if that happened. Arriving at agreeable caregiving is one goal, and becoming closer as siblings is another. Accepting the inherent ambiguity of this situation may help Bill move forward and find ways to get closer to his sister.

Insight can be achieved when the siblings recognize that the conflict over caring for the mother can be a replication of other struggles they have had. For Bill, the question would be, when else were ultimatums made in his family? What happened when their parents divorced in relation to ultimatums and caregiving? Do both siblings want to be closer, or is this only Bill's desire? Further in-depth work would explore what Bill jokingly meant about the oedipal relationships and whether the vestiges of these were somehow poisoning the relationship now.

For others, looking at intergenerational aspects of closeness would be helpful. How connected were and are the other family members to one another? Is this a family that embraces emotional closeness or is more distant? Have boundaries been drawn in the past that led to members being excluded? Family events can sometimes interrupt closeness and pull people apart, as demonstrated in earlier chapters with examples of financial disputes, criminal actions, and interpersonal squabbles. Insight would come in relation to whether past events are being repeated in the present.

Satir's communication model could be used if Bill wanted to approach his sister with a specific and clear request for closeness. He could say to her, "I know our relationship has waxed and waned, and I know that we disagree about what to do about Mom. I would like to be closer to you, though. What can I, or we, do to work on this?"

We have described using Bowen's genogram, but some therapists prefer using an ecomap, one that shows the family's current ecology.[23] If family history is not a productive way to pursue, an ecomap could be drawn that included potential resources and systems that are helping or hurting the family. In Bill's situation, this is when a nursing home or home health aide could be drawn in as a potential strength and resource, with geographic distance added as a barrier. Hoarding behavior would also be both a barrier to moving and an impetus for moving if the home environment were unsafe.

Finally, are there models for closeness that the sibling/client has seen that she or he wants to emulate? Interventions can then be constructed that can help achieve some version of that vision, depending on the constraints of the personalities involved.

Cutoffs

In chapter 5 we discussed the reasons for cutoffs. In chapter 7, Ron was presented as a case example of someone cut off from both his brother and his sister. As we explained earlier, cutoffs can be the result of long-standing family issues reaching back to childhood, such as parental favoritism and childhood relations. But they can also have more recent origins, originating as disputes about inheritance, acceptance of in-laws, philosophical differences, or betrayal of trust.

The reasons for the cutoff may naturally suggest the actions to be taken to resolve them. Education about cutoffs would help the client gain a cognitive understanding of their prevalence and how and why they develop. Defining them is the first step, as what one family may call and experience as a cutoff, another family may call a distant relationship. Are the cutoffs complete with no contact, as are a small percentage in our research, or are they more laissez-faire, in which siblings are no longer making an effort to contact one another but still show up at funerals and weddings? Is one sibling cut off from all the other siblings and the parents, or are all members of the family cut off from all the others? Is one sibling cut off from the other siblings but not from the parents or from the parents but not from the siblings? The larger the family is, the more likely will be some form of cutoff.

Reading about well-known people's cutoffs may be instructive. Singers Phil and Don Everly were emotionally cut off from each other even while on tour together. For a period of time, they never looked at each other on stage even while singing in perfect harmony. They later reconciled. Advice columnists Ann Landers and Abigail Van Buren did not speak for years while continuing in the exact same profession—ironically, counseling letter writers how to improve their relationships. They also reconciled later.

Again, insight into why the cutoff occurred can be facilitated by looking at intergenerational family patterns. In one research study of a clinical population, 220 adults rated their own relationship with their siblings as calm, neutral, or tense and then rated their parents' relationship with each of their siblings in the same way. As might be expected, the patterns of the parents' sibling relationships were replicated in the respondents' sibling relationships.[24] Although this study was looking at the mood of the interactions, it also shows how past behavior patterns may unfold. A "cutoff-centric" genogram would examine whether the older generations had cutoffs and how, if at all, they were resolved. If they were resolved, the way they were resolved could be important. If they were not resolved, further insight into the causes of this generation's cutoffs is necessary, which might be helped by gaining insight into previous generations' unresolved cutoffs. In our research we found that the reasons for cutoffs include parental favoritism, an active rejection of partners, and mental health or substance abuse issues.

It also is important to learn how the cutoff is affecting the family. Is the cutoff causing the family great stress? Families from cultures that are more collective will be more upset by cutoffs and may push for resolution more ardently than will families that value individualism more.

To resolve the cutoff, one sibling must reach out to the other sibling or siblings. By definition, these are examples of disengaged, rather than enmeshed, relationships. The client could be the person cut off from the other siblings, one member of a two-sibling set who wants more contact with his or her only sibling, or one of a number of siblings who is unhappy with a single sibling's drifting away. To help with the change, family boundaries may have to be redrawn, as one or more siblings most likely have established an emotional wall to protect himself or herself from the other sibling. Family members may have to be convinced that it is worthwhile for them to reengage with one another in a meaningful way. But some may conclude that it is too painful and not worth the effort. This is where understanding the ambivalent and ambiguous nature of the relationship becomes so important. The family members must accept that resolution may not be possible and still move forward in viewing themselves as a family, although not the version of the family they might have preferred.

Sometimes the next generation fights the battle for a parent. This happened to Verna, a sixty-six-year-old Bostonian who is cut off from one of her sisters and had a particularly disagreeable incident with that sister's daughter.

> I am very close with all my sisters except one who is the oldest. We had a falling out over the family business, so we aren't as close as we once were. It is complex and sad. My brother, the chief florist, died of a heart attack. My oldest sister worked as a manager and thought that she should get part of the business; my oldest brother worked in the greenhouse and thought he should get part of it and sued the sister-in-law [the widow of the brother who died] and her son, who was the florist left living. I was subpoenaed by one of the brothers as a character witness, and when we were leaving the courthouse, one of the brother's daughters spit on me for taking sides. She has not spoken to me since. She said I was a vile person and dishonorable. I am a peacemaker and don't do well with conflict, so it was very hard. I tried to get the nieces together, and it was difficult. There has been a rift since between those nieces and me.

Is it worth the effort for Verna to work on the relationship? She has tried and failed. Both sides would have to agree to forgive in order to make a relationship possible. Seminal family events (deaths and weddings) may offer an opportunity to broach the possibility of becoming closer. Growing older and gaining a more mature outlook, as we have heard from many we interviewed, can make reaching out easier.

While adult siblings must resolve their own issues, if their parents are actively involved in causing the cutoff, their participation in an intervention should be considered as well. Teaching parents to behave differently with their children can help redraw the boundaries to allow for new alliances to be formed.

Expecting siblings to become best buddies after a significant cutoff is unrealistic. Asking to be able to attend a family function without a fistfight breaking out is a more realistic goal if there has been great acrimony. If difficulty between a niece and an aunt (Verna's case) or accepting an in-law or partner has been at the root of the cutoff, meeting without the niece or the in-law present is a possible first step, with clear, nonblaming communication being the frame for requesting a rapprochement. If one sibling has been cut off, asking the family what will have to change in order for the cutoff to be resolved is another approach.[25]

In this chapter we have described different and specific therapeutic ways to approach these relationships when one or all the siblings want to improve them. Because they are highly idiosyncratic and complicated, we do not want to overlook their inherent ambivalence and ambiguity. Such problems cannot be handled neatly and will not always be resolved completely. To believe that they can be will only lead to more struggles and more disappointment.

WHAT ADVICE DO SIBLINGS GIVE?

What Should Siblings Do?

It is not just therapists who can offer suggestions, of course, for improving sibling relationships. We ended the interviews by asking what advice these siblings could offer others. Of the 262 people we interviewed, many provided both insight and concrete suggestions based on their experiences. We read each response and grouped them thematically.

The suggestion given most often, by more than one-third of the respondents, centered on the importance of communication, whether it was deep and meaningful or casual. "Talk to each other," "Keep in touch," and "Be honest with each other" were commonly given responses in this category. Satir would approve.

The suggestion given second most frequently, by one-third, centered on forgiveness and acceptance. The essential message was to rise above whatever had happened in the past and to accept the sibling, warts and all, in the present. Our respondents told us to "accept differences in each other," "apologize if needed," "forgive each other," and "respect each other and don't be judgmental." While these are important goals, they clearly would be difficult for some siblings to achieve based on what may have occurred between them.

Third, and given by about one-quarter of the respondents, was the suggestion to put effort into the relationship to make it functional. The advice here pertained to taking specific actions like "show up and see your sibling," "work at the relationship," "make time for each other," and "have the necessary but difficult talks." As Mick said in chapter 9, "Be deliberate about it." The reasoning behind these responses is quite insightful: that relationships will not improve on their own but require attention and action.

A smaller number of siblings recommended therapy, as exemplified in the epigraph at the beginning of this chapter, said, in part: "I think it's openness and sitting and talking. That's the most important. When there are any issues, sit and try to work it out. If you cannot work it out, go to family therapy." A few others took a page from Minuchin and recommended having boundaries and giving "each other space."[26]

The following seven statements about advice illustrate these:

Life is long; there are a lot of things that happen. There are a lot of ups and downs in every relationship or family. Particularly when there were strains in relationships, I would find it important to look at the big picture. I can remember one time when my sister wasn't talking to my brother and I would have to say that I might not agree with what he is doing right now, but in the whole, he would be the first one to come and help you if you need it. I am not going to dismiss my brother because he is acting like a jerk right now. Even with your parents. They might have done something you still resent years later, but the big picture is they did everything they could to help you. Keep the big picture in view, and don't sweat the small stuff.

I strongly feel that the moment there is discontent, you need to act on it. Don't let things fester or bother you for long. Like every relationship, you need to work on your sibling relationship, too. Call frequently and stay in touch. The conversations don't have to be long. We usually have short conversations, but once a week or once every other week we catch up.

In order to have a close relationship with a sibling, you have to be open-minded and reach out to each other. Sibling relationships are a form of trust and security and are also a form of having the kind of interaction where you enjoy each other's company. You have to create activities to do together or find a way to go to some event or activity together. Maybe through that activity you can create a connection. Creating connections is the first stage of bonding.

How about being nice to each other? [Laughs.] I think improving any kind of relationship can be traced back to lessons from kindergarten. You need to share and speak kindly to each other. There's no need to berate one another if you disagree. I've always allowed my sisters to be their own people. We all have different personalities, but we all learn to accept the differences and find strengths in each other. It's funny because, sometimes, my sisters will do or say something and it will remind me of my mother or father. We are all products of our parents, and we respect our parents and each other by remaining close and supporting one another.

You need to listen to each other. You can't just hear what you want to hear; you need to hear what the other sibling is saying. I have tried to communicate better with my brother, and maybe I don't do a good job, but I also feel like he doesn't hear me—he just hears what he wants to, which is probably his little brother whining and complaining. It's important to be humble and admit when you're wrong. I would say that if your sibling does reach out, open up both arms and create a place where the sibling feels like he or she can speak candidly. This is your sibling—you grew up with this person. If you can't be honest with your sibling, that's sad.

I like to write letters. I don't do it often. There's something about a handwritten letter. Even with my youngest brother, if I sit down and I talk to him and I say "Hey, this is what's going on, let's talk man-to-man," it turns into a heated argument. There have been a few times where I've written a letter to him. You can sit and read it. You can't get defensive about it. There are times when I've started out the letter saying, "My main goal with this letter is to become closer as brothers and for us to live better lives, and this is what I'm thinking right now. I'm not talking down to you." A lot of times he's called me and said he appreciated the letter and was going to take it to heart.

Finally is the advice from one of four sisters about the importance of boundaries:

I talk to each of them separately. Even if one sister tells me some news about the other, I still call her to hear it from her. I don't just take another sister's word for it. I want to give each sister her own time and space to tell me things—not just blow off a conversation because I may have heard something from another sister.

Ultimately, resolving any difficult sibling relationship requires some vulnerability on the part of those involved. It requires humility and accepting that one sibling's perception may not be the same for another sibling. Finally, it requires the instillation of hope that, with effort, a better relationship can be achieved.

CHAPTER 13

Looking Forward to Fostering Better Sibling Relationships

TAILORED PRESCRIPTIONS AND GRAND PROGNOSTICATIONS always run the risk of being either too specific or too general and therefore of limited utility. With those caveats, we have learned important lessons from our research that may be helpful to siblings struggling with their relationships. Many of our concluding suggestions and reflections support the tenets of family systems theory, that family members are linked to one another ineluctably and for better and worse. The art is learning how to maximize relationships for mutual benefit.

EFFECTS FROM CHILDHOOD AND IMPLICATIONS
FOR PARENTS OF YOUNG CHILDREN

Some of our most important research findings, presented in chapter 4, illustrate the strong link between how parents raise their children and its effect on those children's relationships with one another in adulthood. Our respondents' perceptions of their parents' favoritism, interference, and protection during their childhood were correlated with worse relationships on a number of measures in their adulthood. These findings have implications for parents raising children today.

As we have stressed throughout this book, favoritism is a double-edged sword; it can hurt both those favored and those not favored. In our egalitarian society (with the exception of cultures that privilege firstborn children or males), parents should know that favoritism may be damaging. Indeed, any parent with a sibling with whom she or he vied for attention will understand that favoritism can cause emotional damage. From our interviews, we learned that siblings may resent parents and siblings, distance themselves emotionally for self-protection, become resigned to favoritism being shown to another, dismiss a parent's behavior, and feel guilty for being favored.

Although sometimes a child needs extra attention, that attention should not be confused with favoritism, and the other child or children may need help to understand that. When a parent purposefully gives extra attention to a child in need, it should be within reason and with the awareness that the other children may get less. All the children should know why the child is getting more attention, or else a cycle will be set up that will lead to unclear expectations about the meaning of the attention. Parents showing the most common kinds of favoritism (aligning with one child because of common interests, personality similarities, birth order, or gender) should examine their own behavior, thoughts, and feelings. Parents showing disfavor toward a more difficult child should consider separating the child's displeasing behavior from the child as a person.

There is a fine line, which varies in different cultures and in different families, between interfering in children's relationships and letting them work things out on their own. Where that line is drawn cannot be determined from afar. Of course, children need protection from one another when those fighting are markedly unequal (physically, emotionally, and intellectually) or when harm is being inflicted. But interference and protection can also be intrusion into children's time together when they are having fun, by a parent attaching too closely to the children so they do not have the opportunity to build relationships on their own terms, or by a parent hovering over the children at all times. Instead, parents should look for opportunities to bring their children together in projects, such as making dinner, playing games, and teaming up, while recognizing that this might be easier at some developmental stages than others. For example, support for the relationship might be a game of Monopoly in which two children have their own pieces but can conspire against the parent so that if one of them wins at the end, they both win. Or in golf, they could play their best ball against a parent's only shot.

Parents' active support of the relationship in childhood carries over into adulthood. Nuance is important. Telling children too aggressively to be close can be perceived as interference or denial of differences that the children may be feeling toward one another. Conversely, a passive approach may miss an opportunity to help children form a lifelong and life-sustaining relationship. When opportunities arise, children can be encouraged to be close. If the opportunities are not presenting themselves, they should be initiated.

EFFECTS FROM ADULTHOOD AND IMPLICATIONS FOR PARENTS OF ADULT CHILDREN

We also found in our research a similarly strong connection between parental favoritism, interference, protection, and support in adulthood and the adult siblings' relationships. These findings have implications for older parents and their adult children.

Although children are subject to their parents' parenting behaviors, in middle and later adulthood the power shifts to either a more equal relationship or a reverse hierarchy in which, if parents are ill or highly dependent, the adult children are in charge. Adults are more capable than children of deciding how they want to respond to parents favoring an adult sibling, as they do in a quarter of our sample. Redrawing boundaries can reduce the amount of favoritism. For example, and as we suggested earlier, the favored sibling can ask the parent to stop showing favoritism. Or all the siblings can agree to not "listen" when a parent talks excessively (positively or negatively) about another sibling. They can retrain the parent by asking Mom or Dad to not talk about the other children unless it is to share basic information and to keep the conversation directed to the present.

Parents can also take responsibility. Their children should not have to retrain them if they are capable of making the changes themselves. In fact, parents might realize that their fostering better relationships among their children will most likely lead to better care for them as they age. Unclear wills and health care directives may exacerbate sibling discontent and not benefit their own well-being or enhance their legacy.

At this stage of the family life cycle, siblings should not depend on their parents for reinforcement to the extent they did when younger. But they can send a strong message to the next generation by taking responsibility for repairing the broken pieces of the family and show affection, support, and healthy communication.

Fathers

When fathers were perceived as being very close to their own siblings, as 36 percent of our sample perceived their fathers to be, our respondents also tended to be closer to their siblings. But when mothers were perceived as being very close to their own siblings, as 53 percent of our sample perceived their mothers to be, it was not a predictor of sibling closeness in our respondents. We offered one reason for this in chapter 4: Because it was unusual for fathers in the early and middle part of the twentieth century to display emotions and express closeness, when they did, it had a profound impact on the children. Since then, men's and women's behavior and role expectations, both inside and outside the family, have changed. Emotional expressiveness in men is certainly more common now. As a result, fathers' showing closeness may have less impact on today's children while still being important in role modeling for their children.

The potential influence of a father's closeness to his own siblings on his children's closeness gives him a unique opportunity to be a role model. Although we assume that this role modeling should begin as early as possible, this should not preclude an older father of adult children from becoming closer to his siblings and affecting his children's relationships with one another. Mothers' and fathers' role modeling of healthy relationships with their own siblings is paramount in fostering well-being in their children's relationships with one another.

Age

People mellow with age. Our oldest cohort felt less competitive and jealous than did the younger cohorts. Past differences that loomed so large when young did not seem to matter as much in later life. Yet the oldest cohort retained certain vestiges of the period in which they were raised and felt less comfortable than did the younger cohorts talking about certain topics. They also visited with one other less. Other research has described the hourglass of closeness: that siblings are closer when young, gain more distance in adulthood, and then grow closer again in later life.[1] Many of those we interviewed mentioned becoming close to their siblings only in middle and older adulthood, a linear trajectory of getting closer as the differences in ages narrow and they began to appreciate one another as adults.

As each generation of siblings ages and change becomes inevitable, a number of events are anticipated: parents die; the siblings' children become independent and better able to care for their parents; the siblings become less mobile; and they may have greater physical and emotional need for one another as the number of living family members of their generation diminishes. For siblings wishing to improve their relationships, age and these inevitable life events may be the impetus to become closer. The need could be even greater for those who are single and without children nearby. Although a sibling with a large family of his own may not feel the same need for reconciliation, he still may want to send a message to his children about the importance of sibling togetherness as a part of the family legacy.

For siblings in early and middle adulthood who despair of ever becoming closer to distant or difficult siblings, simply remembering that most sibling relationships wane and wax in closeness throughout life may help reduce their anxiety and increase their openness to both changes that may come with effort and those that may evolve more naturally. This requires becoming comfortable with the ambivalence that characterizes many sibling relationships.

Gender

We suspect that younger brothers are becoming increasingly involved in what used to be the sister's role of taking care of aging parents and facilitating communication among the sibling set. Now that more women are working outside the home and men are more comfortable expressing their feelings physically and emotionally and helping more with the housework,[2] families should not assume that a sister will be responsible for cleaning up and facilitating conversation, that a brother should manage the family money, or that the brother's wife will take care of Mom. Our research findings indicate that younger brothers (those forty to fifty years old) communicate more frequently and share more secrets with their sisters than do the older brothers. While this is a narrow age span and a small sample, we suspect that if we had asked younger adult siblings, for example, those twenty-one to thirty-nine, the same questions, they would have shown the same trend toward greater and more in-depth communication, which would suggest that other roles are now more equally divided. More fluid gender roles allow more people to take care of parents and permit communication to be facilitated by whoever feels most comfortable.

It will be interesting to see if, in the future, the more fluid gender dynamics will make sister-to-brother relationships as powerful as sister-to-sister relationships[3] and brother-to-brother relationships.[4] One possibility is that sibling relationships, for so long restricted by gender expectations, will take on new, as yet to be defined, meaning.

For our middle and older siblings, keeping in mind that their assumptions about gender roles may be contributing to the tension in their family may help ease any tension that flows from those assumptions. For example, asking sisters if they are comfortable with their caretaking roles may help brothers grow closer to their sisters, even when the sisters are comfortable with their roles. Inviting brothers to participate more actively in caretaking may give them an opportunity to move closer to their siblings and parents.

The Past

Karen Gail Lewis described the frozen roles and crystallized images from the past that affect us today. Murray Bowen taught us how family patterns repeat themselves in subsequent generations. Our research shows the strong influence of parental behavior during childhood on sibling relationships forty, fifty, and even sixty years later. Whatever approach is used to repair a sibling relationship, the past must be considered when trying to understand the present. Not all events can be traced to the past, but those that can may be alive in the present and could influence future generations. Children need to know their family history and whether they are stuck looking at their siblings through only one lens, a lens formed by their parents' behavior, by interactions with their siblings, or both.

Communication

Communicating clearly and through "I" messages can help undo past patterns of people not sharing their feelings or relying on blaming, distracting, and placating. But sharing feelings and talking openly requires being willing to listen to the other sibling's response and then working toward growth in the relationship. Conversely, many siblings rely on maintaining distance in their relationships and choosing their words judiciously, rather than opening up everything for discussion. Much of the advice from siblings centers on learning to accept differences and not trying to change a sibling at this age. As such, siblings must choose which direction to go in with their communication, as sharing comes with higher risks and rewards. Greater closeness may not be the goal of all the siblings, especially if they cannot forgive what has happened in the past.

Forgiveness

Not easy to do but, at some point, siblings may have to let go of past slights, injustices, favoritism, and hurts in order to build a relationship. This may not be possible if the past behavior has been too egregious. Everyone weighs relationships on balance. Am I willing to have this person in my life, given what has happened? Will I be putting in more than I will get out of the relationship? Do I feel that I am being untrue to myself and my children if I reestablish a relationship with a sibling who has broken a significant trust? If their decision is to forgive, if they are going to put the past to rest, siblings should consider what the future relationship may look like.

Putting Effort Into the Relationship

Many of those we interviewed talked about the importance of putting in time, working on the relationship, and "being there." Maintaining sibling relationships takes effort, as Utrecht University sociologists Marieke Voorpostel and Tanja van der Lippe found. Job and family demands often intervene, and if the siblings were never particularly close, it can be difficult to make the effort to establish a relationship. Some brothers and sisters just drift away, especially if there are many of them, without any specific reason. They must be willing to make the initial effort and then a continued commitment to reignite the relationship and keep it alive.

New Experiences

To build better relationships, siblings should consider trying new experiences together. New activities help people break out of their old ways of relating and allow them to take a different view of one another. For example, people often regress to old ways of relating when they return home for holidays, but experimenting with new environments can help siblings break out of uncomfortable interpersonal expectations. And as comforting as the old experiences might be, they may not be sufficient to adapt to new family challenges, such as a parent's becoming ill, that will need innovative responses.

Stepsiblings and Half Siblings

Relationships with stepsiblings and half siblings often are complicated, as they frequently begin in the context of family loss and are usually not as satisfying or as committed as full-sibling relationships. The societal imperative to improve them is not as clear. Many of our earlier suggestions for where to begin fit here: understanding the family history and how the family developed, redrawing boundaries, improving communication, weighing the benefits and costs of reaching out, and envisioning how the relationships should work. Families with step- and half siblings are becoming more prevalent and more diverse within the family. These families are no longer only dealing with the addition of a new person to their family; they may be dealing with a new person from a different culture. Therapists will increasingly need a culturally responsive life-span perspective to understand and be sensitive to how family members might deal with their differences.

Affection

The majority of our sample felt positively toward their siblings and valued their relationships with them. Affection exists in many relationships. Siblings can look for ways to express appreciation for one another, thank one another for taking care of a parent, arrange a family get-together, or ask about or help a niece or nephew. Some families feel comfortable with demonstrations of physical affection. Others value other forms of personal expression. Siblings should take every opportunity to be gracious to one another in ways that feel comfortable so that the relationship can be improved. Quick fixes for sibling issues are few and far between. As we heard from those we interviewed, communication, acceptance of the other sibling, and putting effort into the relationship are vital.

Ambivalence

For many, these are not always easy relationships. Even though siblings share experiences growing up, no two siblings are raised in the same family, particularly those with step- and half siblings.[5] Not only do siblings go through life on different trajectories, but their relationships with one another experience ups and downs, run hot and cold, and are a mixture of joy and sadness. As we noted, ambivalence is a common feature of adolescent relationships,[6] and it also continues into middle and late adulthood.

Some people come to realize that their sibling relationship is not as good as they would like. One woman in her sixties whom we interviewed remarked how sad she was that she and her sister were not as close as some other sisters are. They can relate to each other as they used to be but not as they are now. They can recycle the past but have trouble building a future, leaving her with a bitter-sweet feeling. Scott Myers's aptly titled article, "I Have to Love Her, Even If Sometimes I May Not Like Her," epitomizes this push-pull. Sometimes, obligation based on family upbringing and geographic proximity keeps the siblings close.[7] At other times, it is a cultural imperative or the family history's idiosyncratic ebb and flow that pulls siblings together, maintains their loyalty to one another, and causes them to downplay disagreements, hurts, and perceptions of unequal treatment by parents and other siblings.

Ambivalent feelings need to be recognized as normal and then to be sorted through. The focus for siblings can then shift to the parts of the relationship that are working and not to the parts that are less satisfactory.

Ambiguity

We cannot know everything about everybody, even our closest sibling. Much about another's behavior will always remain a mystery. Why a sibling acts in the way that she or he does may remain unexplained. Indeed, learning to live with that ambiguity may be essential to improving, or even maintaining, those relationships.

The interdependence, reliance on, and connection to our siblings last a lifetime. The journey we take with them may not always be easy but if we know they are riding along with us, we feel safer, the bumps along the way may be smaller, and the ride a lot more fun.

Study Methodology and Implications for Future Research for Clinical Work

DATA COLLECTION

The data for this book are drawn from interviews conducted by us, the authors, between 2011 and 2014 and in three distinct waves by trained, master's level, student interviewers in 2011, 2012, and 2013. A mixed-methods approach was employed in which respondents forty years old and older with at least one living sibling were given a 101-item questionnaire[1] (which is reproduced at the end of this appendix) to complete and then were interviewed qualitatively. The respondents answered questions about "siblings" (their sibling set as a whole) and also about their individual relationships with each sibling. The questions and items on the questionnaire and in the qualitative interview changed from one wave to the next as we learned more about the topic from our respondents. This resulted in a nonrandom and nonclinical sample size of 262 individual siblings with completed questionnaires, giving us data on more than seven hundred sibling relationships, as most respondents had more than one sibling. The qualitative interviews were conducted almost exclusively with individuals and, with sibling sets, exclusively by the authors. Two of these sibling-set interviews appear as separate chapters. The sibling sets in these two chapters were asked to read and approve the description of their family interaction to check the accuracy of our reports of those interviews and also to permit follow-up questions after the interviews. Names and other identifiable information have been changed throughout all the interviews to maintain confidentiality.

We also conducted a survey of mental health practitioners in 2012. In 2014, when we completed the data analysis, we interviewed clinical experts to gain their perspectives on various topics, including our findings. When these experts are quoted, their names are given in the text. Both studies received IRB approval from the University of Maryland.

The student interviewers were enrolled in the MSW program at the University of Maryland School of Social Work. All completed online training in confidentiality and ethics before we trained them on how to conduct interviews. For their training, all the students also completed IRB training and were then oriented to the topic of sibling relationships through readings, videos, and in-class discussions and lectures. They next were trained in qualitative interviewing and in administering a survey questionnaire. First, they practiced interviewing one another and then were asked to interview a respondent who met the study criteria who was not a family member. They returned to class to discuss the interview process and to refine their approach if a question was not clear to them or the respondent. They then interviewed five more adults with siblings. When they completed their interviews, they discussed the meaning of the collected data. Each made a class presentation and submitted a paper. This gave us an opportunity to constantly reevaluate our own understanding of sibling relationships. The student interviewers ranged in age from the twenties to the fifties. They are a demographically diverse group and tended to interview people from backgrounds similar to their own. This approach to getting a sample offered us a nonclinical (typical) convenience sample of siblings, some of whom had wonderful sibling relationships and others of whom suffered with their sibling relationships. In addition, the students' eyes and ears on the data provided multiple meanings for the interviews. Although their work helped inform ours, all the analyses are our own.

The questionnaire data were analyzed using SPSS Version 22. We and one research assistant coded the qualitative interviews. Guided by Deborah Padgett's[2] work, we read each interview twice, and when there were differences in coding, the team met to resolve them. The agreement on the coding was significant, nearly 85 percent.

ANALYTIC STRATEGY

For all the analyses, the criteria for reporting and discussing findings were two-tailed statistical significance at a 95 percent confidence level ($p < .05$) and for discussing a finding as a "trend," statistical significance at a 90 percent confidence level ($p < .10$). We used two analytic strategies for the reported analyses. When comparing groups, for example, by gender or age, we used independent samples T Tests that compare the means for a survey item for each group to determine whether there is a statistically significant difference between those means. When examining whether two survey items covaried, or were associated with each other, we used Pearson correlations with the criteria for reporting findings—the statistical significance criteria as just detailed—and also a correlation above .20 for a mild association, between .30 and .40 for a moderate association, and above .40 for a strong association.

All 262 respondents were included in analyses when appropriate, as they were in the analyses examining differences in adult sibling relationships across age or gender. For some analyses, however, we used only some of the respondents. In chapter 6, on sibling sets that included half, step-, or adopted siblings, our sample contained forty-nine respondents. In chapters 4 and 5, on parental influence and sibling sets that struggled significantly with their relationships, we did not include the respondents who reported having half, step-, or adopted siblings, for two reasons. First, we did not want to confound those findings with our findings in chapter 6, analyzing the dynamics in sibling sets with half, step-, or adopted siblings. Second, we anticipated the complex relationships in such blended families would also confound the findings for our analyses of the effects of problematic parenting dynamics on adult sibling relationships.

This nonrandom, moderately sized, cross-sectional sample does not give us a representative sample of siblings in the United States, nor does it allow for concluding cause-and-effect relationships. When we describe the findings from our sample, they are unique to this group and should not be interpreted as being true of all sibling relationships. When we report that variables were associated or were predictive, it means that they covaried in our data but not that one variable leads to the other. Even when time implies causality, as when one variable took place in a respondent's childhood and the other variable in his or her adulthood, it is still possible that both could be, for example, the result of a third, unmeasured variable. What the findings do provide is a highly descriptive snapshot of sibling relationships that is, for some of the data, remarkably similar to other research on siblings.

We interviewed only one sibling from almost all these families. We think this more clearly reflects who comes in for treatment: usually one adult family member talking about issues with other family members. We also believe that the respondents would have been less honest if several siblings had been interviewed together about their relationships. More fundamentally, we believe that there is no "truth" to any family, that each member has her or his own experiences and perspective. Trying to find the truth in some family event, and admitting that memory can be faulty over the years, may be a mission impossible, given siblings' multiple perspectives.

In addition, the limitations of our research include the use of different student interviewers who may have asked questions in slightly different ways[3] and our use of a convenience sample drawn largely from people living in the mid-Atlantic region. In chapter 3, we examined how age may affect the development of sibling relationships in adulthood. In presenting our findings, we described, in part, what appear to be age, gender, and parental influences on siblings' thoughts, feelings, and behaviors toward one another, but this may be correlation and not causation. Also, feelings toward siblings at any time in their life, but especially in middle and late adulthood, are not shaped *only* by parental behavior in childhood and adulthood, age, and gender. Life is much too complex for that. People have multiple identities as they cross from one context to the next. Significant life events, both positive and negative (gaining autonomy / entering adulthood,[4] getting married or finding a partner, having a child, succeeding at work and school, becoming seriously ill, etc.) diminish the impact of parental treatment on sibling relationships over time. In other words, as time passes from when siblings lived together and were subject to what the structural family therapists call the parental "executive subsystem," the potential for social environment factors and personal change to influence sibling relationships apart from the family of origin dynamics continually increases.

In addition, parent-child dynamics are mutually causal, a two-way street. Parents are influenced by the emerging personalities and feedback they receive from their children across the life span. In the literature, this process is referred to as "child-based effects."[5] When one member of the system behaves in a particular way, other members are influenced by that behavior and may adjust their own behavior in reaction. Thus parents, not only children, are influenced by the feedback they receive from all members of the family across their life span. Difficult relationships between parents and children or between siblings can also affect the relationship between parents, which can then affect how the parents raise their children. It is not just that siblings and parents influence children separately, they also make conjoint contributions.[6] The chicken-and-egg nature of a family's relationships is difficult for researchers and clinicians to discern; still, the roles people play often endure into adulthood and can be very hard to escape.

Using this systemic understanding, aging parents also are influenced by their adult children's behavior. This may be why parents, for example, sometimes decide to help out one adult child with emotional or financial needs and not help another one. Adult children often regress when they return home, as certain roles (e.g., youngest, middle, and oldest; the good child, the troublemaker) are hard to escape. As Murray Bowen did with his trainees, we asked our master's students to study their own family's behavior around the dining-room table on Thanksgiving. As predicted, many of these young adults, who were doing very difficult and critical work as social workers during the rest of the year, found themselves pulled back into childhood roles when they were with their siblings and parents.

Of course, and as an aside, talking about child-based effects does not absolve parents of responsibility for their own behavior or for setting the atmosphere and safety in a family. The family theories we chose place this responsibility primarily on parents, albeit in a broader context. This is often the basis of therapy with adults who are trying to understand how their childhood has affected the rest of their lives. As psychologist Stephen Bank wrote about his own therapeutic work with adult sibling issues: "Here lies the art of therapy: to help patients take responsibility for relationships while understanding their family's powerful effects, to help them understand that parents, while responsible, are also victims of a family system."[7] To further explain his position, Bank, citing his own research, stated that

> extreme disturbances in the sibling relationship are usually associated with serious parental problems. When rivalry becomes abuse, when envy leads to humiliation, when sexual interest becomes incestuous abuse, when identification leads to a loss of boundaries, parents have been unable or unwilling to see what is going on or are incapable of monitoring or intervening in the situation between their children.[8]

No two parents raise their children in the same way, nor can they agree all the time on every parenting decision. Each, as Bowen teaches, has his or her own personality and history at work. Sometimes the father is more involved, other times the mother. Each parent, as our findings show, has different influences on children.

Finally, we presented analyses of cross-sectional data from a nonrandom convenience sample. Caution is warranted in generalizing our findings to all adult siblings, as the statistically significant patterns we reported can be confidently ascribed only to the respondents in our sample. Future research is needed with other samples, ideally randomly chosen and including the collection of longitudinal data for more robust generalizability and cause-and-effect conclusions. Nonetheless, we believe that the research described in this book represents a significant step forward in our knowledge of an understudied yet central relationship across the life span. Interviews, with the exception of those siblings presented in chapters 7, 8, and 9, were conducted at one point in time. So even though they represent siblings' perceptions at that time, the perceptions and sibling relationships may have changed since then.

Therefore, in presenting our findings, we paid attention to parents' influence while realizing that many others were influential. With these warnings, we hope to draw attention to patterns that therapists can use in helping adult siblings sort out their relationships.

SURVEY OF CLINICIANS

Both the California Society for Clinical Social Work and the Greater Washington Society for Clinical Social Work agreed to let us publish a link to a SurveyMonkey instrument asking about their clinical work with adults. The twenty-five-item survey asked how frequently, compared with other significant relationships, siblings were discussed in treatment, as well as how important maintaining adult sibling relationships was to their clients. The survey also asked respondents to identify areas that clients raised in treatment regarding their siblings. We received 120 responses, an estimated 15 percent rate of return for those in the two organizations who were likely to have received the e-mail with the link. A follow-up e-mail was sent to each organization asking them to forward the link again to their members. While this rate of return is low, it is difficult to know how many recipients read the e-mail from any one organization.

Our findings from this clinician survey are perhaps the most helpful to discovering what types of relationships are talked about in therapy, a topic on which there is surprisingly little research. We found no particular differences between the West Coast and the East Coast samples on the demographic characteristics of the samples. The relevant findings appear in chapter 12.

DESCRIPTION OF THE SAMPLE

Of the 262 respondents in our sample, 150 (57 percent) were females and 112 (43 percent) were males. Of the 704 living siblings they described to us, 376 (53 percent) were sisters and 328 (47 percent) brothers. The median age of the respondents was fifty-three, and their average age was fifty-four. The oldest person we interviewed was ninety, and the youngest was 40. The respondents had, on average, 2.69 siblings, with two siblings being the most frequent configuration ($n = 78$), and nineteen had six or more siblings. The age range of sibling sets with all biological siblings was, on average, eight years, ranging from zero (a set of twins) to twenty-eight (a set of three siblings with the youngest in the thirties and the other two in their fifties or sixties). For the blended families (with half, step-, or adopted siblings), the average age span was thirteen years, ranging from two (two sibling dyads, one with an adopted sibling and one with a stepsibling) to thirty-eight (a set of six siblings including full, half, and adopted siblings). Nineteen percent ($n = 49$) reported having half, step-, or adopted siblings. Within this group, thirty-six had at least one half-sibling, fourteen had at least one stepsibling, and five had at least one adopted sibling. This is more than forty-nine, as some families had siblings in different categories. Seventy-five percent had children ($n = 195$), with the average number of children being 2.3. Sixty-nine percent ($n = 183$) currently had a partner. In regard to the racial and ethnic breakdown, 70.5 percent of the respondents were white, 17.3 percent were African American, 6.1 percent were Latino, 3.8 percent were Asian, and the remaining 2.2 percent were mixed/other/Pacific Islander, or Native American.[9] We asked the respondents to self-report their religious affiliation: slightly fewer than half said Protestant (48.3 percent), with the rest Catholic (27.3 percent), Jewish (8.4 percent), Sikh (2.4 percent), spiritual (2.4 percent), Muslim (0.8 percent), or another religion (0.5 percent). About one in ten (9.6 percent) described themselves as agnostic or atheist.

The sample is skewed in terms of educational attainment, with 21.2 percent having a high school diploma or less, 11.2 percent having some college, and the remainder having finished college and not continuing (36.7 percent) or having at least some graduate education (30.9 percent). By comparison, about one-third of the U.S. population in this age range has a high school diploma or less, and 12 percent have some graduate education.[10] As predicted by their education, when asked to describe their family income level (on a five-point scale), 12 percent indicated they were lower class or lower-middle class; 48.8 percent, middle class; 35.7 percent, upper-middle-class; and the remaining 3.5 percent, upper class. As expected given our sample's education range, about 25 percent were professionals: teachers, therapists, nurses, social workers, and lawyers. Ten percent were managers and business people, and 14 percent were retired, which was not surprising, given the age range.

IMPLICATIONS FOR FUTURE RESEARCH TO ASSIST CLINICIANS WORKING WITH ADULT SIBLINGS

1. Because of the increasing diversity within extended families, clinicians need to know more about how different backgrounds and cultures interact within the same family. For example, Cicirelli argued that sibling relationships in industrialized societies are more likely to be discretionary and more obligatory in nonindustrialized societies.[11] How do these differences play out in the treatment of siblings?

2. As life spans lengthen, older siblings will increasingly work together to take care of older parents as well as their fellow aging siblings. How can cooperation between these older siblings best be facilitated,[12] and how might electronic media and the changes in health care delivery help them?

3. Our research found that fathers' relationships with their siblings were correlated with their children's better sibling relationships. While we have hypothesized why this is the case, more research is needed on the father's role in modeling this process and how that behavior can be encouraged in families.

4. We found that parents' interference, favoritism, protection, and support are related to siblings' helping one another, trusting one another, and becoming close.[13] All these family processes are very difficult to operationalize, particularly across cultures, but are key components of and powerful forces in many family therapy theories. More research on how these processes change during the life span is needed.

5. Ambivalence must be better understood as a therapeutic framework. Connidis and Bedford have made substantial contributions to our psychological and sociological understanding of the concept, and Boss has pioneered work on ambiguity. Learning how these two combine to frame the work in therapy may be useful in a number of settings and clinical issues.

6. Gender differences in our data appeared to be decreasing in the younger respondents. How will men's and women's changing behaviors and roles affect the future behaviors and expectations for the adult brothers and sisters in the family? How will these changes affect treatment?

7. Finally, the best tests for some of the patterns we found in adult sibling relationships require longitudinal data to determine the complex causal mechanisms at play. Even though such research takes many years, given siblings' important and consequential roles in their social and psychological development and outcomes across the life span, such an investment would be very worthwhile.

ADULT SIBLING RELATIONSHIPS: PLEASE COMPLETE THE FOLLOWING QUESTIONS TO THE BEST OF YOUR ABILITY.

1. Your age: ___ 2. Your sex: ___ 3. Your race: _____ 4. Your religion: _____

5. Starting with your youngest sibling, give the age and sex of each of your siblings:
    a. Sibling's age ___ Sex ___ b. Sibling's age ___ Sex ___ c. Sibling's age ___ Sex ___
    d. Sibling's age ___ Sex ___ e. Sibling's age ___ Sex ___ f. Sibling's age ___ Sex ___
6. Are any of these half, step-, or adopted siblings? No ___ (go to #7) Yes ___ (go to #6a)
    a. The following are half siblings (write in letters): _____
    b. The following are stepsiblings (write in letters): _____
    c. The following are adopted siblings (write in letters): _____
7. Are you married or in a long-term partner relationship? Yes ___ No ___
8. Years of education completed (high school = 12; college degree = 16): _____
9. What type of work do you do? _____
10. What is the level of your total family income?
    a. Lower   b. Lower middle   c. Middle   d. Upper middle   e. Upper
11. Do you have any children? If so, give ages: _____ (indicate if step- or adopted children)
12. Are you usually comfortable with the level of support you have from your sibling(s)?
    Very comfortable ___ Somewhat comfortable ___ I would like more support ___
13. Are you comfortable with the level of support you have from your spouse/partner?
    Very comfortable ___ Somewhat comfortable ___ I would like more support ___
    Does not apply ___
14. If your parent(s) need care, is one sibling usually responsible for the care?
    No care is needed___ We share the care___ One sibling has responsibility ___
    (give sibling's age)___
15. How often do you and your sibling(s) agree on how to care for your parent(s)?
    Very often ___ Somewhat often ___ Occasionally ___ Never ___
    Parents are deceased ___
16. Using the scale, to what extent do you agree with the following statements about you and your sibling(s) when you were young?
    Strongly agree = 5, Agree = 4, Neither agree nor disagree = 3, Disagree = 2, Strongly disagree = 1
    a. We competed more than most ___
    b. We were jealous of each other more than most ___
    c. Our parents always played favorites ___
    [Answer *only* if your parents played favorites]: My parents favored me over my sibling(s)___
    d. One sibling excelled much more than another ___
    e. We could trust one another ___
    f. We fought or argued frequently ___

17. Using the scale, to what extent do you agree with these statements about you and your sibling(s) *now*?
    Strongly agree = 5, Agree = 4, Neither agree nor disagree = 3, Disagree = 2,
    Strongly disagree = 1, DNA = 0
    a. We compete more than most ___
    b. We are more jealous of one another than most ___
    c. Our parents always play favorites ___
    [Answer *only* if your parents play favorites]: My parents favor me over my sibling(s)___
    d. One sibling excels much more than another ___
    e. We trust one another ___
    f. We fight or argue frequently ___

18. Using the same scale, to what extent do you agree with these statements about your parent(s) when you were growing up:
    a. They interfered in our relationship ___
    b. They often tried to protect one of us from the other ___
    c. They were highly upset by it ___

19. Using the same scale, to what extent do you agree with these statements about your parent(s) when you and your sibling(s) became adults:
    a. They interfere(d) in our relationship ___
    b. They often try(ied) to protect one of us from the other ___
    c. They were/are highly upset by it ___

20. Starting with your youngest sibling, describe in a few words your relationship with him/her:
    a. Youngest sibling: _____
    b. Next youngest sibling: _____
    c. Next youngest sibling: _____
    d. Next youngest sibling: _____
    e. Next youngest sibling: _____

21. Starting with your youngest sibling, (a) how many miles apart do you live, and (b) how much contact do you have by Internet (email/texting/Facebook/Skype), face-to-face, and telephone? Check each that is applicable.

		Frequent contact	Occasional contact	No contact
a. Youngest: miles apart:_____	Internet	_____	_____	_____
	Face-to-face	_____	_____	_____
	Telephone	_____	_____	_____
b. Next youngest: miles apart:_____	Internet	_____	_____	_____
	Face-to-face	_____	_____	_____
	Telephone	_____	_____	_____
c. Next youngest: miles apart:_____	Internet	_____	_____	_____
	Face-to-face	_____	_____	_____
	Telephone	_____	_____	_____

d. Next youngest: miles apart:_____   Internet   _____   _____   _____
                                         Face-to-face   _____   _____   _____
                                         Telephone   _____   _____   _____
e. Next youngest: miles apart:_____   Internet   _____   _____   _____
                                         Face-to-face   _____   _____   _____
                                         Telephone   _____   _____   _____

22. Were your parents (to the best of your knowledge) close to their siblings?
    a. Mother: Very close _____Somewhat close/mixed _____Not close _____DNA _____
    b. Father: Very close _____Somewhat close/mixed _____Not close _____DNA _____
    _____
    _____

Now we want to learn about your relationship with two of your siblings. If you only have one, skip #24.

23. This next series of statements is based on your relationship with a sibling that has had a *positive* impact on you [see Riggio 2000]. If no sibling has had a positive impact, still answer the question. Use the following scale:
    Give the sibling's sex: _____ and age: _____
    Strongly agree = 5, Agree = 4, Neither agree nor disagree = 3, Disagree = 2, Strongly disagree = 1
    1. My sibling makes me happy ___
    2. My sibling's feelings are very important to me ___
    3. I enjoy my relationship with my sibling ___
    4. I am proud of my sibling ___
    5. My sibling and I have a lot of fun together ___
    6. My sibling frequently makes me very angry ___
    7. I admire my sibling ___
    8. I like to spend time with my sibling ___
    9. I presently spend a lot of time with my sibling ___
    10. I call my sibling on the telephone or email frequently ___
    11. My sibling and I share secrets ___
    12. My sibling and I do a lot of things together ___
    13. I never talk about my problems with my sibling ___
    14. My sibling and I borrow things from each other ___
    15. My sibling and I "hang out' together ___
    16. My sibling talks to me about personal problems ___
    17. My sibling is a good friend ___
    18. My sibling is very important in my life ___
    19. My sibling and I are not very close ___
    20. My sibling is one of my best friends ___
    21. My sibling and I have a lot in common ___
    22. I believe I am very important to my sibling ___
    23. I know that I am one of my sibling's best friends ___

24. My sibling is proud of me ___
25. My sibling and I spend our free time in very different ways ___
26. My sibling and I do not hold similar views about how to parent ___

_____

_____

24. This last series of statements are based on your relationship with a sibling that has had a *negative* impact on you. If no sibling has had a negative impact, still answer the question. Use the following scale:
Give the sibling's sex: _____ and age: _____
Strongly agree = 5, Agree = 4, Neither agree nor disagree = 3, Disagree = 2, Strongly disagree = 1

1. My sibling makes me happy ___
2. My sibling's feelings are very important to me ___
3. I enjoy my relationship with my sibling ___
4. I am proud of my sibling ___
5. My sibling and I have a lot of fun together ___
6. My sibling frequently makes me very angry ___
7. I admire my sibling ___
8. I like to spend time with my sibling ___
9. I presently spend a lot of time with my sibling ___
10. I call my sibling on the telephone or e-mail frequently ___
11. My sibling and I share secrets ___
12. My sibling and I do a lot of things together ___
13. I never talk about my problems with my sibling ___
14. My sibling and I borrow things from each other ___
15. My sibling and I "hang out" together ___
16. My sibling talks to me about personal problems ___
17. My sibling is a good friend ___
18. My sibling is very important in my life ___
19. My sibling and I are not very close ___
20. My sibling is one of my best friends ___
21. My sibling and I have a lot in common ___
22. I believe I am very important to my sibling ___
23. I know that I am one of my sibling's best friends ___
24. My sibling is proud of me ___
25. My sibling and I spend our free time in very different ways ___
26. My sibling and I do not hold similar views about how to parent ___

_____

_____

THANK YOU FOR COMPLETING THE QUESTIONNAIRE

PREFACE

1   Nandwanda & Kotach 2009.

1. THE WORLD OF ADULT SIBLINGS

1   Edward 2012.
2   Hemphill 2011, 225.
3   Greif 2009.
4   Kreider & Ellis 2011, reporting for the U.S. Census Bureau.
5   Donrovich, Puschmann, & Mathijs 2014. These Belgian demographers looked
     at the impact that sibling configuration had on life spans in nineteenth- and
     early twentieth-century Antwerp. On the one hand, they write, siblings com-
     peted with one another for limited resources, which were then diluted, but on
     the other hand, they protected one another.
6   Kreider 2008. This figure is often cited but is difficult to pin down exactly. The
     U.S. Census Bureau report states that 79 percent of children under age eigh-
     teen lived with at least one sibling. Clearly, some children do not live with a
     sibling. Also, this is referring to children, not adults. It could be a higher per-
     centage, as birthrates were higher in the past, though older siblings might also
     have died.
7   See, e.g., Davidoff 2012 and Straus, Gelles, & Steinmetz 1980.
8   Jensen et al. 2013.
9   Finzi-Dottan & Cohen 2011.
10   Gold (1989) used intimate, loyal, cordial, apathetic, and hostile as categories;
     also see Stewart et al. 2001.
11   The statements they were asked to agree in the order in which they were read
     were "sibling relationships are highly satisfying with a minimum of conflict.

Sibling(s) feel close to each other and are trusted. If there is geographic distance, attempts are made to stay in contact" (62 percent); "sibling relationships are fairly frequent, but they are strained and not satisfying. There may be anger or resentment that affects interactions" (6 percent); "sibling relationships are not frequent, but they are strained and not satisfying. Anger or resentment may affect interactions" (15 percent); and "sibling relationships are neither highly satisfying nor particularly strained. Siblings feel loyal and act cordial to each other, but the relationship is not very important. Attempts at closeness may have failed, and the sibling is resolved that he or she will not be closer, or there may never have been an attempt to be close because of differences in personality, age, gender, or lifestyle" (17 percent).

12 Bedford 1989.
13 Connidis 2007. For the application of ambivalence to fictional characters, see also Connidis 2011.
14 Bengston et al. 2002, 568.
15 Ibid.
16 Connidis 2007, 483. The previous sentences also draw on 483.
17 The term was originally coined by Boss (2006) for instances of abducted children and soldiers missing in action when there is no physical proof of their whereabouts. The loss cannot be easily resolved because the typical grieving processes, when a body is found, are often not initiated.
18 Boss 2006.
19 Connidis 2007, 484.
20 Sulloway (1996, xiii) noted that siblings born in the same family have almost as different personalities as do those born in different families.
21 Jensen et al. 2013.
22 Kramer 2011.
23 Kramer & Bank 2005, 483. See also Salash, Wood, & Parker 2013, who found a correlation between the way siblings in adolescence resolved their conflicts and how they resolved their conflicts in adulthood with intimate partners.
24 For original writing, see, e.g., Bowen 1974, and for a textbook discussion, see Nichols 2014. Bowen's disciples have a very helpful website, www.thebowencenter.org, that explains his work. The discussion here is drawn from these sources.
25 Nichols 2014, 116.
26 In a large Dutch study, Poortman and Voorpostel (2009) found that siblings in high-conflict families have less contact in adulthood. Thus if parents are

pulling in children to diffuse the conflict between them, the residue of those actions may continue for generations.

27   Nichols 2014, 132.

28   Sulloway (1996) wrote about the connection between birth order and creative success; Kluger (2011), a *Time* magazine reporter, also used a Bowen lens to look at his own family.

29   In writing about work with children, Jenkins and Dunn (2009) described the need to look at the processes underlying more than one sibling dyad per family. We think this approach also can be applied to adults.

30   Nichols 2014. See also Minuchin & Fishman 1981.

31   Bascoe, Davies, & Cummings 2012.

32   Satir 1964; Nichols 2014.

2. SIBLING RELATIONSHIPS

1   Mock & Parker 1997, 308.

2   Ibid., 2.

3   Ibid., vii.

4   As Bedford and Avioli (2012) point out in their excellent review of the sibling literature, the perception of egalitarian treatment by parents goes a long way toward building sibling closeness.

5   Davidoff 2012, 35.

6   Bank and Kahn (1982b) provide an in-depth discussion of the meaning of this fairy tale. Psychotherapists, they write, often treat "Hansels" and "Gretels" who have had to take care of each other when there are no supportive parents in the home.

7   Schomburg 1992.

8   For those interested in delving more deeply into sibling relationships in literature, see Mink & Ward 1993.

9   This would not be surprising. According to Mock and Parker (1997), kin recognition occurs even in larva, in which sibling groups stay together while those who are not related settle randomly.

10   Hemphill 2011, 24–25.

11   Hemphill (2011) treats West Africa as one entity and does not distinguish specific countries or areas of origin.

12   Hemphill 2011, 20.

13   Davidoff 2012, 39.

14   Hemphill 2011, 29.

15   The term *Latino* is used to describe a grouping of a number of distinct Spanish-speaking cultures, with Mexican being the largest in the United States.

16   For more information on Latino families, see, e.g., Webb's 2001 book.

17   Hemphill 2011, 170. She further writes that although there was greater equality between the roles of sisters and brothers in northern families, a patriarchal society was more common in the South and West.

18   Greif 2009.

19   Connidis & Campbell 1995.

20   Davidoff 2012, 40.

21   Irish 1964.

22   Troll 1971.

23   Pfouts 1976.

24   Dunn 1983.

25   Ibid.

26   Ainsworth & Bowlby 1991.

27   For those interested in the long trajectory of Dr. Bowlby's work leading up to the development of attachment theory, a great place to start is his 1951 World Health Organization report, *Maternal Care and Mental Health.*

28   For a description of the careers of both John Bowlby and Mary Ainsworth in their development of attachment theory, see Bretherton 1992.

29   Bretherton 1992.

30   Ainsworth 1989.

31   Drawing on more recent research from a Dutch sample, Voorpostel and van der Lippe (2007, 1280) suggest "that siblings do not function as a dormant source of support, ready to be activated when there is a need for it. The sibling relationship needs maintenance." This speaks to the need to nurture sibling relationships.

32   Feeney & Humphreys 1996; Doherty & Feeney 2004.

33   Myers & Bryant 2008.

34   Canary et al. 1993.

35   Van Volkom, Machiz, & Reich 2011.

36   Cicirelli 1989. In addition, and consistent with other research, Gilligan, Suitor, and Nam (2015), analyzing data from the Within-Family Differences Study II, found that respondents chose sisters over brothers "as the siblings to whom they felt the most emotional closeness" (173).

37   Finzi-Dottan & Cohen 2011. Note that the gender difference in the Israeli culture may have been at play here.

38   Jensen et al. 2013.

39   Boll, Ferring, & Filipp 2003.

40   Gilligan et al. 2013.

41   We have selected only a few health issues, but several others could be reviewed for their impact on siblings. For example, schizophrenia, which usually develops in adulthood, also takes a significant toll on siblings and the family. For research on this topic, see, e.g., Smith & Greenberg 2008 and Friedrich, Lively, & Rubenstein 2008.

42   Degeneffe & Olney 2008.

43   Orsmond & Seltzer 2007.

44   Hodapp & Urbano 2007.

45   Degeneffe & Olney 2008.

46   Degeneffe & Lynch 2006.

47   Degeneffe & Olney 2010.

48   Kempson & Murdock 2010.

49   Robinson & Mahon 1997.

50   For more on attachment and sibling loss in young adulthood and from a psychoanalytic perspective, see Charles and Charles (2006), who surveyed thirty-four college students who had experienced the death of a sibling.

51   Cicirelli 2009.

52   Hayes, Gold, & Pieper 1997.

53   D'Epinay, Cavalli, & Guillet 2009–2010. The size of the sample went down over time owing to the subjects' deaths.

3. SIBLING RELATIONSHIPS IN MIDDLE TO LATE ADULTHOOD

1   For a description of her scale, see Riggio 2001.

2   For example, a fifty-year-old who was the youngest child and had many older siblings would be placed in an older sibling set than would a fifty-year-old who was the oldest and had many younger siblings. Of course, friends of siblings can have an influence, too. Grace McMillan, the research assistant for this book, offered the following example, which shows both the differences in sibling age sets and how friends could be the same age but be influenced by their own sibling set, which could influence the friendship.

> My sister, Carrie, and her best friend from high school, Joyce, both were born in 1964, but Joyce is the youngest of six while Carrie is the oldest, by seven and a half years, of two. Joyce's oldest sibling is eighteen years her

senior, with three siblings twelve or more years older than she, and because her next oldest was born in 1958, her sibling set's mean age is 59.9. Carrie has a mean sibling set age of forty-five and a half. Even though Joyce and my sister are the same age, their sibling set mean age is fifteen years apart.

3   The greatest generation was born before the silent generation and was not a significant part of our sample.

4   The actual age cutoff for the oldest baby boomers would have been sixty-seven at the time of our study. In order to increase the sample size for the oldest age category and because retirement age is often considered to be sixty-five, we set the age limit at sixty-five.

5   Because the interviews were conducted between 2011 and 2013, a fifty-year-old could have been born from 1961 to 1963. To even out the sample sizes for analysis, therefore, we placed them with the younger siblings.

6   Krieder & Fields 2002. Since 2000, the rate of divorces has declined, according to the CDC, *National Marriage and Divorce Rate Trends, 2000–2011*.

7   Hobbs & Snoope 2002.

8   Bureau of Labor Statistics Report 2004.

9   Bedford, Volling, & Avioli 2000.

10 Voorpostel & Blieszner 2008.

11 Riggio 2000.

12 Cicirelli 1995.

13 Gold 1989. In addition to intimate, loyal, and cordial, Gold has two other categories of sibling relationships, apathetic and hostile. Bank and Kahn (1982a) wrote earlier about loyalty as a major theme or dimension in sibling relationships (251).

14 Gold 1987.

15 Myers 2011. Other reasons are that we are relationally close; we have a similar construct; we give each other support; we share similar or common experiences; we are friends; and I love my sibling.

16 Stewart et al. 2001.

17 Our wording of the question is open to interpretation. A sibling could be very comfortable with the level of support, indicating closeness to the sibling, but not have or want any relationship with that sibling.

18 Note that one-quarter of the interviewees had only one living sibling, so their responses to the global questions referred to the same sibling they described for single-sibling specific questions, whereas those with multiple siblings may

have been thinking of different siblings when responding to the different types of questions.

19 Riggio 2000. This scale was developed based on responses of 711 undergraduate and graduate students with a mean age of twenty-three and a half, significantly younger than our sample's mean age. It contains questions about child and adult sibling relationships in three areas: affective, cognitive, and behavioral. We chose to include the adult items on the questionnaire. For a more recent analysis of her scale using a larger sample, see Riggio 2006.

20 For waves 1 and 2, the responses were very positive when respondents were asked to complete only one scale. We wondered whether we were capturing the full range of relationships, even though the scale asked the respondent to "answer the following questions regarding the sibling that has had the greatest impact on your life, positive or negative." For wave 3, we phrased the question as follows for the completion of the first Riggio scale: "This next series of statements is based on your relationship with a sibling that has had a positive impact on you. If no sibling has had a positive impact, please answer the questions thinking of the sibling with whom you currently have your most positive or least negative relationship." We then asked the respondents to complete a second scale with the following wording:

> This last series of statements is based on your relationship with a sibling that has had a negative impact on you. If no sibling has had a negative impact, please answer the questions thinking of the sibling with whom you are least close or with whom you occasionally have conflict.

21 We compared Riggio's (2000) mean subscale scores with our sample by both all respondents and by gender. For the feelings subscale, Riggio reported a mean of 30.9, while our sample was 32.3; on the beliefs subscale Riggio reported 29.2, and our sample was 31.3; and for the behavior subscale Riggio reported 25.2; while our sample was 24.9. The mean age of Riggio's sample was 23.5, and the mean age of our sample was 54.2. Therefore on the feelings and beliefs subscales, our sample reported modestly higher and more positive responses. But on the behavior subscale, our sample reported slightly lower levels, which reflect our finding that older respondents are more likely, for example, to report spending time together and borrowing things from each other. We found a very similar pattern by gender across the two samples: sisters report more positive feelings, behaviors, and beliefs in regard to a sibling than brothers do.

22 These next sets of findings are based on our analyses using the LSRS.

23 These two questions are part of our survey and not the LSRS.

24 In a sample of people fifty-four years old and older, Folwell and colleagues (1997, 846) also found variation in sibling relationships. When there was little or no closeness, tragedy and never being close were mentioned as reasons for the current state of the relationship.

25 A sample size of eighty-one for the third sibling, forty-eight for the fourth, and thirty-two for the fifth.

26 Madden et al. 2013.

27 A 2000 Pew Research Center study, "Tracking OnLine Life: Women's Different Online Lives," reported that siblings with an email relationship communicated that way more than by telephone. Breakdowns were not available in relation to age, so we offer this finding with caution, given the age of the research.

28 We combined "strongly agreed" and "agreed."

29 This is consistent with Stewart and colleagues' 2001 findings.

30 Bedford's 1998 work suggests that siblings' early positive experiences with one another are related to later well-being.

31 In one study of older adults (Connidis 1994), a majority of respondents believed their siblings would be there for them in a crisis. In Stewart and colleagues' 2001 work, 56 percent were described as "supportive" or "longing," both positive characterizations of relations, although contact does not occur as often with a "longing" sibling relationship. Safer (2012, 2) stated that "at least one-third of the adult siblings in America suffer serious sibling strife . . . the number rises significantly, to 45%, when therapists probe more deeply." Regardless of how we tried to get at this information, this is a higher percentage of troubled relationships than when we asked respondents to place themselves in categories and found that about 20 percent were not especially close or hostile.

32 In a further analysis of our qualitative interviews, sixty-six respondents were located who had provided enough information for us to create common patterns that siblings followed after the death of one or both parents. These siblings were grouped into eight patterns, ranging from becoming closer to more distant. We called them Even closer; Just us now; New roles, responsibilities, and relationships; Unsettled estate; Never close; From bad to worse; Back together again, temporarily; and No change (Greif & Woolley 2015).

33 Folwell and colleagues (1997) found that of their sample of sixty-one subjects who were fifty-four years old and older, 70 percent said their closeness had varied; 23 percent said no change had occurred, that they always had been close; and 7 percent said they had never been close.

34 Folwell et al. 1997.

4. THE PERCEIVED IMPACT OF PARENTS ON SIBLING RELATIONSHIPS

1 Angier 1995.

2 It is interesting to go to Amazon and see how many books on siblings have a variation of this in their title or subtitle.

3 For an excellent overview of how siblings differ, even though they were raised in the same family, see Dunn & Plomin 1991.

4 For more on how a sibling death can play out in therapy, see Kempson & Murdock 2010 and our discussion in chapter 2.

5 We found many statistically significant correlations between having one sibling excel more than the others and reports of more parental favoritism, protection, and interference.

6 Jensen et al. 2013.

7 Leavitt et al. 1999.

8 When studying advanced directives, Khodyakov and Carr (2009) found that if the living will was not clear, relationships between siblings suffered. They improved if someone other than a family member was given power of attorney. Despite the hypothesis that a parent's death reactivates negative feelings from childhood that were submerged during the parent's life, Khodyakov and Carr found differences that were based on how the end-of-life planning was handled.

9 Halgunseth, Ispa, & Rudy 2006.

10 Tucker et al. In Press. The researchers used a fairly broad definition of victimization, including being hit, beaten, or attacked as well as being called names or being told that they were not wanted around.

11 Myers and Bryant (2008) found that one of the myriad ways that siblings show commitment is by protecting one another from parents and outsiders.

12 Ballantine 2013.

13 Monahan 2010.

14 Instances of reported sexual abuse were reported to the departments of social service in the state in which they occurred.

15 Some of the shifts took place in those who were neutral toward its occurrence in childhood.

16 Note that interference became significant in adulthood but not in childhood.

17 In the statistical relationships between parenting and sibling relationships that we discuss in this chapter, we used the same analysis and criteria. First, we did not include respondents with half, step-, or adopted siblings because those sets of relationships are discussed in another chapter and because such blended

family issues complicate and confound the parenting issues that are the focus of this chapter. Therefore, the sample here is 213. All analyses were bivariate correlations between the survey items of interest, with the criteria for discussion being a statistical 95 percent confidence $p < .05$ if the relationship found is true. In magnitude, all the correlations we discuss are above .02, with many being between .03 and .05, so they are moderate to large, given our sample size.

18 Boll, Ferring, & Filipp 2003; Suitor et al 2009. The specific findings from Boll et al. are discussed in chapter 2.

19 Jensen et al. 2013.

20 E.g., Cicirelli 1995, both 73 and endnote xxii.

21 Another example of an intergenerational behavior pattern regarding siblings comes from Donley and Likins's 2010 research. They found that siblings whose parents had a tense relationship were more likely to have tense relationships themselves with their siblings.

22 We do not know to what extent the mother is also reaching out to the father's siblings to bring them closer. We believe that given when our respondents were raised, the mother would be more likely to do this than the reverse, the father reaching out to the mother's siblings. Nearly 20 percent of the respondents perceived that both parents were close to their siblings.

23 Bank 1988.

24 Suitor et al. 2009.

25 In reviewing the literature, Cicirelli 1995 reported that in one study, 45 percent of those studied felt sibling rivalry in adulthood. Wagner, Hunter, and Boelter (1988) made the case that rivalry is normal in families with children and, when problematic, can be handled strategically through role reversal.

26 Other research suggests that children learn about friendships from same-sex parents, too, so it would be plausible to assume that learning about sibling relationships from parents also is possible (Greif 2009).

27 For a good review of the literature, see, e.g., Van Volkom 2006, and for an earlier review, see Cicirelli 1989.

5. WHEN SIBLING RELATIONSHIPS ARE IN SERIOUS TROUBLE

1 Agllias 2011, 108.

2 In wave 3, we asked the respondents this specific question about Internet, telephone, and face-to-face contact for each of their siblings.

3 Personal communication with Scott Myers, April 12, 2014.

4 Personal communication with Victoria Hilkevitch Bedford, April 18, 2014.

5 Markowitz 1994, 29, 66.

6 Fuller-Thomson 1999–2000.

7 Ingersoll-Dayton et al. 2003.

8 Boss 2006.

9 Bedford & Avioli 2001.

10 Campbell, Connidis, & Davies 1999.

11 A sister is often viewed as the sibling who works the hardest to maintain relationships (Bedford & Avioli 2012). In research conducted in Germany with 902 adults, same-sex siblings were identified as the most important (Buhl 2009), leading us to hypothesize that relationships with opposite-sex siblings would be more likely to be cut off. Sisters also do most of the caregiving of parents (e.g., Willyard et al. 2008), giving them a more central role in the family.

12 Bedford & Avioli 2012. Fingerman, Hay, and Birditt (2004) found that family relationships are more likely to arouse feelings of ambivalence than platonic friendships are and that parents and children raise more ambivalent feelings than siblings do.

13 Agllias 2011, 110–111.

14 Step- and half-sibling families were not included in the count of cases.

6. ADULT SIBLING RELATIONSHIPS WITH STEP- AND HALF SIBLINGS

1 Shattuck & Kreider 2013.

2 Pew Research Center 2011.

3 Note that second marriages end less often than do first marriages, according to a 2004 U.S. Census Bureau report, table 125. For example, a father remarries a woman with children. Those children and the father's children become stepsiblings. But then that marriage breaks up. That makes them ex-stepsiblings, even though they still may remain close if they had formed a close relationship.

4 White & Riedmann 1992, 197.

5 Voorpostel,, van der Lippe, & Flap, 2012.

6 Pollet 2007.

7 Visher & Visher 1988.

8 Rosenberg 1988.

9 Asian, Pacific Islander, Native American, or mixed race.

10 Because of the sample size, we did not indicate whether the respondent was, for example, an only stepsibling or a half sibling who was speaking about a sibling set or whether the respondent was one of a number of full siblings who was speaking about a single or a number of step- or half siblings.

7. WHEN SIBLINGS CUT OFF CONTACT

1   Bank 1988, 342.
2   Parker-Pope 2010.
3   See, e.g., Cicirelli 1989, 214.
4   Cicirelli 1995.

8. COPING WITH THE DEATH OF A SISTER (A TWIN) AND OTHER LOSSES

1   Kluger 2011, 251.
2   Mauthner 2002, 3–4. For two other books dedicated to sisters' relationships, see Apter 2007 and Kuba 2011.
3   Kuba 2011, 28.
4   Cicirelli 1982.
5   As we mentioned in the first chapter, our initial intention in writing this book was to compare sibling relationships with friendships. After much consideration, we determined that a friendship lens was not the correct lens for us to use. For one discussion of the similarities, see Voorpostel & van der Lippe 2007.
6   Mauthner (2002) described twins Annabelle and Chloe, in their early twenties, as having a relationship that was rife with anger and jealousy when they were younger but that is now characterized by mutual appreciation of each other. It was a crisis, the illness of one of the twins' best friends, which caused them to connect more meaningfully.
7   Ross & Milgram 1982, 228. In chapter 7, we noted that Bank (1988) made a similar point about the legacy of early family upbringing.
8   Consider the three sisters who have run the Argosy bookstore in Manhattan since their parents died and whose relationship was described in a 2014 *New Yorker* article by Janet Malcolm. Those sisters became closer when a potential source of their distance, their father's lack of attention, was no longer a factor. As the middle sister explained in Malcom's article,

> We really get along . . . but more since our father died. When he was alive, we were always vying for his attention and compliments, and there wasn't enough to go around. He was very chintzy with his compliments. It was embarrassing for him to say a nice word. . . . But after he died we really stuck together. We have always been equals here. (73)

9 Ross and Milgram (1982) interviewed seventy-five adults across the life span and found that 23 percent cited shared values and 22 percent cited communication as important to keeping the relationship strong. The next most frequently mentioned were shared goals and interests, 18 percent, and shared family traditions, 15 percent.

9. THREE BROTHERS WHO GET IT RIGHT

1 Kluger 2011, 292.
2 Bedford & Avioli 2006.
3 Emanuel 2013, 25.
4 Greif 2009.
5 We followed up the interview with e-mail and telephone contact to clarify some points and obtain additional information.
6 Kluger 2011, 272.
7 Edward 2013.

11. DEALING WITH ADULT SIBLINGS IN AN EMERGENCY HEALTH CRISIS

1 Shulman 2005.
2 Scott & Caughlin 2012.
3 Khodyakov & Carr 2009.
4 Kinrade, Jackson, & Tomnay 2011.
5 Shulman 2005.
6 Lamas 2014.
7 Erikson 1963.
8 Ibid.
9 Kinrade, Jackson, & Tomnay 2011.
10 Cooper, Bernacki, & Diva 2011.
11 Ibid.
12 Bergman 2013.
13 Scott & Caughlin 2012.
14 Quinn et al. 2012.
15 Kinrade, Jackson, & Tomnay 2011.
16 Lamas 2014.

12. THERAPY WITH SIBLING ISSUES

1   See, e.g., Caspi 2011, Kahn & Lewis 1988, Kluger 2011.

2   Both Cicirelli and Hilkevitch Bedford have produced a body of groundbreaking and highly accessible work that began more than twenty-five years ago; see references. Caspi's 2011 edited book, primarily focused on younger ages, is an important source for working with children.

3   We searched PsychINFO July 10, 2014, by inputting (1) parent AND therapy, 20,267 cites; child AND therapy, 66,183 cites; parent-child AND therapy, 4,008 cites; and sibling AND therapy, 1,418 cites. Adult siblings AND therapy produced 17 hits. Six of those cites were published between 2004 and 2014. They included a description of a bereavement-group approach for surviving siblings (Zampitella 2011); clinical work with adult survivors of sibling sexual abuse (Monahan 2010), which we discussed earlier; a dissertation on siblings in their twenties, with a prominent athlete sibling; an article on developmental disabilities and siblings by Orsmond and Seltzer (2007), which we talked about in chapter 2; a review of a book on siblings with autism; and a case study of five siblings in their twenties whose sister died after a lengthy terminal illness.

4   The California Society for Clinical Social Work and the Greater Washington Society for Clinical Social Work. The members were surveyed in 2012, and 121 therapists completed the SurveyMonkey instrument; see Greif & Woolley 2012. We asked about adult clients, not clients specifically forty and older. We also presented our research from the siblings study at the Council on Social Work Education (Woolley, Greif, & McMillan 2014) and Society for Social Work Research (Woolley, Greif, & McMillan 2015).

5   The choices were "more than 75%," "75%," "50%," "25%," and "10%"; 85 percent of therapists said that 50 percent or more talked about parents; 63 percent said that 50 percent or more talked about children; and 60 percent said that 50 percent or more talked about their siblings. Friends and then colleagues were the least talked about in therapy.

6   In interviews with 103 well siblings, with an average age of thirty-nine, related to siblings with serious mental illness, Leith and Stein (2012) found that only 20 percent were the primary caregivers, yet the well siblings still suffered great personal loss in relation to their ill sibling. In chapter 2, we discussed some of the research on siblings with a struggling sibling. For more on adult siblings with a developmentally or intellectually disabled sibling, see Burke et al. 2012. The website/listserv group SibNet@yahoogroups.com might be helpful as well.

7   Personal communication, April 25, 2014. See also Watson 1998 and Watson & McGoldrick 2011. For those interested in differences in sibling relationships among ethnic groups, see the research by Voorpostel and Schans (2011), who, drawing on a sample of 2,573, compared the experiences of Dutch natives with Moroccan, Surinamese, Antillean, and Turkish immigrants to the Netherlands.

8   See the research by Voorpostel and van der Lippe (2007) about the need to nurture sibling relationships.

9   Bedford 1989.

10 See, e.g., Apter 2007 for the application of attachment theory, Mauthner 2002 for the application of feminist theory, and Kuba 2011 for the application of feminist family therapy. Kluger (2011) wrote from a reporter's perspective about the relationships of brothers, including his own, and Colt (2012) also looked at brothers historically as well as his own. We examined attachment theory in chapter 2.

11 Kahn & Lewis 1988.

12 *Ghosts You Live With* is in progress, as reported in a personal communication, January 27, 2014. Dr. Lewis sent us a draft of the first two chapters of the book.

13 Edward 2013.

14 As we pointed out in chapter 4, references were occasionally made to physically and emotionally abusive sibling relationships during childhood that went beyond typical sibling fighting. In our nonclinical sample, these were not frequently mentioned as driving problems for siblings in middle and later adulthood, although the legacy of the abuse could still affect the relationships. We cited the work of others, e.g., Ballantine 2012 and Monahan 2010, who have greater expertise in the area of sexual abuse and encourage therapists who are working with clients with this history to refer to departments of social services.

15 We did not ask whether fathers or mothers were more likely to show favoritism or if half or stepparents were more likely to show favoritism. Jensen and colleagues (2013) found being less favored by fathers was related to more depressive symptoms in young adulthood, whereas being less favored by mothers was correlated with fewer depressive symptoms. Jensen and colleagues hypothesized that mothers may give more help to their most needy children, but if these children are not receiving favored treatment from their mother, they may be less needy. Fathers, they believe, may withdraw somewhat from needy children, so more depressed children may receive less from fathers.

16 Others, e.g., Agllias 2011, have noted the importance of normalizing sibling experiences as part of the treatment. Gilligan, Suitor, and Nam (2015) interviewed both mothers and their children and found that siblings' closeness tended to vary by whom the mother was perceived to favor and by how favored the child felt. For example, if they did not feel favored by the mother, they tended to feel closer to the sibling whom the mother favored.

17 Kramer & Conger 2009.

18 Kerr 1988, 53.

19 During our interview, Victoria Hilkevitch Bedford suggested reappraisal as an important step in rebuilding relationships.

20 Kerr 1988, 57–58.

21 We asked this question only in wave 3 and found twelve cases in which caregiving was not shared and the family had at least one brother and one sister. Only one of those twelve had a brother taking primary care of the parents. Hequembourg and Brallier (2004) interviewed eight pairs of brothers and sisters, with a mean age of 47.1, and also found that the sisters took much more responsibility for caregiving than the brothers did.

22 On working together as a team, see Khodyakov & Carr 2009. Because the elderly may also be financially abused, this should be guarded against as well. This responsibility should be given to the outside person assigned to assist the family preemptively (Gibson & Qualls 2012).

23 See, e.g., Freeman 1993.

24 Donley and Likins 2010.

25 For other intergenerational interventions, see Freeman 1993. Allen, Blieszner, and Roberto (2011) found kin loss, a concept similar to a cutoff, to be a result of divorce or relocation. In one case example, two siblings were cut off from their grandmother after their father died. Their parents had been divorced.

26 We did not see any particular trends between suggestions and responses to other items on the questionnaire, with one exception: a few people who had poor relationships with their siblings said they had no advice to offer.

27 A handful said they had done nothing to improve their relationship, and a few others said they did not need to improve their relationship. For example, one said,

> They've done nothing. Over the years I have tried to be a good person and tried to help my brother and be there for my sister, but it never seems to work. I've stopped trying, as you can tell. But I guess that's what happens over time when you get treated poorly.

13. LOOKING FORWARD TO FOSTERING BETTER SIBLING RELATIONSHIPS

1 E.g., Cicirelli 1995.
2 According to Coontz (2014), since 1977, husbands have doubled the time they spend doing housework. She also noted that since the 1990s, college-educated parents have increased the amount of time they spend with their children.
3 E.g., Mauthner 2002 and Apter 2007.
4 E.g., Bedford & Avioli 2006.
5 See, e.g., Dunn & Plomin 1991 as well as our discussion in chapter 1.
6 Kramer 2011.
7 Using a telephone survey sample of people with an average age of nearly forty-five, Lee, Mancini, and Maxwell (1990) made this point.

APPENDIX

1 This figure is for 2013; the number of questions varied from one wave to the next.
2 Padgett 2008. Strauss and Corbin's 1998 work also was influential.
3 For the same limitation, see also Folwell et al. 1997. They also say that the use of multiple students could be a strength, as they offer more and varied perspectives when locating subjects.
4 Myers and Bryant (2008) talk about breaking away from the family, and sibling relationships taking a backseat to other relationships, as a normative stage of emerging adulthood.
5 In describing the reciprocal influence of parent and child on each other, Ulbricht and colleagues (2013) talk about child-based effects and also "evocative child effects."
6 Tucker & Updegraff 2009.
7 Bank 1988, 344.
8 Ibid., 344–45.
9 When our respondents were young, the United States had a higher percentage of whites. For example, according to various census reports, in 1970 Latinos comprised 4.7 percent of the population, and whites, more than 80 percent. Now Latinos are the country's largest minority, at close to 17 percent.
10 U.S. Bureau of the Census 2013.
11 Cicirelli 1994, 7.
12 See also Ingersoll-Dayton et al. 2003 and Van Volkom 2006.
13 For this point in relation to favoritism shown by fathers, see Suitor et al. 2009.

REFERENCES

Agllias, K. (2011). No longer on speaking terms: The losses associated with family estrangement at the end of life. *Families in Society, 92*, 107–113.

Ainsworth, M. D. S. (1989). Attachments beyond infancy. *American Psychologist, 44*, 709–716.

Ainsworth, M. D. S., & Bowlby, J. (1991). An ethnological approach to personality development. *American Psychologist, 46*, 333–341.

Allen, K. R., Blieszner, R., & Roberto, K. A. (2011). Perspectives on extended family and fictive kin in the later years: Strategies and meanings of kin reinterpretation. *Journal of Family Issues, 32*, 1156–1177.

Angier, N. (1995). New view of family: Unstable but wealth helps. *New York Times*, August 29. Retrieved from http://www.nytimes.com/1995/08/29/science/new-view-of-family-unstable-but-wealth-helps;html.

Apter, T. A. (2007). *The sister knot: Why we fight, why we're jealous, and why we'll love each other no matter what.* New York: Norton.

Ballantine, M. W. (2012). Sibling incest dynamics: Therapeutic themes and clinical challenges. *Clinical Social Work Journal, 40*, 56–65.

Bank, S. (1988). The stolen birthright: The adult sibling in individual therapy. In M. D. Kahn & K. G. Lewis (Eds.), *Siblings in therapy: Life span and clinical issues* (341–355). New York: Guilford.

Bank, S. P., & Kahn, M. D. (1982a). Intense sibling relationships. In M. E. Lamb & B. Sutton-Smith (Eds.), *Sibling relationships: Their nature and significance across the lifespan* (251–266). Hillsdale, NJ: Erlbaum.

Bank, S. P., & Kahn, M. D. (1982b). *The sibling bond.* New York: Basic Books.

Bascoe, S. M., Davies, T., & Cummings, E. M. (2012). Beyond warmth and conflict: The developmental utility of a boundary conceptualization of siblings relationship processes. *Child Development, 83*, 2121–2138.

Bedford, V. H. (1989). Ambivalence in adult sibling relationships. *Journal of Family Issues, 10*, 211–224.

Bedford, V. H. (1998). Sibling relationship troubles and well-being in middle and old age. *Family Relations, 47,* 369–376.

Bedford, V. H., & Avioli, S. (2001). Variations on sibling intimacy on old age. *Generations, 25*(2), 34–40.

Bedford, V. H., & Avioli, S. (2006). "Shooting the bull": Cohort comparisons of fraternal intimacy in midlife and old age. In V. H. Bedford and B. F. Turner (Eds.), *Men in relationships* (81–101). New York: Springer.

Bedford, V. H., & Avioli, S. (2012). Siblings in middle and late adulthood. In R. Blieszner & V. H. Bedford (Eds.), *Handbook of families and aging* (2nd ed., 125–153). New York: ABC-CLIO.

Bedford, V. H., Volling, B. L., & Avioli, S. (2000). Positive consequences of sibling conflict in childhood and adulthood. *International Journal of Aging and Human Development, 51,* 53–69.

Bengston, V., Giarrusso, R., Mabry, J. B., & Silverstein, M. (2002). Solidarity, conflict, and ambivalence: Complementary or competing perspectives on intergenerational relationships? *Journal of Marriage and Family, 64,* 568–576.

Bergman, E. J. (2013). Surmounting elusive barriers: The case for bioethics mediation. *Journal of Clinical Ethics, 24,* 11–24.

Boll, T., Ferring, D., & Filipp, S. H. (2003). Perceived parental differential treatment in middle adulthood: Curvilinear relations with individuals' experienced relationship quality to sibling and parents. *Journal of Family Psychology, 17*(4), 472–487.

Boss, (2006). *Loss, trauma, and resilience: Therapeutic work with ambiguous loss.* New York: Norton.

Bowen, M. (1974). Theory in the practice of psychotherapy. In J. Guerin (Ed.), *Family therapy: Theory and practice* (314–342). New York: Gardner Press.

Bretherton, I. (1992). The origins of attachment theory: John Bowlby and Mary Ainsworth. *Developmental Psychology, 28*(5), 759–775.

Buhl, H. M. (2009). My mother: My best friend? Adults' relationships with significant others across the lifespan. *Journal of Adult Development, 16,* 239–249.

Bureau of Labor Statistics Report. (2004). *100 years of U.S. consumer spending: 1950.* Washington, DC: U.S. Government Printing Office.

Burke, M. M., Taylor, J. L., Urbano, R., & Hodapp, R. M. (2012). Predictors of future caregiving by adult siblings of individuals with intellectual and developmental disabilities. *American Journal on Intellectual and Developmental Disabilities, 117,* 33–47.

Campbell, L. D., Connidis, I. A., & Davies, L. (1999). Sibling ties in later life. *Journal of Family Issues, 20*, 114–148.

Canary, D. J., Stafford, L., Hause, K. S., & Wallace, L. A. (1993). An inductive analysis of relational maintenance strategies: Comparisons among lovers, friends, and others. *Communication Research Reports, 10*(1), 5–14.

Caspi, J. (Ed.). (2011). *Sibling development: Implications for mental health practitioners.* New York: Springer.

Charles, D. R., & Charles, M. (2006). Sibling loss and attachment style: An exploratory study. *Psychoanalytic Psychology, 23*, 72–90.

Cicirelli, V. G. (1982). Sibling influence throughout the lifespan. In M. E. Lamb & B. Sutton-Smith (Eds.), *Sibling relationships: Their nature and significance across the lifespan* (267–284). Hillsdale, NJ: Erlbaum.

Cicirelli, V. G. (1989). Feelings of attachment to sibling and well-being in later life. *Psychology and Aging, 4*, 211–216.

Cicirelli, V. G. (1994). Sibling relationships in cross-cultural perspective. *Journal of Marriage and Family, 56*, 7–20.

Cicirelli, V. G. (1995). *Sibling relationships across the lifespan.* New York: Plenum Press.

Cicirelli, V. G. (2009). Sibling death and death fear in relation to depressive symptomatology in older adults. *Journals of Gerontology: Series B: Psychological Sciences and Social Sciences, 64B*, 24–32.

Colt, G. H. (2012). *Brothers: On his brothers and brothers in history.* New York: Scribner.

Connidis, I. A. (1994). Sibling support in older age. *Journals of Gerontology Series B: Psychological Sciences & Social Sciences, 49*, 309–317.

Connidis, I. A. (2007). Negotiating inequality among adult siblings: Two case studies. *Journal of Marriage and Family, 69*, 482–499.

Connidis, I. A. (2011). Ambivalence in fictional intergenerational ties: The portrayal of family life in freedom. *Journal of Family Theory & Review, 3*, 305–311.

Connidis, I. A., & Campbell, L. D. (1995). Closeness, confiding, and contact among siblings in middle and late adulthood. *Journal of Family Issues, 16*, 722–745.

Coontz, S. (2014, July 27). The new instability: Women expect more, while men can provide less. *New York Times*, Sunday Review, 1, 7.

Cooper, Z., Bernacki, R. E., & Diva, M. (2011). Chronic critical illness: A review for surgeons. *Current Problems in Surgery, 48*, 12–57.

Davidoff, L. (2012). *Thicker than water: Siblings and their relations—1780–1920.* New York: Oxford University Press.

Degeneffe, C. E., & Lynch, R. T. (2006). Correlates of depression in adult siblings of persons with traumatic brain injury. *Rehabilitation Counseling Bulletin, 49,* 130–142.

Degeneffe, C. E., & Olney, M. F. (2008). Future concerns of adult siblings of persons with traumatic brain injury. *Rehabilitation Counseling Bulletin, 51,* 240–250.

Degeneffe, C. E., & Olney, M. F. (2010). "We are the forgotten victims": Perspectives of adult siblings of persons with traumatic brain injury. *Brain Injury, 24,* 1416–1427.

D'Epinay, C. J. L., Cavalli, S., & Guillet, L. A. (2009–2010). Bereavement in very old age: Impact on health and relationships of the loss of a spouse, a child, a sibling, or a close friend. *Omega: Journal of Death & Dying, 60,* 301–325.

Doherty, N. A., & Feeney, J. A. (2004). The composition of attachment networks throughout the adult years. *Personal Relationships, 11,* 469–488.

Donley, M. G., & Likins, L. (2010). The multigenerational impact of sibling relationships. *American Journal of Family Therapy, 38,* 383–396.

Donrovich, R., Puschmann, P., & Mathijs, K. (2014). A life course approach to the impact of sibship composition and birth order on later life mortality risk, Antwerp (1846–1920). *Demographic Research, 38,* 1167–1198.

Dunn, J. (1983). Sibling relationships in early childhood. *Child Development, 54,* 787–811.

Dunn, J., & Plomin, R. (1991). Why are siblings so different? The significance of differences in sibling experiences within the family. *Family Process, 30,* 271–283.

Edward, J. (2012). *The sibling relationship: A force for growth and conflict.* London: Jason Aronson.

Edward, J. (2013). Sibling discord: A force for growth and conflict. *Clinical Social Work Journal, 41,* 77–83.

Emanuel, E. (2013). *Brothers Emanuel: A memoir of an American family.* New York: Random House.

Erikson, E. (1963). *Childhood and Society.* New York: Norton.

Feeney, J. A., & Humphreys, T. (1996, November). *Parental, sibling, and romantic partner relationships: Exploring the functions of attachment bonds.* Paper presented at the Fifth Australian Research Conference, Brisbane.

Fingerman, K. L., Hay, E. L., & Birditt, K. S. (2004). The best of ties, the worst of ties: Close, problematic, and ambivalent social relationships. *Journal of Marriage and Family, 66,* 792–808.

Finzi-Dottan, R., & Cohen, O. (2011). Young adult siblings relations: The effects of perceived parental favoritism and narcissism. *Journal of Psychology, 145,* 1–22.

Folwell, A. L., Chung, L. C., Nussbaum, J. F., Bethea, L.S., & Grant, J. A. (1997). Differential accounts of closeness in older adult sibling relationships. *Journal of Social and Personal Relationships, 14,* 843–849.

Freeman, E. A. (1993). *Family treatment: The sibling bond and other relationship issues.* Springfield, IL.: Charles C. Thomas.

Friedrich, R. M., Lively, S., & Rubenstein, L. M. (2008). Siblings' coping strategies and mental health services: A national study of persons with schizophrenia. *Psychiatric Services, 59,* 261–267.

Fuller-Thomson, E. (1999–2000). Loss of the kin-keeper? Sibling conflict following parental death. *Omega: Journal of Death & Dying, 40,* 547–559.

Gibson, S. C., & Qualls, S. H. (2012). A family systems perspective of elder financial abuse. *Generations: Journal of the American Society on Aging, 36,* 26–29.

Gilligan, M., Suitor, J. J., Kim, S., & Pillemer, K. (2013). Differential effects of perceptions of mothers' and fathers' favoritism on sibling tension in adulthood. *Journals of Gerontology Series B: Psychological Sciences and Social Sciences, 68,* 593–598.

Gilligan, M., Suitor, J. J., & Nam, S. (2015). Maternal differential treatment in later-life families and within-family variations in adult sibling closeness. *Journals of Gerontology: Series B: Psychological Sciences and Social Sciences, 70*(1), 176–177.

Gold, D. T. (1987). Siblings in old age: Something special. *Canadian Journal on Aging, 6,* 199–215.

Gold, D. T. (1989). Sibling relationships in old age: A typology. *International Journal of Aging and Human Development, 28,* 37–51.

Greif, G. L. (2009). *Buddy system: Understanding male friendships.* New York: Oxford University Press.

Greif, G. L., & Woolley, M. E. (2012, December). Do adults talk about their siblings in therapy? *News & Views: Greater Washington Society for Clinical Social Work,* 6–7.

Greif, G. L., & Woolley, M. E. (2015). Patterns in adult sibling relationships after the death of one or both parents. *Journal of Social Work in End-of-Life & Palliative Care, 11*(1), 74–89.

Halgunseth, L. C., Ispa, J. M., & Rudy, D. (2006). Parental control in Latino families: An integrated review of the literature. *Child Development, 77,* 1281–1297.

Hayes, J. C., Gold, D. T., & Pieper, C. F. (1997). Sibling bereavement in late life. *Omega: Journal of Death and Dying, 35,* 25–42.

Hemphill, C. D. (2011). *Siblings: Brothers and sisters in American history.* New York: Oxford University Press.

Hequembourg, A., & Brallier, S. (2004). Gendered stories of parental caregiving among siblings. *Journal of Aging Studies, 19,* 53–71.

Hobbs, F. & Snoope, N. (2002, November). Demographic trends in the 20th century. Census 2000 Special Reports. Washington, DC: U.S. Census Bureau.

Hodapp, R. M., & Urbano, R. C. (2007). Adult siblings of individuals with Down syndrome versus autism: Findings from a large-scale US study. *Journal of Intellectual Disability Research, 51,* 1018–1029.

Ingersoll-Dayton, B., Neal, M. B., Ha, J., & Hammer, L. B. (2003). Collaboration among siblings providing care for older parents. *Journal of Gerontological Social Work, 40,* 51–66.

Irish, D. (1964). Sibling interaction: A neglected aspect in family life research. *Social Forces, 42,* 279–288.

Jenkins, J., & Dunn, J. (2009). Siblings within families: Levels of analysis and patterns of influence. In L. Kramer & K. J. Conger (Eds.), *Siblings as agents of socialization. New Directions for Child and Adolescent Development* (vol. 126, 79–93). San Francisco: Jossey-Bass.

Jensen, A. C., Whiteman, S. D., Fingerman, K. L., & Birditt, K. S. (2013). "Life still isn't fair": Parental differential treatment of young adult siblings. *Journal of Marriage and Family, 75,* 438–452.

Kahn, M. D., & Lewis, K. G. (Eds.). (1988). *Siblings in therapy: Life span and clinical issues.* New York: Norton.

Kempson, D., & Murdock, V. (2010). Memory keepers: A narrative study on siblings never known. *Death Studies, 34,* 738–756.

Kerr, M. (1988). Chronic anxiety and defining a self. *Atlantic Monthly, 262* (September), 35–58.

Khodyakov, D., & Carr, D. (2009). The impact of late-life parental death on adult sibling relationships: Do parent's advance directives help or hurt? *Research on Aging, 31,* 495–519.

Kinrade, T., Jackson, A., & Tomnay, J. (2011). Social workers' perspective on the psychosocial needs of families during critical illness. *Social Work in Health Care, 50,* 661–681.

Kluger, J. (2011). *The sibling effect: What the bonds among brothers and sisters reveal about us.* New York: Riverhead Books.

Kramer, L. (2011). Supportive sibling relationships. In J. Caspi (Ed.), *Sibling development: Implications for mental health practitioners* (41–58). New York: Springer.

Kramer, L., & Bank, L. (2005). Sibling relationship contributions to individual and family well-being: Introduction to the special issue. *Journal of Family Psychology, 19*, 483–485.

Kramer, L., & Conger, K. J. (2009). What we learn from our sisters and brothers: For better or for worse. *New Directions for Child and Adolescent Development, 126*, 1–12.

Kreider, R. M. (2008, February). Living arrangements of children: 2004 household economic studies (P70–114). Current Population Reports. Washington, DC: U.S. Census Bureau.

Kreider, R. M., & Ellis, R. (2011, May). Number, timing, and duration of marriages and divorces: 2009 household economic studies (P70–125). Current Population Reports. Washington, DC: U.S. Census Bureau.

Kreider, R. M., & Fields, J. M. (2002, February). Number, timing, and duration of marriages and divorces: 1996 household economic studies (P70–80). Current Population Reports. Washington, DC: U.S. Census Bureau.

Kuba, S. A. (2011). *The role of sisters in women's development.* New York: Oxford University Press.

Lamas, D. (2014). Chronic critical illness. *New England Journal of Medicine, 370*, 175–177.

Leavitt, K. S., Gardner, S. A., Gallagher, M. M., & Schamess, G. (1999). Severely traumatized siblings: A treatment strategy. *Clinical Social Work Journal, 26*, 55–71.

Lee, T. R., Mancini, J. A., & Maxwell, J. W. (1990). Sibling relationships and adulthood: Contact patterns and motivations. *Journal of Marriage and the Family, 52*, 431–440.

Leith, J. E., & Stein, C. H. (2012). The role of personal loss in the caregiving experiences of well siblings of adults with serious mental illness. *Journal of Clinical Psychology, 68*, 1075–1088.

Madden, M., Lenhard, A., Duggan, M., Cortesi, S., & Gasser, U. (2013, March 13). Teens and technology 2013. Washington, DC: Pew Research Center.

Malcolm, J. (2014, June 23). The book refuge. *New Yorker*, 64–73.

Markowitz, L. M. (1994). Shared passages. *Family Therapy Networker*, January/February, 19–29, 66–69.

Mauthner, M. L. (2002). *Sistering: Power and change in female relationships.* New York: Palgrave Macmillan.

Mink, J. S., & Ward, J. D. (Eds.) (1993). *The significance of sibling relationships in literature.* Bowling Green, OH: Bowling Green State University Popular Press.

Minuchin, S., & Fishman, C. (1981). *Family therapy techniques.* Cambridge, MA: Harvard University Press.

Mock, D. W., & Parker, G. A. (1997). *The evolution of sibling rivalry.* New York: Oxford University Press.

Monahan, K. (2010). Themes of adult sibling sexual abuse survivors in later life: An initial exploration. *Clinical Social Work Journal, 38,* 361–369.

Myers, S. A. (2011). "I have to love her, even if sometimes I may not like her": The reasons why adults maintain their sibling relationships. *North American Journal of Psychology, 13,* 51–62.

Myers, S. A., & Bryant, L. E. (2008). The use of behavioral indicators of sibling commitment among emerging adults. *Journal of Family Communication, 8,* 101–125.

Nandwana, S., & Katoch, M. (2009). Perception of sibling relationship during middle adulthood years: A typology. *Journal of Social Sciences, 21,* 67–72.

Nichols, M. (2014). *The essentials of family therapy* (6th ed.). Boston: Allyn & Bacon.

Orsmond, G. I., & Seltzer, M. M. (2007). Siblings of individuals with autism or Down syndrome: Effects on adult lives. *Journal of Intellectual Disability Research, 51,* 682–696.

Padgett, D. (2008). *Qualitative methods in social work research* (2nd ed.). Thousand Oaks, CA: Sage.

Parker-Pope, T. (2010, May 3). When the ties that bind unravel. *New York Times,* D5.

Pew Research Center (2000). Tracking online life: How women use the Internet to cultivate relationships with friends and family. Retrieved April 15, 2015, from http://www.pewinternet.org/files/old-media//Files/Reports/2000/Report1 .pdf.

Pew Research Center (2011). A portrait of stepfamilies. Retrieved June 15, 2013, from http://www.pewsocialtrends.org/2011/01/13/a-portrait-of-stepfamilies/.

Pfouts, J. (1976, May). The sibling relationship: A forgotten dimension. *Social Work, 21,* 200–204.

Pollet, T. V. (2007). Genetic relatedness and sibling relationship characteristics in a modern society. *Evolution and Human Behavior, 28,* 176–185.

Poortman, A-R., & Voorpostel, M. (2009). Parental divorce and sibling relationships: A research note. *Journal of Family Issues, 30,* 74–91.

Quinn, J. R., Schmitt, M., Baggs-Gedney, J., Norton, S. A., Dombeck, M. T., & Sellers, C. R. (2012). Family members' informal roles in end-of-life decision making in adult intensive care units. *American Journal of Critical Care, 21,* 43–51.

Riggio, H. R. (2000). Measuring attitudes toward adult sibling relationships: The Lifespan Sibling Relationship Scale. *Journal of Social and Personal Relationships, 17,* 707–728.

Riggio, H. R. (2001). Relations between parental divorce and the quality of adult sibling relationships. *Journal of Divorce and Remarriage, 36,* 67–82.

Riggio, H. R. (2006). Structural features of sibling dyads toward sibling relationships in young adulthood. *Journal of Family Issues, 27,* 1233–1254.

Robinson, L., & Mahon, M. M. (1997). Sibling bereavement: A concept analysis. *Death Studies, 21,* 477–499.

Rosenberg, E. (1988). Step-siblings in therapy. In M.D. Kahn & K. G. Lewis (Eds.), *Siblings in therapy: Life span and clinical issues* (209–227). New York: Guilford.

Ross, H. G., & Milgram, J. I. (1982). Sibling influence throughout the lifespan. In M. E. Lamb & B. Sutton-Smith (Eds.), *Sibling relationships: Their nature and significance across the lifespan* (225–249). Hillsdale, NJ: Erlbaum.

Safer, J. (2012). *Cain's legacy: Liberating siblings from a lifetime of rage, shame, secrecy, and regret.* New York: Basic Books.

Salash, F. M., Wood, N. D., & Parker, T. S. (2013). Our problems are your sibling's fault: Exploring the connections between conflict styles of siblings during adolescence and later adult committed relationships. *American Journal of Family Therapy, 41,* 288–298.

Satir, V. (1964). *Conjoint family therapy.* Palo Alto, CA: Science and Behavior Books.

Schomburg, C. R. (1992). To survive whole, to save the self: The role of sisterhood in the novels of Toni Morrison. In J.S. Mink & J.D. Ward (Eds.), *The significance of sibling relationships in literature* (149–157). Bowling Green, OH: Bowling Green State University Popular Press.

Scott, A.M., & Caughlin, J. (2012). Managing multiple goals in family discourse about end-of-life health decisions. *Research on Aging, 34,* 496–518.

Shattuck, R. M., & Kreider, R. M. (2013). Social and economic characteristics of currently unmarried women with a recent birth: 2011. Washington, DC: U.S. Census Bureau.

Shulman, S. C. (2005). The changing nature of family relationships in middle and later life: parent caring and the mid-life developmental opportunity. *Smith College Studies in Social Work, 75,* 103–119.

Smith, M. J., & Greenberg, J. S. (2008). Factors contributing to the quality of sibling relationships for adults with schizophrenia. *Psychiatric Services, 59*, 57–62.

Stewart, R. B., Kozak, A. L., Tingley, L. M., Goddard, J. M., Blake, E. M., & Cassel W. A. (2001). Adult sibling relationships: Validation of a typology. *Personal Relationships, 8*, 299–324.

Strauss, A., & Corbin, J (1998). *Basics of Qualitative Research: Techniques and procedures for developing grounded theory.* Thousand Oaks, CA: Sage.

Straus, M., Gelles, R., & Steinmetz, S. (1980). *Behind closed doors: Violence in the American family.* Garden City, NY: Anchor Books.

Suitor, J. J., Sechrist, J., Plikuhn, M., Pardo, S. T., Gilligan, M., & Pillemer, K. (2009). The role of perceived maternal favoritism in sibling relations in midlife. *Journal of Marriage and Family, 71*, 1026–1038.

Sulloway, F. J. (1996). *Born to rebel: Birth order, family dynamics, and creative lives.* New York: Vintage Books.

Troll, L. (1971). The family of later life: A decade review. *Journal of Marriage and Family, 33*, 263–290.

Tucker, C. J., Finkelhor, D., Turner, H., & Shattuck, A. M. (In Press). Sibling and peer victimization in childhood and adolescence. *Child Abuse & Neglect.*

Tucker, C. J., & Updegraff, K. (2009). The relative contributions of parents and siblings to child and adolescent development. In L. Kramer & K. J. Conger (Eds.), *Siblings as agents of socialization. New directions for child and adolescent development* (vol. 126, 13–28). San Francisco: Jossey-Bass.

Ulbricht, J. A., Ganiban, J. M., Button, T. M. M., Feinberg, M., Reiss, D., & Neiderhiser, J. M. (2013). Marital adjustment as a moderator for genetic and environmental influences on parenting. *Journal of Family Psychology, 27*, 42–52.

U.S. Census Bureau (2004). Survey of Income and Program Participation (SIPP) Reports, Number, timing and duration of marriages and divorces: 2004. Washington, DC: U.S. Government Printing Office.

U.S. Census Bureau (2013). Table 1. Educational attainment of the population 18 years and over, by age, sex, race, and Hispanic origin: 2013. Retrieved from http://www.census.gov/hhes/socdemo/education/data/cps/2013/tables.html.

Van Volkom, M. (2006). Sibling relationships in middle and older adulthood: A review of the literature. *Marriage & Family Review, 40*, 151–170.

Van Volkom, M., Machiz, C., & Reich, A. E. (2011). Sibling relationships in the college years: Do gender, birth order, and age spacing matter? *North American Journal of Psychology, 13*, 35–55.

Visher, E. B., & Visher, J. S. (1988). *Old loyalties, new ties: Therapeutic strategies with stepfamilies.* New York: Brunner/Mazel.

Voorpostel, M., & Blieszner, R. (2008). Intergenerational solidarity and support between adult siblings. *Journal of Marriage and Family, 70,* 157–167.

Voorpostel, M., & van der Lippe, T. (2007). Support between siblings and between friends: Two worlds apart? *Journal of Marriage and Family, 69,* 1271–1282.

Voorpostel, M., & Schans, D. (2011). Sibling relationships in Dutch and immigrant families. *Ethnic and Racial Studies, 34,* 2027–2047.

Voorpostel, M., van der Lippe, T., & Flap, H. (2012). For better or worse: Negative life events and sibling relationships. *International Sociology, 27,* 330–348.

Wagner, V.S., Hunter, R., & Boelter, D. (1988). Sibling rivalry and the systemic perspective: Implications for treatment. *Journal of Strategic and Systemic Therapies, 7,* 67–71.

Watson, M. F. (1998). African American sibling relationships. In M. McGoldrick (Ed.), *Revisioning family therapy* (282–293). New York: Guilford.

Watson, M. F., & McGoldrick, M. (2011). Practice with siblings in a cultural context. In J. Caspi (Ed.), *Sibling development: Implications for mental health practitioners* (59–81). New York: Springer.

Webb, N. B. (Ed.). (2001). *Culturally diverse parent-child and family relationships.* New York: Columbia University Press.

White, L. K., & Riedmann, R. (1992). When the Brady bunch grows up: Step/half and full sibling relationships in adulthood. *Journal of Marriage and the Family, 54,* 197–208.

Willyard, J., Miller, K., Shoemaker, M. & Addison, (2008). Making sense of sibling responsibility for family caregiving. *Qualitative Health Research, 18,* 1673–1686.

Woolley, M. E., Greif, G. L., & McMillan, G. (2014). Differences in sibling relationships between late and middle adulthood: implications for practice. Poster presented at the Council on Social Work Education Annual Program, October, Tampa.

Woolley, M. E., Greif, G. L., & McMillan, G. (2015). Parenting and relationship predictors of adult siblings collaborating in the care of aging parents. Paper presented at the Society for Social Work Research, January, New Orleans.

Zampitella, C. (2011). Adult surviving siblings: The disenfranchised grievers. *Group, 35,* 333–347.

Printed in the USA
CPSIA information can be obtained
at www.ICGtesting.com
JSHW011824120624
64690JS00015B/398

9 780231 165174